The
Photoshop
Plug-ins
Book

The
Photoshop
Plug-ins
Category Listings,
Instructions & Examples
Book

Daniel Gray

VENTANA

The Photoshop Plug-ins Book
Copyright © 1997 by Daniel Gray

Library of Congress Cataloging-in-Publication Data

Gray, Daniel, 1961-
  The Photoshop plug-ins book /Daniel Gray.--1st ed.
    p. cm.
  Includes index.
  ISBN 1-56604-718-8
  1. Computer graphics. 2. Adobe Photoshop (Computer file).
I. Title.
T385.G7385 1996
006.6'86—dc21   97-25468
                                                              CIP

First Edition 9 8 7 6 5 4 3 2 1

Printed in the United States of America

Ventana Communications Group
P.O. Box 13964
Research Triangle Park, NC 27709-3964
919.544.9404
FAX 919.544.9472
http://www.vmedia.com

Ventana Communications Group is a division of International Thomson Publishing.

President
Michael E. Moran

**Director of Acquisitions
and Development**
Robert Kern

**Editorial Operations
Manager**
Kerry L. B. Foster

Production Manager
Jaimie Livingston

Brand Manager
Jamie Jaeger Fiocco

Art Director
Marcia Webb

Creative Services Manager
Diane Lennox

Acquisitions Editor
Christopher D. Grams

Project Editor
Jennifer Huntley Mario

Development Editor
Michelle Corbin Nichols

Copy Editor
Judy Flynn

CD-ROM Specialist
Ginny Phelps

Desktop Publisher
Lance Kozlowski

Proofreader
Alicia Farris

Indexer
Timothy Griffin

Interior Designer
Patrick Berry

Cover Illustrator
Leigh Salmon

About the Author

Daniel Gray is the Marketing Communications Manager for PrePRESS SOLUTIONS and writes for several graphics and Web-related publications. He is the author of *Web Publishing With Adobe PageMill 2*, and co-author of *The Official Palace Tour Guide*, *Looking Good Online*, and *The Comprehensive Guide to CorelWEB.GRAPHICS Suite* (all by Ventana), among other books in the computer and graphic arts fields.

Acknowledgments

This book would never have come together without the effort of literally dozens of individuals. When I write a set of acknowledgments, I sometimes feel as if it's an Academy Awards acceptance speech. Rest assured, this one is going to run over. There are many folks to thank…

First and foremost, I'd like to thank Cynthia Johnston, who heads up Adobe's plug-in developer relations team. Cynthia has been a wonderful positive force, and has been instrumental in getting this project done.

The editorial, marketing, and production staff at Ventana has been incredibly supportive, as well. I'd like to thank Chris Grams for acquiring the book; Michelle Nichols for her developmental editing prowess; Jennifer Huntley Mario for patiently shepherding the manuscript; Judy Flynn for her expert copy editing; Ginny Phelps for pulling together a precedent-setting Companion CD-ROM; Diane Lennox, Rebecca Sawyer, and Monica Jackson for their marketing savvy; and the entire print and multimedia production crew for dealing with all of those crazy files. Many thanks to my agent, Martha Kaufman at Adler & Robin, for her advice as well.

The plug-in developers have been a joy to work with. A good number of them went above and beyond the call of duty by contributing their own chapters. My hat goes off to Sam Moore at Fortune Hill; Jot Kailay and John Davis at Plastic Thought; Jan Dyson, Farrah Jinha, and Gary Shilling at Vertigo; Michael Aslett and Craig Kevghas at MEAC; and Carolyne Walton at Altamira for the fine job they've done.

I'd also like to thank all the developers that helped to get their plug-ins out to us, agreed to include demos on the CD-ROM, and dutifully tech edited their chapters. The following folks get the big thumbs up: Greg Hatem and Robert Schwalbe at a lowly apprentice production; Michael Pilmer and Skip Elsheimer at Alien Skin; Lance Gilbert, Keith Mowry, and Pat Mansfield at Second Glance; Dana Cohen and Megan Flinn at Alaras; Patti Duffy at Auto F/X; Cynthia Johnson and Travis Anton at BoxTop; Lorena Peer and Peter Whitehead at Chroma Graphics; Doug Frohman at Digital Frontiers; Mark Law, Mark Mehall, and Diana Smedley at Extensis; Gerry at Human Software; Phil Jackson and Ted Cheney at ImageXpress; Jason Ysais at MetaCreations; Dan Bryndle at Magic Software; Willi Penner at M.M.M. Software; Kimberly Myers at Pantone; Kirk Lyford at Vivid Details; Kermit Woodall at Nova Design; Lotus Chen and Dwight Jurling at Ulead; Craig Burriss, Ian Lombard, and Erin Denny at Xaos Tools; Chris Athanas at DigiEffects; Klaus Schallhorn at digital showbiz; and Erik-Paul Gibson at Cytopia. And many thanks to Andrew Coven at Adobe for checking out the "how they work" appendix.

I've been lucky to work with a talented group of independent contributing authors and artists, as well. I'd like to thank Lynn "Finchy" Finch for the Eye Candy chapter, Eric Coker for the Kai's Power Tools chapter, Jeanne Taylor for the Paint Alchemy chapter, and Mike "King of All Scanners" Paternoster for the Seven Steps Appendix. The doggy artwork in the Eye Candy chapter was created by Skip Proffitt. A very special thank you to Barry Burns at Andromeda for allowing us the use of his beautiful artwork.

In all, I hope that *The Photoshop Plug-ins Book* becomes a constant work-in-progress. With a little luck, we'll keep this baby updated on a regular basis—both online and in print. If you've purchased this book, you have my heartfelt thanks. And if you're thinking about plunking down your hard-earned cash, I know you'll find this to be a fabulous resource.

And as always, my family deserves a multitude of thanks. (Yes, it's finally time for Daddy to come "out of the computer room"!)

Contents

PART II

Optimizing Images for the Web

PART III

Streamlining Your Workflow

PART IV
Bust Loose With Creative Filters

PART V
Plug Into the Third Dimension

P A R T   V I

Appendices

Introduction

I have a confession to make. I'm not a Photoshop god. I'm just Joe Average Photoshop User. While I love the program to death and have been using it for years, I haven't come close to absorbing the vast depth of power that it allows. Like many folks, my strong suit has never been in executing complex procedures with clinical precision. Thankfully, that's where Photoshop plug-ins come into play. They enable us to perform amazing effects with incredible ease. Just drop in a plug-in, take the time to learn a bit about how it works, and your cohorts will look at you (and your artwork) in awe.

When I was a little kid, we had a marvelous general store in my hometown. This place had everything, including a meat counter, produce, groceries, newspapers, and a soda fountain. Most importantly, it had a wonderful case full of penny candy; it was stuffed full of all the goodies that made a little kid's heart pound. The proprietor of the general store, Edna Robotti, was a wonderful lady. She would let the kids she knew come around to the back of the counter to pick their candy out of the case themselves. For a five-year-old, it was an exhilarating experience.

From the moment I first began talking with Ventana about writing this book, there was never a doubt in my mind that I had to do it. For once again, I've become the proverbial kid in a candy store. And the best part is that I get to share all my candy with you!

Who Needs This Book?

The Photoshop Plug-ins Book is intended for all users of Adobe Photoshop—from beginner to expert. Whether you're an artist, designer, retoucher, scanner operator, desktop publisher, educator, illustrator, printer, publisher, prepress person, or student preparing images for print, the Web, presentations, multimedia projects, or just for fun, you'll find this book to be an invaluable asset.

It's important to note that you don't even have to have Photoshop to make this book worth your while. In many cases, you can use any one of a range of paint programs that can use Photoshop plug-ins, including:

- Adobe PhotoDeluxe
- Color It
- Corel Photo-Paint
- Equilibrium DeBabelizer
- Fractal Design Painter
- GraphicConverter
- Live Picture
- Macromedia xRes
- Micrografx Picture Publisher
- Paint Shop Pro
- Ulead PhotoImpact

And that's just a start—if you're an Adobe Illustrator or Macromedia FreeHand user, you can apply plug-in filters there too!

What's Inside?

This book does something that's never been done before. It is a virtual encyclopedia of third-party Photoshop plug-ins. While other books may touch on the subject in a different context, this book's raison d'être is to present the entire spectrum of choices. We won't waste your time covering PageMaker plug-ins or the plug-ins that are part of the standard Photoshop package. Instead, you'll learn about all the commercial plug-ins. By using this book as a reference, you'll discover what each and every plug-in does and which one might be the best choice for your project at hand.

Each plug-in is detailed with a "what it does/how it does it" section, starting with an easy-to-read listing:

Creator
Cinematte

Components (if more than one)
Cinematte
Kill Transparency

Purpose
Blue/green screen compositing for Photoshop

Platforms
Windows 95/NT

Hardware/software requirements
Same as Photoshop

URL/contact info for creator of plug-in
http://members.aol.com/dgdominion

Products that the plug-in works with
Photoshop 3.04 - 4.0

And perhaps best of all, the CD-ROM that accompanies this book is a treasure trove of commercial demos and shareware plug-ins, giving you an unprecedented opportunity to "try before you buy." We've spent untold hours packing it full of goodies for both Macintosh and Windows platforms.

How This Book Is Organized

The Photoshop Plug-ins Book is arranged in five basic sections:

■ **Part I: Optimizing Images for Print.** Part I is intended for those who can't seem to get their scans to print properly. These products make it easy for anyone to tweak scanned images for the highest reproduction quality. You'll learn how to optimize images for different printing technologies, from low-end black-and-white through high-end four-color (and beyond!). This is essential stuff for anyone designing for print.

- **Part II: Optimizing Images for the Web.** If you're building Web pages, you'll want to ensure that your images download quickly, while looking their best. The plug-ins covered in this part of the book deal with the infamous image quality/file size dilemma. Be sure to check out these plug-ins...whether you're creating Web images for fun or profit.

- **Part III: Streamlining Your Work Flow.** This part of the book covers the plug-ins designed for folks who work in Photoshop all day long. These products will make your image editing go more smoothly. This section covers batch operations and production issues. It's important for folks in high-volume scanning operations, including publishers, service bureaus, and printers.

- **Part IV: Bust Loose With Creative Filters.** Here is where all the fun is. Are you looking for a little magic? In this section, we get into the fun aspects of plug-in filters. These products allow you to create wild cutting-edge imagery with a few simple clicks. This genre generates the most excitement with experienced artists and newbies alike.

- **Part V: Plug Into the Third Dimension.** The final section is intended for artists that want to delve into 3D without investing the time to learn a complicated 3D app. These plug-ins will help you to achieve cool 3D effects without the pain. They appeal to artists and designers that create for Web, video, and print.

As a bonus, there are four appendices:

- **Appendix A: About the Companion CD-ROM.** So you can see all the goodies on the disc.

- **Appendix B: More Great Plug-ins!** We sneaked these plug-ins into the book just under the wire!

- **Appendix C: How Plug-ins Work**. This appendix touches on the basics behind the plug-in architecture.

- **Appendix D: Seven Steps to Quality Color.** Need some basic scanning and color tips? Check out Mike Paternoster's seven steps to scanning nirvana!

CD-ROM/Online Updates

As hard as we've tried to make our information current, the truth is that new plug-ins will be released as soon as this book goes to press (and continually thereafter). We're committed to keeping you updated! That's why the

Companion CD-ROM is linked to the Ventana Web site (www.vmedia.com/updates.html). There, you'll find plenty of real live examples of the plug-ins covered in this book.

The Photoshop Plug-ins Book Companion CD-ROM contains the ultimate compendium of demo plug-ins. We've included plug-ins from Altamira, Alien Skin, Alaras, Andromeda, Auto F/X, BoxTop, ChromaGraphics, Digital Dominion, Digital Frontiers, Extensis, Fortune Hill, MetaCreations, MMM Software, Pantone, ScanPrepPro, Second Glance, Ulead, and Vertigo, among others. You'll save days of searching and downloading! We're also proud to include Adobe's official System Developers Kits for Photoshop and Premiere. Be sure to check out Appendix A for a complete rundown on all the plug-ins.

Hardware & Software Requirements

If you're already working with Adobe Photoshop or another paint editor (see the list earlier), it's likely that your Macintosh or Windows computer is beefy enough to work with third-party plug-in filters. With Photoshop, the bare minimum is pretty much 16MB of RAM and a 68030 (Mac) or 80486 (PC) processor. As always, the faster your processor and the more RAM your computer has, the happier you will be. If you're serious about image editing, you'll be working on a Power Macintosh or Pentium PC. Each paint editor is likely to have its own requirements, so the best advice is to double-check the manual.

Your video card is one place where you definitely don't want to scrimp. For the most pleasurable image editing experience, you should be working in 16.7 million colors (also referred to as 24-bit color). You might get by with thousands of colors, but you should always avoid working in 256-color mode.

TIP *If your video card has a meager amount of video RAM, try switching to a lower resolution to see if you can achieve a higher color level. While you'll fit less on the screen, the color will be much more pleasing.*

Plug In!

Are you ready to step into the candy store? *The Photoshop Plug-ins Book* is one that you'll want to visit over and over. With this book and your favorite image editor (and plenty of hard drive space), you're bound to have a wonderful time discovering cool new effects, as well as uncovering deadline-beating convenience. And remember—you can never be too rich, too thin, or have too many plug-ins!

Part I

Optimizing Images for Print

chapter 1

A Lowly Apprentice Production's PlateMaker

Creator
a lowly apprentice production, inc.

Purpose
DCS 2.0 file format support

Platforms
Macintosh

Hardware/software requirements
Same as Photoshop

URL/contact info for creator of plug-in
www.alap.com
a lowly apprentice production, inc.
5963 La Place Court
Suite 206
Carlsbad, CA 92008
760/438-5790 voice
760/438-5791 fax

Products that the plug-in works with
Adobe Photoshop 2.0.1 or later

Do you create high-end process color print jobs that include multiple varnishes, foil stamping, embossing, and other niceties? Are you looking for a better way to create spot color masks? A lowly apprentice production's PlateMaker brings Desktop Color Separation (DCS) 2.0 file format to Adobe Photoshop, thereby making it possible to create an unlimited number of spot color plates.

Who Should Use a lowly apprentice production's PlateMaker?

If you work on print projects that include extra plates for spot colors, varnishes, bump plates, and other processes, PlateMaker will make your life a whole lot easier. This plug-in fits with high-end designers, graphic artists, commercial printers, silk screen printers, specialty printers, color trade shops, service bureaus, and prepress shops, among others.

What a lowly apprentice production's PlateMaker Does

With PlateMaker, you can create as many extra plates as you'll ever need, even for the most intricate print job. With PlateMaker and the DCS 2.0 format, you can export 16 extra plates, complete with clipping paths—one for each Photoshop channel—when working with CMYK images. And if you're working with an indexed color image, PlateMaker allows you to create a whopping 256 spot plates.

Why Use a lowly apprentice production's PlateMaker?

In the bad old days, extra finishing procedures such as varnishes, foil stamping, and embossing tacked on extra expense in the prepress phase. Masks were either created by hand or on expensive proprietary workstations. Thankfully, those days are over! PlateMaker allows you to handle these tasks within Photoshop, saving you time and money. PlateMaker's 24-bit PICT preview provides a good look at how your piece will print.

How a lowly apprentice production's PlateMaker Does It

PlateMaker is a file export plug-in. After you've prepared your image in Photoshop, choose File | Export | PlateMaker from Photoshop's menu bar. PlateMaker's DCS 2.0 Format dialog box appears, as shown in Figure 1-1. Here, you can specify which plates will separate as well as their screen angles, frequencies, and dot types. You can name each plate with a descriptive title in addition to specifying clipping paths and flatness.

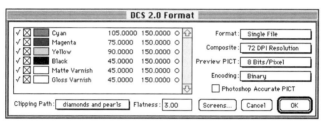

Figure 1-1: The DCS 2.0 Format dialog box allows you to set all of the separated file's attributes quickly.

The DCS 2.0 Format dialog box includes four drop-down menus:

■ **Format**. Choose either single or multiple files.

■ **Composite**. Choose none, 72 dpi, or full resolution.

■ **Preview PICT**. Choose none, 1, 8, or 24 bits per pixel. You can also specify a Photoshop Accurate PICT.

■ **Encoding**. Choose from Binary or ASCII.

When you click the OK button, another dialog box appears. This dialog box allows you to name the file and assign either accurate or conventional screening (or no screening). Once you've exported your file in DCS 2.0 format, you can import it into QuarkXPress or Adobe PageMaker.

Second Glance LaserSepsPro

Creator
Second Glance

Purpose
Creates stochastic separations

Platforms
Macintosh

Hardware/software requirements
System 7.0.1 or later, 2 megabytes of RAM in addition
to the Photoshop minimum

URL/contact info for creator of plug-in
http://www.secondglance.com
Second Glance
7248 Sunset Avenue NE
Bremerton, WA 98311
360/692-3694 voice
360/692-9241 fax

Products that the plug-in works with
Adobe Photoshop 3.0.1 (or later)

W ant to create stochastic separations of your process color images, yet you lack the screening option on your imagesetter? Second Glance LaserSepsPro provides an alternative means to create stochastic seps, at an expense far less than an imagesetter RIP upgrade.

Who Should Use Second Glance LaserSepsPro? _____

Second Glance LaserSepsPro was developed to create stochastic separations for process color printing. The audience for LaserSepsPro includes commercial printers, silk-screen printers, color trade shops, service bureaus, graphic artists, designers, desktop publishers, and newspapers.

What Second Glance LaserSepsPro Does _____

Second Glance LaserSepsPro is an export filter that renders stochastic separations within Adobe Photoshop rather than at the imagesetter's RIP (raster image processor). The plug-in provides control over CMYK tone curves and exports files in DCS format. The DCS files—which are dramatically smaller in file size than conventional separations—are then placed into QuarkXPress or Adobe PageMaker. The separated files remain completely editable within Photoshop.

Why Use Second Glance LaserSepsPro? _____

Stochastic separations provide a broader dynamic range than conventional halftone separations. The technique came into vogue a number of years ago. This screening method—also referred to as *frequency modulated* screening— differs from conventional halftone screening in that it uses an irregularly spaced pattern of spots instead of a static grid. Since they are random in nature, stochastic separations are free from the rosette patterns and moirés of conventional screening. The zoomed up views in Figures 2-1 and 2-2 demonstrate the difference between conventional and stochastic screening.

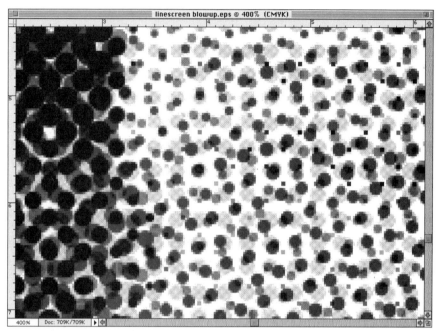

Figure 2-1: A conventional halftone screen. Note the ordered rows of dots.

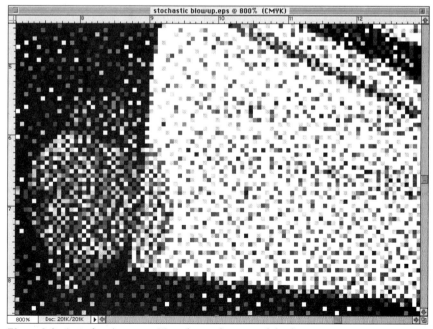

Figure 2-2: A stochastic screen. Note the randomness of the dots.

While most imagesetter manufacturers have their own flavors of stochastic screening—Agfa has CristalRaster, Scitex has FULLtone, Linotype-Hell has Diamond Screening, and PrePRESS SOLUTIONS has ESCOR-FM—the hardware RIPs on older imagesetters are often incapable of being upgraded. Second Glance LaserSepsPro provides the means to create stochastically screened images that can be output on these older devices.

How Second Glance LaserSepsPro Does It

Second Glance LaserSepsPro is a file export plug-in. Once your image is ready to be separated, choose File | Export | LaserSepsPro from the Photoshop menu bar. LaserSepsPro uses a little dialog box along with four preview windows, as shown in Figure 2-3, to provide you with the means to adjust your separation. The Control dialog box lets you fine-tune the curves for each of the four process color channels. There are three ways to adjust the curves: You can click and drag in the grayscale area to adjust the gamma, click and drag individual points on the curve, or enter the percentages numerically. Selecting the Master check box allows you to adjust all four channels simultaneously.

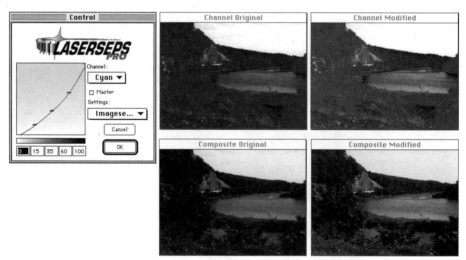

Figure 2-3: With four previews, LaserSepsPro delivers a high level of interactivity.

As you tweak your image, LaserSepsPro's four preview windows let you keep a close eye on what's happening. The preview windows demonstrate how the image will appear before and after color curve modifications.

- **Channel Original**. How the specific channel looked before you made a change.
- **Channel Modified**. How that channel looks after you've tweaked it's curve.
- **Composite Original**. How the whole image looked before you made a change.
- **Composite Modified**. How the whole image looks after you've done your tweaking.

The Settings drop-down menu lets you assign attributes for specific output devices. While LaserSepsPro ships with a handful of settings, you'll want to create your own settings so that you can calibrate to your specific output devices. Once you've tweaked the curves to perfection, click the OK button. A new dialog box will appear, as shown in Figure 2-4. This dialog box lets you name your separated file and specify either Photoshop or DCS formats. It also gives you the option of printing both a white plate and a flash plate.

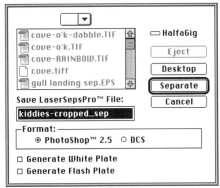

Figure 2-4: If you're going to be printing directly, choose the Photoshop format. But if you plan on bringing the image into QuarkXPress or Adobe PageMaker, choose the DCS format.

chapter 3

Second Glance PhotoSpot

Creator

Second Glance

Purpose

Color reduction, spot color separation

Platforms

Macintosh

Hardware/Software requirements

System 7.0.1 or later, 1 MB of RAM in addition to the Photoshop minimum, QuickTime recommended

URL/Contact info for creator of plug-in

http://www.secondglance.com
Second Glance
7248 Sunset Avenue NE
Bremerton, WA 98311
360/692-3694 voice
360/692-9241 fax

Products that the plug-in works with

Adobe Photoshop 1.07 or later, other programs that support the Photoshop plug-in standard

D o you create artwork for spot color printing? Need a better method for creating spot color separations from your scans? Second Glance PhotoSpot gives you the tools you need to perform intricate color reductions and create beautiful seps.

Who Should Use Second Glance PhotoSpot?

If you work on spot color print projects, Second Glance PhotoSpot will provide a handy selection of color separation tools. The audience for PhotoSpot includes graphic artists, designers, desktop publishers, quick printers, commercial printers, silk-screen printers, color trade shops, service bureaus, and newspapers.

What Second Glance PhotoSpot Does

Second Glance PhotoSpot includes the PhotoSpot export filter along with three wittily named color reduction filters to perform expert spot color photo separations: Acetone, PaintThinner, and Turpentine. Acetone provides quick and automatic color reduction, while PaintThinner offers a high level of control for hand-tuned results. Turpentine is specifically intended for creating eight-color diffusions.

Why Use Second Glance PhotoSpot?

Let's say that a new client walks into your shop and asks you to design a new brochure or perhaps a T-shirt design. He doesn't have any existing electronic artwork but provides you with a printed copy of his multicolor logo. With PhotoSpot, you can quickly convert a scan of his logo into a color separated image.

How Second Glance PhotoSpot Does It

Ready to get down to the nitty-gritty? Let's take a look at how the three-color reduction filters operate before we tackle the subject of file export. The color reduction filters work only when the original image is in RGB mode, as it is when you first acquire it from your scanner.

Using Acetone

To start Acetone, choose Filter | Second Glance | Acetone from Photoshop's menu bar. Enter the initial number of colors in the dialog box that appears. Specify the number of colors in your final printed piece, plus one (to allow for white). Add one more color if you need to drop out a background. When you click OK, Acetone analyzes the color content in the image. After it has completed analyzing the image, Acetone displays Original and Thinned views, as shown by Figure 3-1. The Thinned view provides an instantaneous preview of how the image will look with the current settings.

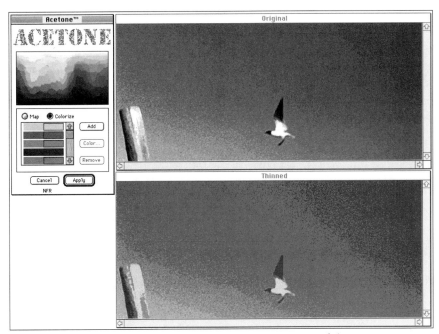

Figure 3-1: That sky needs a little work. We'll use Acetone to smooth it out.

The initial colors in the Acetone dialog box will be fairly neutral. You'll probably want to alter them to get a better preview of how the final printed piece will appear. By choosing a color and then clicking the Color button, you can alter the color with the system's color picker. In addition, you can use the eyedropper tool to select colors from the original image, or you can select them from the hue bar in the Acetone dialog box. As you alter the colors, the Thinned view changes to depict the alterations. To achieve more depth and realism, you may want to create additional colors. To add a new color to your image, click the Add button. To remove a color, select it and then click the Remove button.

While Acetone does a good share of the work for you, there's plenty of room for adjustments. To remap a color, select it from the list in the Acetone dialog box, and use the eyedropper to select the color you want to remap it to from the Original view. Once you have your image looking the way you want it to look, click the Apply button to apply the color changes. We'll learn how PhotoSpot will create the separated image files shortly.

Using PaintThinner

To start PaintThinner, choose Filter | Second Glance | PaintThinner from Photoshop's menu bar. When it starts, PaintThinner automatically uses a dithering algorithm to reduce the image's color palette to a maximum of 256 colors. After building a histogram of the image, the large PaintThinner dialog box appears. The preview area dominates the dialog box. The four buttons at the bottom of the dialog box allow you to switch between Original, Thinned, Selected, and Remaining color previews.

The Source Palette grid at the right side of the dialog box displays the original image colors, while below it, the scrolling Target Palette menu displays the thinned image colors. When the dialog box first appears, the Target palette will be empty, as shown in Figure 3-2. Notice that the colors in this image were reduced with Photoshop *before* launching PaintThinner, hence the limited palette.

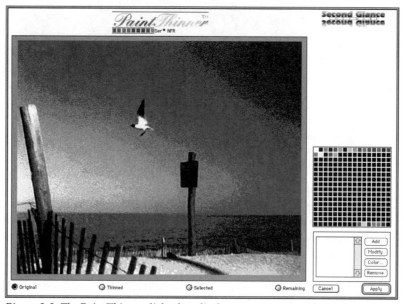

Figure 3-2: The PaintThinner dialog box displays a generous preview image, while the Source and Target palettes allow you to plow through the color reduction process with precision.

TIP *To avoid excessive dithering, you can use Photoshop's built-in color reduction feature by choosing Image | Mode | Indexed Color from Photoshop's menu bar; use an adaptive palette with the dithering option turned off. After you've converted to indexed color, you'll have to switch back to RGB mode to work with PaintThinner. You can also try Photoshop's Posterization option or Second Glance's own Chromassage for more intricate color palette manipulation.*

Thinning colors is a manual procedure. It's up to the operator to determine which source colors should be assigned to each target color. As with most things in the Photoshop realm, if you possess an eye for color and a good understanding of the printing process, it will definitely be to your advantage. Let's take a look at how to reduce the colors:

- **Creating new target colors**. You can select colors by clicking in the Source Color palette or by using the eyedropper tool in the preview window. Shift+click to select a range of colors, or use Command+click to select a number of individual colors. (Clicking on a currently selected color will deselect it.) Then, click the Add button to create the new target color. Once a source color has been assigned to a target color, a slash will appear through that color in the Source Color palette.

- **Editing existing target colors**. To edit an existing target color, choose that color in the Target Color palette and then click the Modify button. You can then add or remove source colors. As you click through the Target Color palette, you'll notice that the slashes on the Source Color palette colors will flip to the right if they make up part of the chosen target color.

- **Changing the hue of a target color**. You'll probably want to tweak the way that your target colors appear. Choose the color you want to change in the Target Color palette and then click the Color button to access the system color picker.

- **Removing target colors**. Do you have an extra target color? Just choose the color you want to delete in the Target Color palette and then click the Remove button to purge it from the Target Color palette.

TIP *Holding down the Command key while using the eyedropper will deselect the color (the eyedropper will turn upside down).*

Figure 3-3 shows our beach scene reduced to only six target colors, in a Thinned view. When you click the Apply button, the color reduction is applied to the original image.

Figure 3-3: Reduced to six colors, this scene might make a nice silk-screened T-shirt design.

Using Turpentine

Turpentine creates eight-color stochastic separations by adding red, green, blue, and white to the CMYK colors. There are no options to this filter. To start Turpentine, choose Filter | Second Glance | Turpentine from Photoshop's menu bar. Once Turpentine has converted your image into an eight-color stochastic-screened image, you'll use the PhotoSpot export function to create the separated files.

Exporting Files With PhotoSpot

To export your file with PhotoSpot, choose File | Export | PhotoSpot from Photoshop's menu bar. PhotoSpot analyzes the image and presents its color separation list for your approval. PhotoSpot is even polite enough to go to the trouble of assigning fairly descriptive names to your colors, as shown in

Figure 3-4. You can override the names with names of your own liking, or you can use numbers instead. You can also specify which individual plates you want to export from the scrolling menu.

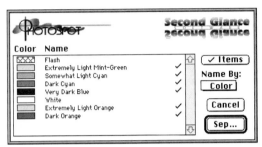

Figure 3-4: The PhotoSpot dialog box automatically assigns names to each color.

TIP *Always create your images at the exact size and resolution that will be used in the destination application to avoid any chance of distortion in the printed piece.*

When you click the Sep button, you'll be given the option of exporting the colors as separate files in either EPS, TIFF, or Photoshop format. Separations saved in EPS format offer the advantage of a single file that easily drops into the layout program. Most layout software will automatically add the colors in the EPS to the color palette, thereby allowing you to match other layout elements to the colors in the EPS.

If you choose multiple TIFF file separations, you will be able to match the PhotoSpot colors to existing colors in your layout. While we won't go into the specifics of setting up the separations in each application, let it suffice to say that this method requires importing, colorizing, stacking, and aligning the multiple images.

TIP *The PhotoSpot export filter can also be used to create index color separations. By using standard Photoshop techniques, you can reduce the number of colors in the image. PhotoSpot is then used to automate the actual separation process.*

chapter 4

Extensis
Intellihance 3.0

Creator
  Extensis

Purpose
  Instant image enhancement

Platforms
  Macintosh, Windows 95/NT 4.0

Hardware/Software requirements
  System 7.5 or higher, FPU

URL/Contact info for creator of plug-in
  http://www.extensis.com
  Extensis Corporation
  1800 SW First Ave, Ste. 500
  Portland, Oregon 97201
  503/274-2020 voice
  503/274-0530 fax

Products that the plug-in works with
  Mac: Adobe Photoshop 3.0.4 or later, Windows: Adobe Photoshop
  3.0.5 or later

Need to tune up your images in a hurry? No time to fiddle with levels, curves, balance, contrast, and a bunch of filters? No sweat! Extensis Intellihance lets you tweak your images like a pro—without forcing you to go through a printer's apprenticeship program. You might not end up with a union card, but you'll definitely end up with better looking images!

Who Should Use Extensis Intellihance?

Extensis Intellihance is appropriate for anyone working with RGB, CMYK, LAB, and grayscale images—from family photographers to print professionals. It appeals to the widest range of Photoshop users, including adverting agencies, designers, desktop publishers, graphic artists, hobbyists, multimedia developers, newspapers, quick printers, real estate offices, students, and Web developers.

What Extensis Intellihance Does

Extensis Intellihance provides one-button enhancement for print and online images. In addition to providing automatic descreening and despeckling controls, it automatically adjusts image contrast, brightness, saturation, cast, and sharpness. These attributes are fully adjustable to compensate for specific images and applications. This allows you to create custom presets to suit a specific printing press and paper stock.

Why Use Extensis Intellihance?

Preparing images for print can be an exhaustive process, as you plod through each individual step. Extensis Intellihance can make you more productive and free you from the drudgery. It lets you produce the best-looking photographic images in the least amount of time.

TIP *If you only prepare images for the Web and other online environments, check out Extensis PhotoTools. It includes Intellihance Lite, which is suitable for working with RGB images, although it lacks the descreening and cast removal controls found in the full version.*

How Extensis Intellihance Does It

Enough words! It's time to show you exactly what Intellihance can do. Let's open up a family in Photoshop—one that needs a bit of help. The kids in Figure 4-1 may be cute as buttons, but with an image this flat, soft, and dark, it's hard to tell. The original scanned image just doesn't cut it. After applying Intellihance's default settings, you can see (in Figure 4-2) that the little girl is a darling little ham and the boy is a precocious little imp. And how about that hair!

Figure 4-1: The original, unadjusted grayscale image.

Figure 4-2: The image after applying Intellihance's default settings.

At its simplest, the only piece of Intellihance you need to see is the QuickEnhance dialog box, shown in Figure 4-3. The Enhance Image button applies the last-used settings. Once you have your preferences set up, it's a one-click affair. To adjust Intellihance's settings, click the Preferences button.

Figure 4-3: For many images, the QuickEnhance dialog box is about as much of Extensis Intellihance as you'll have to see.

Setting General Preferences

The Preferences dialog box, shown in Figure 4-4, makes image optimization a
snap. The large preview area lets you toggle between corrected and original
views of the image, and the zoom tool and grabber hand provide a closer look.

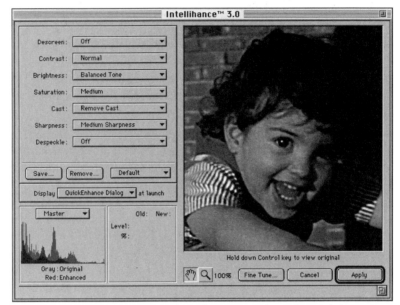

*Figure 4-4: The Preferences dialog box allows you to choose from existing presets
and make adjustments.*

At the bottom left, there's a before and after histogram and densitometer.
The set of seven drop-down menus at the top left of the dialog box allow you
to make general adjustments. These adjustments include:

- **Descreen**. Use this device to remove moirés from previously printed
  artwork. The settings here—Off, Auto Descreen, Newspaper, Magazine,
  and Fine Art—let you compensate for different kinds of halftone screens.

- **Contrast**. How much punch do you want to add to your image? You can
  choose from Off, Soft, Normal, Snappy, Hard Contrast, Flatten Shadows,
  and Flatten Highlights.

- **Brightness**. Where does your image need accentuation? Select from Off,
  Deeper Shadows, Shadow Emphasis, Balanced Tone, Midtone Emphasis,
  or Highlight Emphasis.

- **Saturation**. Do you want a little color or a lot? The Saturation controls can be set to Off, Low, Medium Low, Medium, Medium High, or High.

- **Cast**. We're not talking about that plaster of paris monstrosity from your skateboard accident in junior high—we're talking about color casts! These settings—Off, Purify Gray Balance, Remove Cast, and Aggressive Cast Removal—let you pull out the color skew from your image.

- **Sharpness**. Is your scan looking a little fuzzy and soft? This feature provides simplified unsharp masking controls and can be set to Off, Soft, Medium Sharpness, Hard Sharpness, or Extra Hard.

- **Despeckle**. This control lets you smooth out your image by removing extra noise. It can be set to Off, Overall, Dark Tones Only, or Light Tones Only.

Once you've dialed in your settings and have previewed them to your heart's content, you can save them to use over again. Just click the Save button to save the settings as a Preference preset. To apply Intellihance's settings to your image, click Apply.

TIP *If you're an inveterate image tweaker, you can set Intellihance to display Preferences or Fine Tune rather than QuickEnhance at start-up.*

Fine-Tuning Images

If your image needs just a little more adjustment than the general controls provide, it's time to click the Fine Tune button. A tabbed dialog with Fine Tune controls for Cast, Descreen, Despeckle, Saturation, Sharpness, and Tone will appear. (Cast and Saturation do not apply to grayscale images.)

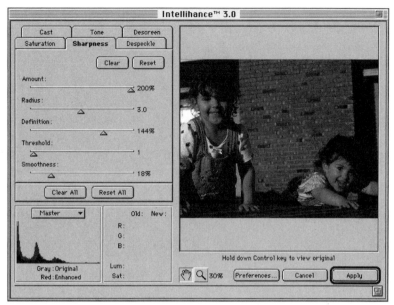

Figure 4-5: The Fine Tune controls let you take total command of your images.

With these controls, you'll need to know just a little bit more about image optimization, as they allow for more precision than the simplified menu choices:

■ **Cast**. You *can* eliminate those Martian greens and out-in-the-sun-too-long reds! The Cast controls allow you to adjust your image's overall hue, and it works in either RGB, CMYK, or Lab color modes. The eyedroppers let you quickly neutralize highlight, midtone, and shadow samples, while the sliders let you fine-tune each setting.

■ **Descreen**. This option aims to eradicate halftone dots by blending the original image with a blurry version of the image. You can adjust the descreening Amount and Radius controls. Try leaving the Amount setting on 100% while fiddling with the Radius slider.

■ **Despeckle**. Like Descreen, the Despeckle control blends a blurry image into the original. You can adjust the Threshold (edge recognition), Amount (blur), and Limits (both dark and light) settings.

■ **Saturation**. To lessen the amount of saturation (if there's too much color in the image), drag the slider to the left. To increase the amount of saturation (if the image is washed out), drag the slider to the right.

- **Sharpness**. Do you like your images mild or extra crispy? The Sharpness tab lets you control the amount (overall), radius, definition (in the shadows and midtones), threshold, and smoothness (excess noise) of your image.

- **Tone**. Need to tweak the overall Brightness and Contrast settings? The Tone tab lets you set the black point, the midtone, and the white point of your image, providing total control from the shadows through the highlights. Use the eyedroppers to set these attributes roughly and then fiddle with the individual sliders as necessary. There's even an Intelligent Light Meter that lets you select the image's foreground elements in order to let Intellihance know which are the most important sections of the image.

chapter 5

Magic Separator

Creator
Magic Software

Purpose
One-button RGB-to-CMYK conversion

Platforms
Macintosh

Hardware/software requirements
Same as Photoshop

URL/contact info for creator of plug-in
http://www.magicsoftware.com
Magic Software Company
360 Delaware Ave. #300
Buffalo, NY 14202
716/855-0295 voice
716/855-0299 fax

Products that the plug-in works with
Adobe Photoshop VERSION or later, as well as other programs that
support Photoshop VERSION's (or later) plug-in standard, including
Live Picture, and Equilibrium DeBabelizer

N eed to create process color separations for SWOP printing? Lack the four-color experience or the time necessary to do the very best job? Magic Separator pulls the rabbit out of the hat for laymen and journeymen alike. This export plug-in's approach to converting RGB files to CMYK files has won industry praise.

Who Should Use Magic Separator?

Magic Separator is appropriate for anyone who needs to create CMYK TIFF separations for SWOP printing, including printers, service bureaus, graphic artists, designers, prepress shops, newspapers, and other publications.

What Magic Separator Does

Magic Separator provides one-button, yet fully tweakable, RGB-to-CMYK conversions upon file export. It provides for a number of key separation functions, including gray component replacement (GCR), unsharp masking, and skeleton black generation.

Why Use Magic Separator?

Although Photoshop lets you perform RGB-to-CMYK conversion by merely switching color modes, the program does not optimize images in the process. It takes a significant amount of color knowledge and time to set up Photoshop for the best RGB-to-CMYK conversions. Magic Separator allows anyone to create great-looking four-color separations without the hassles.

How Magic Separator Does It

Magic Separator works as a TIFF export filter. Once you have your image looking great in the RGB color space, you merely choose File | Export | Magic Separator from Photoshop's menu bar. The plug-in will launch as it computes the best gamut and builds an image preview for the file at hand. The Magic Separator dialog box, shown in Figure 5-1, is relatively uncluttered, providing a simple approach for optimizing images.

TIP *This plug-in relies heavily on your having a calibrated display. The documentation provides instructions for performing internal, external, and average calibrations. The manner in which your monitor is calibrated has great bearing on Magic Separator's on-screen previews.*

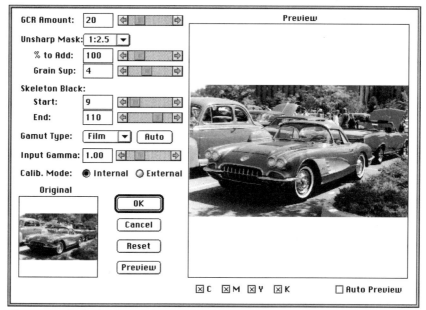

Figure 5-1: If it looks good in the Magic Separator dialog box, just click OK!

Once Magic Separator has computed its gamut setting and built an image preview, you can go ahead and click OK to create the CMYK TIFF, or you can tweak the individual controls. The settings include:

- **GCR Amount**. Gray component replacement removes equal amounts of cyan, magenta, and yellow and replaces them with black. This reduces the amount of ink on the page and can provide more shadow detail. This slider allows you to apply from 0 to 100% GCR.

- **Unsharp Mask**. While you can apply unsharp masking with the standard Photoshop filter, Magic Separator uses a different approach, letting you apply it on the fly while exporting your image. You can use different apertures (1:1.5, 1:2.0, 1:2.5, and 1:3.0), set the percentage from 0 to 500%, and apply grain suppression from 0 to 10.

■ **Skeleton Black**. Need to pump up the shadows? The Skeleton Black Start and End sliders let you add more detail and depth.

■ **Gamut Type**. You can manually set the Gamut Type—to Video, Film+, Film, Film-, or Print—or you can click the Auto button and let Magic Separator automatically calculate it for you.

■ **Input Gamma**. Although the Input Gamma slider can be adjusted from 0.50 through 2.50, Magic recommends sticking with a 1.0 setting.

■ **Calibration Mode**. Choose Internal or External, depending on whether you're separating images from your scanner or from various files, respectively.

The CMYK check boxes below the image preview area allow you to view individual separations as well as color composites. When you view individual plates, they are displayed as grayscale images. Flipping between the composite separations will make you feel as if you're looking at a transparency proof! Be forewarned, however: It's a good idea to use the Preview button and leave the Auto Preview check box unchecked, especially on slower Macs.

chapter 6

PANTONE MC-P/CoCo & Channel 24 by VISU Technologies

Creator

VISU technologies b.v.

Purpose

Advanced color correction tools, multichannel separation support

Platforms

Macintosh

Hardware/Software requirements

PowerPC processor, System 7.5 or later, 16MB of RAM

URL/Contact info for distributor of plug-in

http://www.pantone.com
Pantone, Inc.
590 Commerce Blvd.
Carlstadt, NJ 07072-3098
201/935-5500 voice
201/896-0242 fax

Products that the plug-in works with

Adobe Photoshop 3.0.4 or later

Want more control over RGB and CMYK color correction, with better softproofing? Do you work on high-end print jobs with bump and varnish plates? Would you like to create high-fidelity (Hi-Fi) color and Hexachrome images? MC-P/CoCo & Channel 24, a pair of plug-ins developed by VISU technologies of Amsterdam and distributed by PANTONE, Inc., answers all these questions.

Who Should Use PANTONE MC-P/CoCo & Channel 24?

Folks who work on serious color print projects, including graphic artists, commercial printers, color trade shops, service bureaus, prepress operators, and designers, will find PANTONE MC-P/CoCo & Channel 24 to be of great benefit.

What PANTONE MC-P/CoCo & Channel 24 Do

PANTONE MC-P/CoCo adds advanced color correction tools and soft proofing to Adobe Photoshop. The plug-in lets you make up to 16 independent color corrections. It also allows you to create up to 16 channels of color. Even though you can create additional channels in Photoshop, you cannot accurately view more than four channels of color. MC-P/CoCo lets you make accurate color decisions with additional spot colors. When the file is imported into the page layout application, the accuracy of the preview is controlled by PANTONE Channel 24.

Channel 24 adds Desktop Color Separation (DCS) 2.0 file format support to Photoshop. DCS 2.0 is a godsend for complicated print jobs that contain bump plates, varnishes, and spot colors. PANTONE Channel 24 opens and saves multichannel DCS 2.0 images. As its name implies, Channel 24 gives you the ability to save up to 24 channels with each image.

Why Use PANTONE MC-P/CoCo & Channel 24?

Do you want to avoid the expense and hassle of working with proprietary color workstations on projects that contain bump colors and varnishes? PANTONE MC-P/CoCo & Channel 24 let you attack those high-end print jobs with Adobe Photoshop and your Power Macintosh. This pair of plug-ins let you take control over multichannel projects and allows for Hexachrome six-color process printing.

How PANTONE MC-P/CoCo Does It

PANTONE MC-P/CoCo allows you to apply selective color correction without creating masks. A Preview window of the image will appear, along with the CoCo and Channel floating palettes, as shown in Figure 6-1. The CoCo palette provides up to 16 color corrections in the CoCo drop-down menu. Just select the color (source color) from the image that should be changed and enter color values or move the sliders to determine the destination color. You can also manipulate the range of color to be affected. MC-P/CoCo allows you to acquire color values by plugging into a spectrophotometer, as well. Once you've created a color correction set, you can save it for later use. The Channel palette allows you to add additional inks and view the file as it progresses.

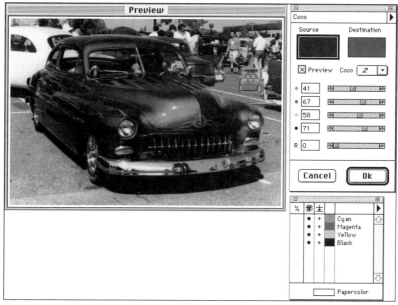

Figure 6-1: MC-P/CoCo's deceptively simple interface packs serious color correction smarts. We've changed this cruiser from burgundy to gold with just a few steps.

MC-P/CoCo's Preferences dialog box allows you to change the sample size—to pixel sample, 3 by 3 average, or 5 by 5 average—as well as control the preview attributes. CMYK composites can be viewed using either of MC-P/CoCo's Digital/Ink algorithms. You can display the preview window in three sizes, with the option of viewing the color channels in color. Digital Ink technology provides a simulation of the file with printed inks. You can display the preview window in three sizes, with the option of viewing the color channels in color.

The ink palette provides instant feedback with regard to color percentages as you move the cursor around in the preview window. You can turn channels on and off, and you can change ink types from transparent to overprint, set a paper color, edit existing color channels, and load inksets.

How PANTONE Channel 24 Does It

PANTONE Channel 24 is a format filter that allows you to load and save DCS 2.0 format files. Once you've created a DCS file, it can be placed into QuarkXPress or Adobe PageMaker. To save an image as a multichannel DCS 2.0 file, choose File | Save As, choose the DCS 2.0 format, and click Save. When the Channel 24/DCS 2.0 Options dialog appears, you'll have the ability to edit the individual color channels. Double-click a channel to summon the Channel dialog box.

The Channel dialog box provides control over the preview appearance of the channel in addition to specifying whether the channel is to be included in the DCS file. Specific colors are assigned to each channel by either adjusting the sliders or double-clicking on the color swatch to summon the Apple color picker. Setting colors with the Apple color picker is the slickest way to go, especially if you're using a spectrophotometer. This allows you to capture actual colors, whether they're from a swatch of custom ink or a swatch of fabric. Two of the most common spectrophotometers are the Light Source Colortron and Xrite Digital Swatchbook. You can control the preview opacity of each color on a scale from 0 (transparent) to 255 (opaque), and you can also prevent a channel from being visible in the preview (as when you're creating a varnish channel).

Channel 24 allows you to load previously created inksets from PANTONE ICISS by VISU Technologies and MC-P/CoCo in addition to those created with Channel 24. Although six channel images are displayed as PANTONE Hexachrome images by default, all inksets are fully editable.

chapter 7

ImageXpress ScanPrepPro

Creator

ImageXpress Inc.

Purpose

Automated image preparation

Platforms

Macintosh, Windows 95/NT (under development)

Hardware/Software requirements

7 MB hard disk space, Mac II or higher, System 7.5 or later, and Adobe
Photoshop 2.5 through 4.0 (68k compatible and PowerMac Native)

URL/Contact info for creator of plug-in

http://www.scanprep.com
ImageXpress Inc.
3545 Cruse Road
Suite 103
Lawrenceville, GA 30044
770/564-9924 voice
770/564-1632 fax

Products that the plug-in works with

Mac: Adobe Photoshop 3.0 or later

Need a helping hand creating images for print? ImageXpress calls ScanPrepPro a "Smart Agent Image Processor," but you can think of this impressive plug-in as a friendly ghost in the machine. ScanPrepPro deftly commandeers Adobe Photoshop and your scanner into producing high-quality, print-ready images.

Who Should Use ImageXpress ScanPrepPro?

ImageXpress ScanPrepPro is a blessing for anyone who needs to create the best scans possible for print work, including desktop publishers, graphic artists, designers, quick printers, and commercial printers as well as businesses such as service bureaus, prepress shops, newspapers, and other publications. ScanPrepPro is also very helpful when optimizing images for multimedia and Web design applications.

What ImageXpress ScanPrepPro Does

This plug-in takes over the helm of Adobe Photoshop, steering it through the tricky waters of print image preparation. Its automated approach works in conjunction with your scanner or digital camera to produce high-quality CMYK separations without the hassles. ScanPrepPro takes the complex jargon of the prepress world and translates it into layman's terms.

Why Use ImageXpress ScanPrepPro?

Are you unhappy with the quality of your process color separations and bogged down with a perplexing and inefficient workflow? ImageXpress ScanPrepPro provides a comprehensive and automated approach for scanning images for print. It removes much of the guesswork and, once configured, can compensate for a lack of in-depth prepress knowledge and operator experience.

How ImageXpress ScanPrepPro Does It

ScanPrepPro lets you sit back and watch as it creates the perfect image. You can work with previously scanned images as well as new scans. Let's take a look at how the plug-in works while scanning a new image. Choose File | Import | ScanPrep from Photoshop's menu bar to summon ScanPrepPro. The plug-in's dialog box, shown in Figure 7-1, allows you to quickly specify the settings for your scans.

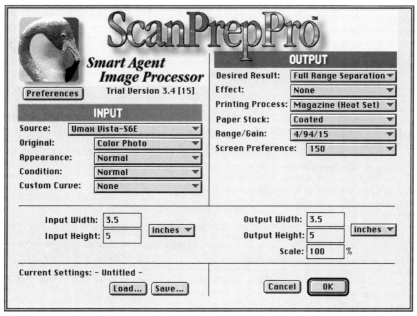

Figure 7-1: ScanPrepPro's dialog box provides a comprehensive list of choices for image optimization.

To achieve the best possible results, it's important to go through the Input and Output specifications methodically (in order). The Input settings include:

- **Source**. You can choose from a wide range of supported flatbed and transparency scanners.

- **Original**. Depending on what type of scanner and original image are at hand, you'll need to specify whether you're working with line art, b&w photo, color photo, transparency, b&w positive, b&w negative, color positive, or color negative.

- **Appearance**. What kind of shape is the original image in? You can choose from very light, light, normal, dark, and very dark.

- **Condition**. How crisp is the original? You can choose from normal, soft/blurry, or grainy. ScanPrepPro can also descreen previously printed images such as those in newspapers, magazines, and brochures.

- **Custom Curve**. Do you have prepress smarts? This is an option to override ScanPrepPro's profile of your selected scanner. If you have plenty of experience in color science, feel free to dive in! The Custom Curve option offers the flexibility that professionals demand from image optimization software.

Just below the Input menus, you'll see the Input Width and Height controls. You can enter the width and height of the original image along with the output width and height (or scaling percentage). By default, ScanPrepPro does not alter the proportions of a scan. The plug-in gets the scan's input width and height from the scanner driver's marquee selection.

The Output menus let you specify half a dozen important attributes:

- **Desired Result**. Depending on your needs, you can set this for line art, copydot/fineline (600 or 1200 dpi), halftone (dropout or full range), separation (dropout or full range), custom separation, RGB color, fax, or RGB archive.

- **Effect**. If desired, you can automatically set this control to provide a 30, 40, or 50 percent ghost image for typeovers.

- **Printing Process**. Choose from newspaper (web offset), magazine (heat set), and brochure (sheet fed) presses as well as a range of proofing devices and film recorders. In addition to the print choices, this setting can also be configured to prepare images for multimedia and Web page use.

- **Paper Stock**. What kind of stock will you be printing the image on? Depending on the press, you can choose from coated, uncoated, or newsprint.

- **Range/Gain**. If you're not sure what highlight and shadow range or dot gain percentages to use, stick with the defaults. If you do know what to use, however, you can specify these settings globally for all four plates, or you can tweak the colors individually.

- **Screen Preference**. What line screen will you use on the printed piece? ScanPrepPro takes an educated guess at the lines per inch (lpi) when you enter the type of printing process, but you can set it to any one of the 12 common screens in addition to specifying custom or stochastic screening.

TIP | *Once you've entered all the specifications, you'll probably want to save the current settings to use on subsequent images. Clicking the Save button will let you save the settings into ScanPrepPro's Custom Setting folder.*

Before you go on, you'll want to fully configure ScanPrepPro by clicking the Preferences button. The Preferences dialog box lets you specify a number of important settings, as shown by Figure 7-2. While many of these settings can ride at their defaults, you don't want to overlook a crucial step.

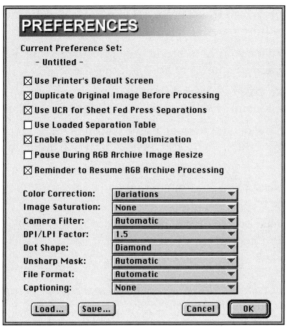

Figure 7-2: The Preferences dialog box allows you to fine-tune ScanPrepPro's automatic processing.

TIP *Intermediate and advanced users should at the very least select Photoshop's Variations color correction option. Anyone with a bit of color experience can use the option's graphic interface to achieve pleasing results.*

The Preferences dialog box includes drop-down menu choices for:

- **Color Correction**. What's your favorite way to color-correct? You can choose from Photoshop's Variations, Color Balance, Curves, Levels, Selective Color, or Replace Color functions. If you don't want to perform any manual color correction, choose None.

- **Image Saturation**. Need more saturation in your digital camera shots? Choose from settings of None, Manual, +5, +10, +15, +20, +25, +30, or +35%.

- **Camera Filter**. Want to knock down digital camera noise? You can choose Automatic, Quantum Mechanic, or None.

- **DPI/LPI Factor**. Which Dots Per Inch/Lines Per Inch ratio meets your needs? Choose from ratios of 1.0, 1.414, 1.5, 1.65, 1.8, and 2.0.

- **Dot Shape**. What's your house style? You can choose from Round, Diamond, Ellipse, Line, Square, or Cross halftone dots.

- **Unsharp Mask**. Need to crispen things up? You can specify Unsharp Masking as Automatic, 1/2 Automatic, 2X Automatic, or None.

- **File Format**. How do you normally save your files? ScanPrepPro lets you save your scans in EPS, PICT, TIFF, Scitex CT, JPEG, or Photoshop formats.

- **Captioning**. Need to add a comment? You can save captions with Photoshop File Info.

When you're finished with the Preferences dialog box, click OK to return to the main ScanPrepPro dialog box.

TIP *Don't forget to save your ScanPrepPro Preferences so that you can reuse them on subsequent scans. Clicking the Save button will let you save the settings into ScanPrepPro's Custom Preferences folder.*

When all the settings are entered, it's time to let ScanPrepPro go to work. When you click OK, ScanPrepPro will launch your scanner plug-in and perform a prescan. Just slide the presized marquee area over the portion of the image you want to scan. Do not resize the marquee lest ScanPrepPro distort the final image. Click your scanner plug-in's Scan (or OK) button, and the image will be acquired.

Once the image opens up in Photoshop, take a good look at it before you start up ScanPrepPro's automated Agent. When the Agent goes on its merry way, you'll feel as if Photoshop is running itself. ScanPrepPro will pause and wait for you to make your subjective color corrections using whichever method you specified in the Preferences dialog box. After you've made your color corrections, resume the Agent; then sit back and watch in awe as it literally flies through a myriad of Photoshop's dialog boxes. When ScanPrepPro is done, Photoshop will sit at the File Save dialog box, patiently wagging its tail as you merely name and save the optimized scan.

ScanPrepPro is equally adept at scanning line art with its copydot/fineline mode and black-and-white photos with its halftone mode. This plug-in is a well-proven partner in the prepress process and has garnered widespread acclaim with a host of five-star reviews.

chapter 8

Vivid Details
Test Strip

Creator
Vivid Details

Purpose
Color correction and proofing

Platforms
Macintosh

Hardware/Software requirements
Power Macintosh, System 7.1 or later

URL/Contact info for creator of plug-in
http://www.vividdetails.com
Vivid Details
8228 Sulphur Mtn. Rd.
Ojai, CA 93023
805/646-0217 voice
805/646-0021 fax

Products that the plug-in works with
Adobe Photoshop 3.0.5 or later, other programs that support the
Photoshop 3.0 plug-in standard in native PowerPC mode

D o you love Adobe Photoshop's Variations plug-in but wish it offered just a little more oomph? Vivid Details Test Strip makes color correction a breeze. The plug-in lets you perform interactive color correction in a "what-if" environment that picks up where Variations drops off.

Who Should Use Vivid Details Test Strip?

Vivid Details Test Strip is appropriate for color-correcting both print and online images. The plug-in should appeal to photographers, large format digital printers, multimedia developers, Web developers, designers, desktop publishers, graphic artists, commercial printers, quick printers, service bureaus, prepress shops, newspapers, and other publications.

What Vivid Details Test Strip Does

Vivid Details Test Strip works its color correction magic with both RGB and CMYK images. It provides five full-screen views of the image at hand, enabling you to interactively adjust an image with control over color balance, single color cast, exposure (brightness and contrast), and saturation. The plug-in lets you see the effects of different color correction settings with big juicy previews because it slices and dices your image into test strips, each with a different percentage of correction applied to it.

Why Use Vivid Details Test Strip?

Are you frustrated by your current color correction methods? Can't seem to get the color "just right"? Vivid Details Test Strip lets you see exactly how those tweaks will look, both onscreen and at your color proofing device.

How Vivid Details Test Strip Does It

Vivid Details Test Strip is both fun and easy to use. Choose Filters | Vivid Details | Test Strip from the Photoshop menu bar to launch the plug-in. The Test Strip dialog box will appear in Color Balance mode, as shown in Figure 8-1. The image will fill the preview area. You can zoom the image up or down with the + and - buttons just below the preview area. Notice how the image has been sliced into labeled strips separated by white lines. Try sliding the Color Balance

Amount slider up or down until you see a noticeable improvement in one of the strips. By rotating the color wheel, color overlays can be repositioned to preview color effects on different portions of the image.

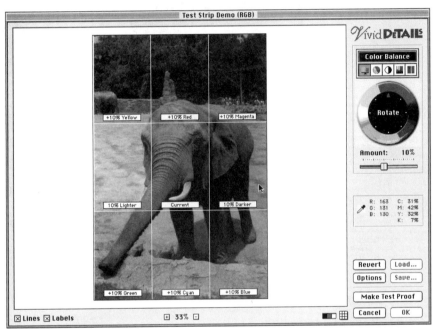

Figure 8-1: The Color Balance controls let you preview changes in single-degree increments from 1 to 25 percent. For greater percentages of change, simply apply multiple edits.

In addition to letting you lighten or darken the image, Color Balance mode allows you to add red, green, blue, cyan, magenta, or yellow. Once you find a Color Balance percentage that suits your fancy, click on that strip to load the correction into the current (center) slot. Then see if you can fiddle with the Color Balance some more. In practice, you might go through a number of Color Balance corrections before you move on to the next phase. Once you're happy with the image, click the One Color button (it's the second button at the top right of the dialog box) to switch to Test Strip's One Color correction mode, as shown in Figure 8-2.

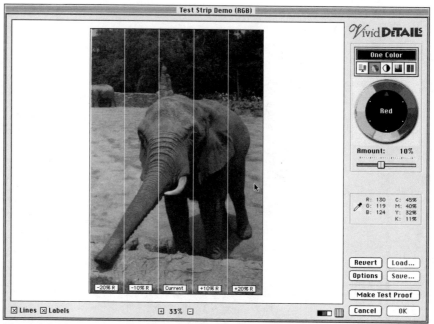

Figure 8-2: The One Color correction preview can be configured to display three or five strips in either horizontal or vertical mode.

TIP *You can check out how your image looks on black, gray, or white backgrounds by clicking on the appropriate square at the bottom right of the Test Strip dialog box.*

The One Color correction mode allows you to dial single colors in or out, providing the means to correct color casts. Just click on the color wheel to select a color, and adjust the Amount slider to an appropriate percentage. When you find a One Color correction mode that looks good, just click on it, and it will be added to the recipe. Take a spin through the color wheel to make sure you've got that image looking its best, and, when you're ready, click the third button at the top right of the dialog box to switch to Exposure mode, as shown in Figure 8-3.

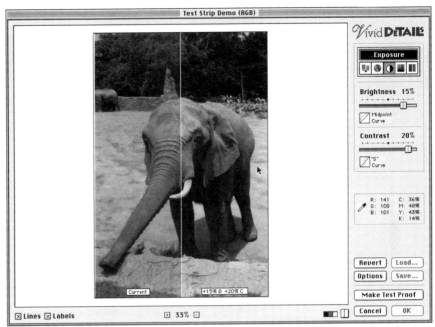

Figure 8-3: The Exposure preview can be configured to display the current and applied strips in either horizontal or vertical mode.

Exposure mode allows you to adjust the image's brightness and contrast. Both the Brightness and Contrast sliders operate from -25 percent to +25 percent. Once the image's exposure settings look right, click the Saturation button (the fourth button) to switch to Saturation mode, as shown in Figure 8-4.

TIP *While Test Strip's interface does not include Undo or Redo buttons, you can still undo and redo changes with a Command+Z or Command+Shift+Z, respectively. The plug-in allows you to perform unlimited undos and redos.*

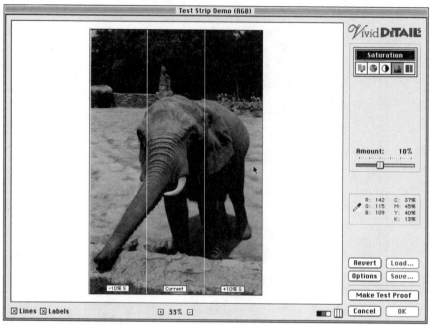

Figure 8-4: The Saturation preview can be configured to display three or five strips in either horizontal or vertical mode.

As a last step, you can adjust the image's Saturation level in one degree increments from 1 percent to 50 percent (in the five strip layout). As with all the other modes, you can use the eyedropper to check specific color percentages. After you're done adjusting the Saturation level, click the last button at the upper right side of the Test Strip dialog box to toggle into Before & After mode, as shown in Figure 8-5.

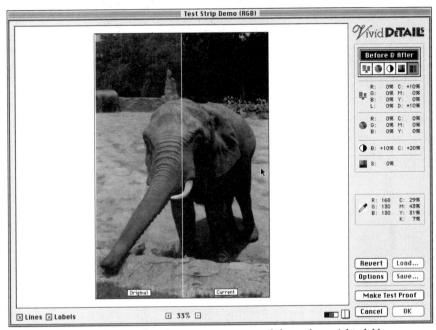

Figure 8-5: Your Before & After changes may appear subtle, or they might clobber you over the head. This is your chance to go back and tweak the settings one more time.

TIP

After you've become comfortable with the way Test Strip operates, you may want to turn the lines and labels off by deselecting the check boxes at the bottom of the dialog box.

The Before & After preview can be quite striking when it is viewed in horizontally or vertically split mode (there's a full image view as well). As you move through the process of color correcting an image, you're looking at just pieces of the image. When you switch to Test Strip's Before & After mode, however, you see the full impact of the cumulative changes you've made. The chart on the right side of the dialog box provides a full report on the changes and provides you with the information you need should you have to go back to fine-tune your color corrections.

To send a proof to a color output device, click the Make Test Proof button. This feature lets you output a Test Strip view to high-end devices, including Iris, Match Print, and Rainbow proofers as well as laser copiers and inkjet plotters. If you're working in a calibrated output environment, you should be able to depend on the Test Strip proofs to make your final tweaks.

Once you've worked with Test Strip for a while, you'll probably want to optimize the dialog boxes to match the way you work. The Options dialog box, shown in Figure 8-6, allows you to control the overall settings as well as the manner in which each mode window appears.

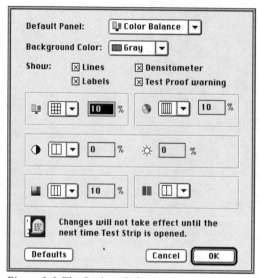

Figure 8-6: The Options dialog box lets you fine-tune Test Strip's interface to suit your working style.

Here's a rundown of the options:

■ **Default Panel**. Which mode do you want as the start-up panel? You can choose from Color Balance, One Color, Exposure, Saturation, or Before & After modes.

■ **Background Color**. Would you prefer to view the previews on a gray, white, or black background?

■ **Show**. Do you want to show lines, labels, densitometer information, or the Test Proof warning?

■ **Color Balance, One Color, Exposure, and Saturation**. How many strips do you want to view? What do you want to use as the default percentage?

■ **Before/After**. Do you want to view a horizontal or vertical split? How about a full image preview?

Part II

Optimizing Images for the Web

chapter 9

Second Glance PhotoCell

Creator

Second Glance

Purpose

Creates GIF and QuickTime animations

Platforms

Macintosh

Hardware/software requirements

Any Macintosh with a 68020 processor or better; System 7.5 or later; QuickTime 2.0 or later; Adobe Photoshop 3.0 or later; 4MB RAM assigned to Photoshop above Photoshop's minimum

URL/contact info for creator of plug-in

http://www.secondglance.com
Second Glance
7248 Sunset Avenue NE
Bremerton, WA 98311
360/692-3694 voice
360/692-9241 fax

Products that the plug-in works with

Adobe Photoshop 3.0 or later

Are you called upon to create GIF and QuickTime animations for Web sites and multimedia projects? Second Glance PhotoCell offers a unique interface that lets you complete your animations without ever leaving the Photoshop environment. With PhotoCell, you can take full advantage of Photoshop's layers to create awesome animation sequences.

Who Should Use Second Glance PhotoCell?

Second Glance PhotoCell will appeal to Photoshop-savvy Web site and multimedia developers who want to create animation without leaving Photoshop for a separate program.

What Second Glance PhotoCell Does

Second Glance PhotoCell lets you use Adobe Photoshop's layers to create anything from the simplest to the most complex animations. Layers provide the same flexibility found in traditional cel-based animation techniques. By using a series of overlaid cels, you can easily set up a background and foreground along with character actions.

Why Use Second Glance PhotoCell?

Most other animation programs require that you leave the Photoshop environment to complete your work. Second Glance PhotoCell, on the other hand, lets you assemble both your images and your animations within Photoshop. You add elements to your animations by simply dragging them from the Layers palette. With PhotoCell, the learning curve is short, and the benefits are enormous.

How Second Glance PhotoCell Does It

Think about your favorite animated cartoon and how it was built. It's likely that each frame of the cartoon uses a number of overlaid images. In most cases, you'll have a background, an actor, and some props. Like traditional animation, Second Glance PhotoCell lets you break each of those elements onto its own layer. This provides a high level of flexibility.

Now think about the animated GIF images you've seen on the World Wide Web—from splash screens to advertising banners. Many of these images are built with a static background that's been overlaid with a number of actors (even if those actors just consist of the words "Click Here!"). PhotoCell gives you the ability to apply traditional animation techniques to Web animations.

Let's take a look at how you might use Second Glance PhotoCell's layering technique to build a typical Web page banner advertisement. We've created a simple example that relies solely on text to get its message across. We started by creating a new Photoshop file with a black background, at the exact size of the banner (468 X 52 pixels). The text tool was used to create the headline. In this banner ad, each word pops into its own layer. We created five additional layers—for a total of six—as illustrated by Figure 9-1.

Figure 9-1: The progressive effect of this advertising banner is effective, yet easy to achieve. Note the WildRiverSSK MagicMask CutOut filter used on the word "through."

Once we completed the design, we saved the file in Photoshop format. PhotoCell is launched by choosing File | Export | PhotoCell from Photoshop's menu bar. PhotoCell looks at the layers in your image and creates its own little floating Layers palette. You'll drag layers from PhotoCell's Layers palette to its Filmstrip palette to build your animation. Figure 9-2 shows our advertising banner as it appears in PhotoCell.

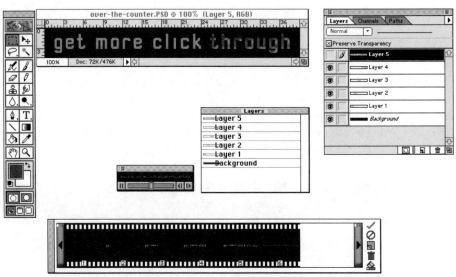

Figure 9-2: The filmstrip metaphor is easy to comprehend. Check out that cute little preview!

TIP *You can quickly create a new cell—complete with a background layer—by double-clicking on the background layer in PhotoCell's Layers palette.*

The Filmstrip palette provides simple controls. You can reorder the cels by simply clicking and dragging them to their new location. At the right side of the palette, the vertical column of icons allow you to:

■ **Create an animation**. Clicking the checkmark builds the animation.

■ **Cancel an animation**. Click on the icon to return to Photoshop.

■ **Create a new cel**. Clicking on this icon adds a blank cel.

■ **Delete a cel**. Click a cel to select it and then click the trashcan icon.

■ **Create a preview**. Click this icon and you'll be rewarded with a tiny little thumbnail preview of your animation.

You can also alter the layering order within each cel. Double-clicking on a cel summons a dialog box that provides the ability to change the stacking order of the layers, as shown in Figure 9-3. You can move each layer up or down, as well as delete layers.

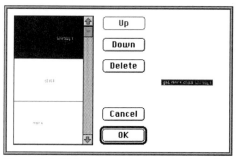

Figure 9-3: Did you want to move that lamp in front of the sofa? No problem! The layer order dialog box makes it easy to rearrange your animation furniture.

After you've previewed your animation and you're ready to make the final file, click the green checkmark icon. A dialog box will appear, allowing you to name your animation and choose from either animated GIF or QuickTime formats. There are different options for each format:

- **Animated GIF**. The frame rate can be set in seconds per frame or frames per second. Animations can be set to loop in HTML browsers and can have white set to be transparent.

- **QuickTime**. The frame rate can be set in seconds per frame or frames per second.

TIP *While PhotoCell is not designed to open existing animated GIF files, you can use it in conjunction with BoxTop PhotoGIF for the ultimate in GIF animation and editing flexibility.*

chapter 10

BoxTopPhotoGIF Plug-in

Creator
BoxTop Software

Purpose
Creates and edits Web-ready GIFs and GIF animations

Platforms
Macintosh

Hardware/Software requirements
Adobe Photoshop 3.0 or greater

Requirements
Same as Photoshop

URL/Contact info for creator of plug-in
BoxTop Software
PO Box 2347
Starkville, MS 39759
601/324-1800 voice
800/257-6954
601/323-7352 fax

Products that the plug-in works with
Any application that is Photoshop 3.0 plug-in compliant

Want to take command over your GIF images? BoxTop's PhotoGIF plug-in creates single image and animated GIF files with the highest degree of control and accuracy.

Who Should Use BoxTop PhotoGIF?

Web site and multimedia developers interested in squeezing and tweaking their GIF files to the nth degree will find this plug-in indispensable.

What BoxTop PhotoGIF Does

PhotoGIF creates Web-ready GIF images, as it takes command over palettes, transparency, and animation attributes.

Why Use BoxTop PhotoGIF?

The standard Photoshop 4.0 GIF export dialog box provides a limited amount of functionality for creating images for the Web. Although it allows you to index colors while exporting, for the best results you'll want to manually convert an RGB image to indexed color (using the Netscape palette) and then cut down the number of colors *before* you save it as a GIF file. Cutting down the size of the palette results in smaller files. Among other niceties, BoxTop PhotoGIF allows you to perform the palette conversion and color reduction as you export the file. This adds a touch of convenience while delivering a much higher degree of control.

How BoxTop PhotoGIF Does It

BoxTop PhotoGIF works magic with file imports as well as exports.

Opening GIF Files

PhotoGIF will open any GIF file, regardless of flavor. And best of all, animated GIF files are a strong suit. Once you've loaded PhotoGIF into the acquire/ export folder, it will automatically open all GIF files using the filter (rather than Photoshop's standard GIF filter). PhotoGIF's import capabilities allow you to open up and edit animations in a variety of ways. Let's take a look at the different options for opening animated GIF files in PhotoGIF:

- **Editing a Single Image.** You'll want to choose this option when you only need to work on one frame of an animation. When you edit a single frame in this manner, the rest of the animation is left intact.

- **Editing a Cell-Strip.** This option lets you see all of a GIF animation's frames at once (either horizontally or vertically). It's particularly useful for comparing the differences between frames.

- **Extract Single Image.** Want to open a single frame of an animation into its own file? Choosing this option will open a new GIF file and leave the original animation file untouched.

- **Extract All Images.** Select this option when you want to open all the frames of an animated file into single frame files.

When you are working with multiframe files, PhotoGIF's Open Image dialog box lets you preview and cycle through the individual frames. And if you open up a multi-image GIF file with multiple palettes, PhotoGIF allows you to choose the specific palette you want to use.

Saving GIF Files

PhotoGIF puts you in the driver's seat by using a series of file export dialog boxes. Once you're done creating your RGB artwork, you'll need to save the image using the PhotoGIF export option. The first dialog box, as shown by Figure 10-1, lets you choose the color reduction and palette settings.

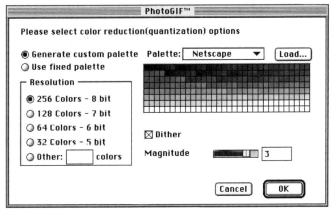

Figure 10-1: The fewer colors you specify, the smaller the exported file should be.

You can generate a custom palette from the image or use a fixed system, grayscale, or Netscape palette. You can also load a custom palette from a GIF or CLUT file. Being able to use a palette from an existing GIF file is a handy option when you need to lock a number of Web page images into the same exact palette.

The Resolution setting governs the size of the palette. PhotoGIF has 8-, 7-, 6-, or 5-bit presets in addition to providing the ability to specify a precise number of colors. Although using more colors may result in a better-looking GIF image, it will increase the size of the file. The plug-in defaults to an 8-bit (256 color) palette.

Dithering will smooth out the shifts in color, although it too will increase the size of the exported image. PhotoGIF provides variable dithering (as opposed to most other applications, which merely allow you to choose between dithering and no dithering). The dithering magnitude can be set anywhere from -5 to 5. You may want to fiddle with this setting to achieve the best results when creating images with lots of color variations. BoxTop recommends a dithering setting between 0 and 3. Once you've specified the dithering magnitude, click OK to bring up the next dialog box, shown in Figure 10-2. BoxTop refers to this as the Single Image Options dialog box.

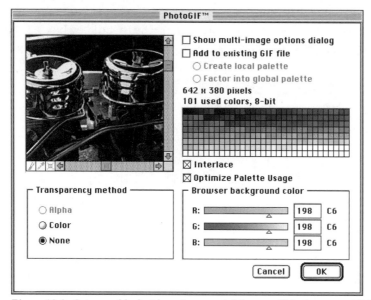

Figure 10-2: Get a good look at how the exported image will look on your Web page.

The Single Image Options dialog box allows you to execute a number of key procedures. Most importantly, the preview window allows you to assign and fine-tune image transparency. You can specify alpha channel, color, or no transparency. If you choose the alpha channel option, a pop-up menu allows you to select an alpha channel (if the image does not contain any alpha channels, this option will be grayed out).

Once you've selected a transparency method, PhotoGIF allows you to use three tools to achieve total control over transparency. In this respect, PhotoGIF far exceeds what you'll see in other GIF export situations. The transparency tools include:

- **Eyedropper tool.** Use this tool to select the dominant transparent color. As you click around the image, the preview window will show how the transparent image will appear on your Web page background.

- **Brush tool.** This tool is great for removing speckles and other anomalies in the transparent area.

- **Edge tool.** Want to get rid of the dreaded "halo" or "dandruff" effect that can result from anti-aliasing? The Edge tool provides an automatic means to a "halo-less" end. Just click around the edges of the image area, and the tool will do the hard work for you!

To the right of the preview window, you'll see the image size and palette along with check boxes for interlacing and palette optimization. Interlacing is cool for single-frame images as it provides that all-too-familiar "fade-in" effect for downloaded Web page graphics. Interlacing is not cool for animated GIFs, however. Use palette optimization to squeeze out duplicate and unnecessary colors, but use it with caution. While it will shave bytes, it may also degrade image quality.

The Show Multi-Image Options Dialog and Add to Existing GIF File options are used when creating (or editing) animated GIFs. If you're working with a single frame GIF file, leave these options unchecked. If you select Show Multi-Image Options Dialog, Photoshop will display this dialog box when you click OK. Selecting Add to Existing GIF File will enable the Create Local Palette and Factor Into Global Palette options. Create Local Palette will save a new palette with each frame, while Factor Into Global Palette will create a super palette that encompasses all the frames in an animation.

At the bottom right of the dialog box, you can set the browser background color to get an accurate preview of how the transparent image will appear on the Web page. This is a welcome touch, as GIF images will appear differently when viewed on disparate backgrounds. As such, it's always best to preview transparent GIFs on the background color that they will be placed upon.

The Multiple Image Options dialog box, shown in Figure 10-3, provides control over GIF animation settings.

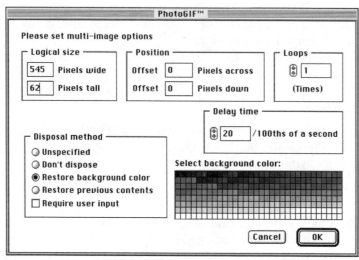

Figure 10-3: PhotoGIF's Multiple Image Options dialog box lets you take charge of your animated GIFs.

These options include:

- **Logical Size.** Defines the height and width of the entire animation space, and should be set to be at least as large as the largest frame.

- **Position.** Controls the horizontal and vertical offset of an individual frame within the animation space. Individual frames are often smaller than the entire space.

- **Loops.** Determines the number of times you want the animation to play before stopping.

- **Disposal Method.** Allows you to choose from Unspecified, Don't Dispose, Restore Background Color, Restore Previous Contents, and Require User Input options for each frame of an animation. These options may or may not be supported by the Web browsers.

- **Delay Time.** Governs the amount of time (in hundredths of a second) that a frame is displayed.

- **Background Color.** Determines the color of the overall image space. This option is essential when creating animation files with individual frames that are smaller than the overall image space.

chapter 11

BoxTop ProJPEG Plug-in

Creator

BoxTop Software

Purpose

Creates progressive JPEG files

Platforms

Macintosh

Hardware/Software requirements

Adobe Photoshop 3.0 or greater

Requirements

Same as Photoshop

URL/Contact Info for creator of plug-in

http://www.boxtopsoft.com
BoxTop Software
PO Box 2347
Starkville MS 39759
601/324-1800 voice
800/257-6954
601/323-7352 fax

Products that the plug-in works with

Any application that is Photoshop 3.0 plug-in compliant

Need to create progressive JPEG files? BoxTop's ProJPEG plug-in provides the control you need to optimize photographs for the Web.

Who Should Use BoxTop ProJPEG?

Web site and multimedia developers that need to create progressive JPEG images will find BoxTop ProJPEG to be quite handy.

What BoxTop ProJPEG Does

Progressive JPEG images are akin to Interlaced GIF images in that they seem to fade into view as a Web page is downloaded. This fade-in effect gives Web surfers the instant gratification of seeing an image before it has finished downloading. ProJPEG creates tight, optimized progressive JPEG images with little fuss.

Why Use BoxTop ProJPEG?

While Photoshop 4.0 includes progressive JPEG import and export capabilities, it delivers only the basics. Earlier versions of Photoshop, as well as other image editing programs, lack progressive JPEG support.

How BoxTop ProJPEG Does It

The ProJPEG Export dialog box, as shown in Figure 11-1, uses an uncluttered and easy-to-comprehend interface. To get a good feel for how the exported image will look, the preview area displays a 100 percent view of the image. As you change the compression-to-quality slider, the preview will change, as will the approximate data size and compression ratio.

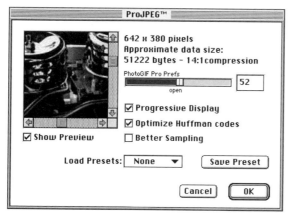

Figure 11-1: With ProJPEG's interactive data size readout, you'll be able to approximate the file size before you export it.

The compression-to-quality slider allows you to fine-tune your images with a range of 0 to 100, although BoxTop recommends using a setting between 10 and 90. The dialog box includes a number of check boxes:

- **Show Preview.** Turning the preview off will speed up the file size/ compression reporting (but since you can't see what the file will look like, you'll probably leave this option selected).

- **Progressive Display.** Deselecting this check box gives you the option of saving as a plain-vanilla (non-progressive) JPEG, should you desire.

- **Optimize Huffman codes.** Selecting this option will compress your file a skoosh more by using an image-specific Huffman compression table. Go the extra mile, squeeze out the last byte, and be prepared to spend a tad more time on the export as the plug-in creates the table.

- **Better Sampling.** Select this option to achieve a higher quality level, but be prepared to take a little hit as the file size increases.

If you're creating a number of similar images, you'll want to check out ProJPEG's presets. You can dial in a specific level of compression (and options) to use on subsequent files. This time-saving feature allows you to avoid the tedium of reconfiguring the dialog box with each export.

chapter 12

Digital Frontiers's HVS JPEG 2.0 Plug-in

Creator

Digital Frontiers

Purpose

High-performance JPEG compression

Platforms

Windows 95/NT, Macintosh

Hardware/Software requirements

Same as Photoshop

Requirements

Same as Photoshop

URL/Contact info for creator of plug-in

http://www.digfrontiers.com
Digital Frontiers
1206 Sherman Ave.
Evanston, IL 60602
847/328-0880 voice
847/869-2053 fax

Products that the plug-in works with

Any application that is Photoshop 3.0 plug-in compliant

Need to create tight JPEG images for the Web? Check out Digital Frontiers's HVS JPEG 2.0. This plug-in provides a high level of control over JPEG file exports.

Who Should Use HVS JPEG?

Web site developers (and other folks) interested in achieving the highest levels of JPEG compression will love HVS JPEG.

What HVS JPEG Does

HVS JPEG uses proprietary HVS preprocessing technology in conjunction with a progressive JPEG encoder, allowing you to create optimized JPEG files. It applies a range of options to the exported JPEG file while leaving the original image untouched.

Why Use HVS JPEG?

JPEG file compression always involves a trade-off between file size and image quality. The trick is to decide how much of one you are willing to give up in order to gain the other. Photoshop's JPEG Options dialog box, shown in Figure 12-1, is fairly limited; it allows you to simply choose a quality level of 1-10 along with some basic options. This may get the job done, but it doesn't provide much in the way of fine-tuning.

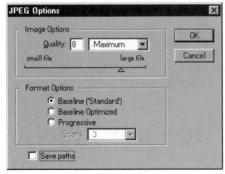

Figure 12-1: Photoshop's JPEG Options dialog box delivers limited export features.

HVS JPEG, on the other hand, provides the highest level of control over JPEG exports, going far beyond the basic capabilities that are built into Photoshop. It does this in a highly interactive dialog box complete with a convenient image preview.

How HVS JPEG Does It

HVS JPEG's preprocessing settings let you modify an image while you export it. Its dialog box, shown in Figure 12-2, provides a flexible range of options. The Prefilter, Q-Table, and Q-Setting options allow you to tweak each image according to content.

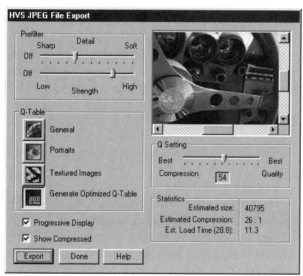

Figure 12-2: The HVS JPEG dialog box lets you preview your JPEG images.

HVS JPEG's Prefilter option does its magic *before* the image is compressed. Proper use of the prefilter enables you to compress images to the highest degree without sacrificing image fidelity. The prefilter softens busy image areas while leaving edges untouched. The less detail, and the smoother an area, the more compression you'll be able to achieve. The Prefilter option is set to trade off between sharpness and softness. Once you determine how much detail you want to preserve, you can experiment with different strength settings.

After you specify the prefilter settings, it's time to set the Q-Table. JPEG compression uses Quality Tables to know how to squeeze an image. The majority of JPEG encoders do not allow you to use specific or customized Q-Tables. HVS JPEG takes the high road by providing three different Q-Table preset options:

- **General.** Use this option when you're content to simply point and shoot.
- **Portraits.** Showing lots of skin? Choose this option to get smooth fleshtones while eliminating sharp details (like those pesky wrinkles).
- **Texture.** Select this option when you need to show lots of fine textures.

For situations when you want the ultimate in control, you should use the Generate Optimized Q-Table option. While your computer may take a little bit of time to crunch the numbers, the resulting file should be worth the few extra seconds.

Setting the Progressive Display option saves files in progressive JPEG format. The progressive JPEG format is supported by the latest versions of Netscape Navigator and Microsoft Internet Explorer. Earlier version of Navigator and Explorer (as well as other browsers) may not support this format.

Clicking the Show Compressed check box allows you to toggle between compressed and uncompressed previews. This comes in handy on smaller displays. On high-resolution displays (with plenty of real estate), you can always position the dialog box so that both the original image and the dialog box are visible.

HVS JPEG lets you choose a Q-Setting (quality setting) from 1-100, thus providing far more control than the built-in Photoshop JPEG export. This delivers 10 times the control (not 10 times the quality).

The Statistics area tells you the estimated size, compression, and load time (with a 28.8 modem) before you export your file. This information is essential for Web designers who are conscious of their visitor's experience. Having these statistics in the dialog box gives you the real-world means to gauge how much compression or quality you're willing to sacrifice. And they save the time you've probably spent exporting, opening, and re-exporting with the standard JPEG filter.

chapter 13

Digital Frontiers's HVS ColorGIF Plug-in

Creator

Digital Frontiers

Purpose

Color reduction and GIF export

Platforms

Windows 95/NT, Macintosh

Hardware/software requirements

Same as Photoshop

URL/contact info for creator of plug-in

http://www.digfrontiers.com
Digital Frontiers
1206 Sherman Ave.
Evanston, IL 60602
847/328-0880 voice
847/869-2053 fax

Products that the plug-in works with

Any application that is Photoshop 3.0 plug-in compliant

Looking for the smallest file sizes and the most accurate color in your GIF images? Digital Frontiers's HVS ColorGIF delivers a host of features that you won't find in Photoshop's indexed color conversion and GIF export filter.

Who Should Use HVS ColorGIF?

Webmasters, designers, and artists looking for an advanced level of control over GIF file exports will find HVS ColorGIF to be of great interest.

What HVS ColorGIF Does

HVS ColorGIF gives you the tools you need to go in and tweak your GIF files to the utmost degree. It consists of two plug-ins: a color reduction filter and a file export filter. This approach differs from most in that it allows you to dissect your Photoshop files by applying the color reduction filter to individual layers or objects. When you're ready to create the GIF file, the export filter provides a high level of control, as well.

Why Use HVS ColorGIF?

Savvy Web developers know that less is always more when it comes to GIF file sizes. The smaller your GIFs, the faster your Web pages will load. HVS ColorGIF offers a unique solution for folks who are fanatical about getting accurate color and the smallest GIF file sizes.

How HVS ColorGIF Does It

There are a handful of key factors that affect the file size of a GIF image. Chief among them is the number of colors in a file's color palette. If you've been creating GIF files for a while, you're probably familiar with Photoshop's Indexed Color dialog box. This dialog box allows you to reduce color depth and apply dithering, but it's a rather blunt tool. The built-in Photoshop color reduction capabilities do not provide an interactive preview, nor do they allow for serious control over the dithering process. And most importantly, they only allow you to apply the changes to the entire flattened image.

In contrast, HVS ColorGIF's two filters allow for a range of flexibility in reducing color palettes while maintaining image quality. By allowing you to work on individual layers and selections, HVS ColorGIF lets you optimize your image. You can apply different dithering and color reduction options to different parts of your image, as required. Let's take a look at how the color reduction filter works.

The HVS ColorGIF Options dialog box, shown in Figure 13-1, puts all the controls close at hand. The preview area at the top right of the dialog box allows you to keep an eye on how the image will look, while file information is provided just below. This provides a running tab on the number of colors, the number of unused colors, the file size, and the compression ratio.

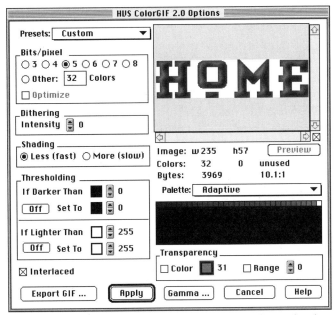

Figure 13-1: HVS ColorGIF's dialog box provides both visual and numerical feedback when performing color reductions.

TIP *You should always pay close attention to the number of unused colors; it's often a clue that you can use a lower number of bits per pixel to slash the file size.*

Here's a rundown on the individual controls:

- **Presets**. After you've created a color reduction profile, you can save it as a preset to subsequently apply it to additional images.

- **Bits/pixel**. You can specify from 3 through 8 bits per pixel in addition to a specific number of colors.

■ **Dithering**. Intensity can be set from 0 (no dithering) to 100. Generally, the less dithering, the smaller the file; and the more dithering, the smoother the shading.

■ **Shading**. Use More Shading with images that contain a number of gradient color transitions for more accuracy. For less demanding images, Less Shading will do the trick.

■ **Thresholding**. These settings provide the means to prevent images from getting too dark or washing out.

■ **Interlaced**. Do you want the image to "fade in" to your Web page or come in all at once? Selecting the Interlaced option turns transparency on.

■ **Palette**. This option allows you to specify either custom, adaptive, Netscape, Mac system, or Windows system palettes. The exact palette is automatically selected when working with an image that contains less than 256 colors. Working on GIF animations or a multimedia project? Select HVS Multi to create a MultiPalette that will factor a number of images to create an optimum palette. This procedure looks at all the images, then builds one palette based upon the colors in all of the images.

■ **Transparency**. HVS ColorGIF offers some interesting transparency options. In addition to being able to assign transparency to one color, the plug-in also allows you to shift-click additional transparent colors from the palette display. You can also dial in a range of transparency—the higher the range, the more transparent the colors. Transparency is only applied to the exported GIF, not the original RGB image.

chapter 14

Ulead's GIF/JPEG SmartSaver

Creator
Ulead Systems

Purpose
GIF and JPEG optimization

Platforms
Windows 95/NT

Hardware/Software requirements
Same as Photoshop

URL/Contact info for creator of plug-in
http://www.ulead.com
Ulead Systems, Inc.
970 West 190th Street
Suite 520
Torrance, CA 90502
310/523-9393 voice
310/523 9399 fax

Products that the plug-in works with
Any application that is Photoshop 3.0 plug-in compliant

When creating images for the Web, small files are where it's at. If you're a Windows-based Web designer, you'll love Ulead's GIF/JPEG Smart Saver. This pair of export plug-ins allows you to quickly experiment with color levels and compression options to achieve the smallest GIF and JPEG files.

Who Should Use GIF/JPEG SmartSaver?

Quality-conscious Windows-based Web site developers that need to create small GIF and JPEG files.

What Ulead's GIF/JPEG SmartSaver Does

Ulead's GIF/JPEG SmartSaver allows you to view a wide range of results before exporting your images in GIF or JPEG format. It uses a convenient batch-processing technique that lets you quickly compare one compressio-recipe to the next. The GIF plug-in also provides a high level of control ove transparency and can accept set transparency using Photoshop layer masks.

Why Use GIF/JPEG SmartSaver?

The faster your Web pages download, the happier your visitors will be. GIF/JPEG SmartSaver lets you create small image files that download quickly. SmartSaver is conveniently sold as one product—providing support for both GIF and JPEG formats—unlike other Web optimization plug-ins that may be sold as separate products.

How Ulead's GIF/JPEG SmartSaver Does It

Although SmartSaver consists of two modules, they share much of the same interface. You'll want to use the GIF module when creating images with lots of flat colors, such as logos and graphics. Use the JPEG module when creating photographic images or artwork with large variations in color. To save an image using a SmartSaver export filter, you'll need to choose File | Export and select the appropriate module.

Let's take a look at how SmartSaver's GIF export works.

Creating GIF Files With SmartSaver

The GIF SmartSaver dialog box, shown in Figure 14-1, puts all the controls easily within reach. Large "before-and-after" previews show how the image will appear, while the compression readout reports on both the size and ratio of the compressed file. A row of buttons below the preview window provides zooming and preview options, including a full-screen preview. You can even specify a GIF Web page background of your choice. This feature is particularly handy when creating transparent GIF images. If you're working with large images, you also have the option of turning the real-time preview off to speed things up.

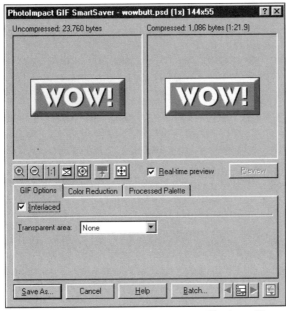

Figure 14-1: Ulead's GIF SmartSaver provides immediate feedback as you manipulate the image controls.

The three dialog tabs display GIF Options, Color Reduction controls, and the Processed Palette.

The GIF Options tab shows options for images to be saved as either interlaced or non-interlaced. Transparency (if desired) can be selected from colors within the image. Multiple colors can be specified to be transparent by Ctrl+clicking (or dragging) with the eyedropper. This lets you take full control over transparency by eliminating any random noise. Transparency can be inverted and may be specified by another GIF file as well.

The Color Reduction tab is where you'll be able to really fine-tune the image for the smallest possible file. Consider these options:

- **Smooth (none-to-10).** Controls how colors blend together. You'll want to experiment with this option, but it's best to keep your choices low on the scale to avoid image distortion.

- **Palette.** Lets you specify a color palette by choosing either an optimized, Netscape Navigator, Microsoft Internet Explorer, or specific palette (from another file). Although an optimized palette will use colors from the original image and will often result in the best-looking file, the Web rule of thumb has been to use the Netscape palette to achieve the most consistent results from browser to browser.

- **Image Colors.** Allows you to specify from 16 to 216 colors, with the smallest numbers of colors producing the smallest files and the largest number of colors producing the largest files. The more colors you use, the more accurate the final image may appear. There are definite trade-offs in file size, however.

- **Dither.** Can be set to Diffusion, Pattern, or None. This setting controls color transitions by simulating the appearance of more colors than are actually present in the chosen palette.

The Processed Palette tab displays each color in the image palette as determined by the settings in the Color Reduction tab. Once you've created a palette, you can save it to use on subsequent images to achieve exact results over a number of files.

One thing that really sets GIF/JPEG SmartSaver apart is its use of batch processing to let you visually select the best output options. Clicking on the Batch button at the bottom of the main dialog box brings up the Batch dialog box. This dialog box allows you to specify the minimum and maximum number of colors in your test images. You can choose to perform either a set number of tests, or you can test by an increment of colors. Figure 14-2 demonstrates how the dialog box can be set up to test from 16 to 216 colors in increments of 16 colors. Once the settings have been dialed in, just click the OK button and let SmartSaver go to work.

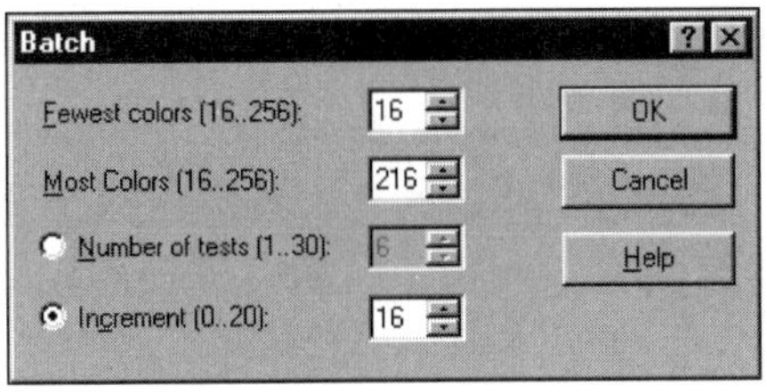

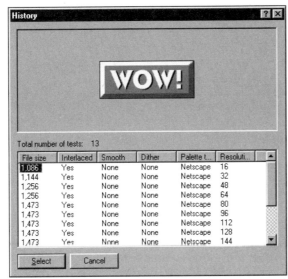

Figure 14-2: The Batch dialog box lets you set up the parameters of your test.

After SmartSaver has finished creating the test images, it will open the batch History dialog box, shown in Figure 14-3. Here you can sort the images by the various options, and thus you are able to quickly compare both the file size and image quality. In this test, we were able to achieve a file size of 1086 bytes at 16 colors. The largest file was almost twice as large, at a size of 1931 bytes at 216 colors. The difference in image quality was negligible since very few colors were actually used in the image. The more colors there are in an original image, however, the more dramatic the size savings (and loss of image quality) will be.

Figure 14-3: The batch History dialog box displays a list of all of the test images.

To save the file, double-click on it in the History list. The History list will go away, and the specified options will appear in the main dialog box. Click Save As to save the new GIF file.

Creating JPEG Files With SmartSaver

JPEG SmartSaver works in much the same manner as its GIF stablemate with regard to image previews and batch operations. The basic difference between the two is that the tabbed GIF dialog is replaced with a set of JPEG compression options, shown in Figure 14-4.

Figure 14-4: SmartSaver's JPEG options allow you to visually gauge the trade-off between compression and quality.

The Compression options far exceed what's built into Photoshop 4.0 and many other image editors. Let's take a look at what each feature provides:

■ **Smooth.** This setting may help you to achieve a slightly higher level of compression on certain images by easing the transition between colors.

■ **Mode.** Choose either Progressive, Standard, or Standard Optimized. Note that early Web browsers do not support progressive JPEG.

■ **Quality.** You can set the quality/compression level by either dragging the slider or entering a specific value. Ulead recommends starting with a quality level of 60 on most images.

■ **Subsampling.** This setting governs how color information is grouped and cast off. Select 4-1-1, 4-2-2, or None. 4-1-1 will provide the most compression, although image quality may suffer. 4-2-2 is the middle ground and usually provides a decent trade-off between file size and compression. Reducing the subsampling (i.e., 4-1-1) is most visible in red colors.

SmartSaver's Batch feature is particularly useful when saving JPEG images. In general, JPEG file size savings are quite dramatic. The Batch feature allows you to quickly browse through the compression options. You can bounce between different Smoothing and Subsampling options, for example, while building a hefty History list from which you'll make your final choice.

And for the ultimate in point-and-shoot ease, SmartSaver even provides a Compress by Size option that allows you to merely plug in a target file size. Just specify how large you want the exported image to be, and SmartSaver will do the math for you, selecting the compression options necessary to meet your goal.

TIP *GIF/JPEG SmartSaver can run as a stand-alone program in addition to working within Photoshop. As a stand-alone tool, it can perform both single file and batch processing chores. To launch SmartSaver as a stand-alone program, you can either choose it from the Windows Start menu or right-click a GIF or JPEG file in Windows Explorer.*

Part III

Streamlining Your Workflow

chapter 15

Alaras Apertura 2.0

Creator

Alaras Corporation

Purpose

Opens portions of any image, reads and writes Scitex files

Platforms

Macintosh

Hardware/Software requirements

Same as Photoshop, Color Quickdraw

URL/Contact info for creator of plug-in

http://www.alarascorp.com
Alaras Corporation
1910 Sedwick Road
Suite 300-D
Post Office Box 14562
Research Triangle Park, NC 27709-4562
919/544-1228 voice
919/544-7772 fax

Products that the plug-in works with

Adobe Photoshop

D o you work with Scitex prepress equipment? Looking for an affordable way to move images to and from the desktop environment? Alaras Apertura lets you acquire and export native Scitex files with your Macintosh. And best of all, it allows you to work on selected portions of an image without waiting to open up the whole image.

Who Should Use Alaras Apertura?

Alaras Apertura is invaluable for anyone working with large images. It is particularly useful for Scitex prepress shops (and their clients) that need to move files from Scitex to Mac.

What Alaras Apertura Does

Alaras Apertura is a set of filters for acquiring and exporting images. It provides the ability to open just a chunk of an image rather than the entire file. This can result in dramatic savings in time when opening, editing, and saving big files. Alaras Apertura conveniently allows you to read and write native Scitex images and supports the following file formats:

- TIFF
- Handshake CT
- Handshake LW
- AccessCT/iRMX
- AccessLW/iRMX
- AccessCT/UFS
- AccessLW/UFS

TIP *Alaras Apertura is sold in various configurations. You'll only want to buy the file modules that pertain to your shop's particular work flow.*

Why Use Alaras Apertura?

There are two basic reasons to use Alaras Apertura, both print related. Let's say you prepare images for process printing. These images are typically quite large—over 30 megabytes for a 300 dpi 8 ½- X 11-inch CMYK TIFF—and they can take ages to open, edit, and save. The first reason to use Apertura is that it allows you to open, edit, and save just a portion of the image for retouching rather than the whole kit-and-caboodle. When you go to save the portion of the image, Alaras Apertura knows where the cropped portion came from and will automatically place it back into the original image (or a copy thereof).

The second reason to use Alaras Apertura is that it lets you easily (and affordably) integrate pricey Scitex systems with (comparatively) inexpensive Macintosh systems. The package allows you to use your Mac to edit images directly from iRMX or UFS formatted Scitex optical disks or shuttles.

TIP *The ability to open an iRMX/UFS LineWork (LW) file is particularly noteworthy for things like fixing last-minute typos and price changes. LW files are usually extremely large and cumbersome to open. Alaras Apertura handles these tasks with aplomb.*

How Alaras Apertura Does It

By allowing you to edit portions of an image, Alaras Apertura makes it possible to quickly make corrections such as fixing a typo or altering line art in a linework image. Once you've loaded Alaras Apertura, you'll find it in Photoshop's Acquire and Export menus. Let's take a look at how it works.

Acquiring Images With Alaras Apertura

To acquire an image with Alaras Apertura, choose File | Acquire | Alaras Apertura. If you have not activated (registered) the program, a demo splash screen will appear. Click the Continue button. A file open dialog box, which is shown in Figure 15-1, will appear. As you scroll through the images, the dialog box reports on the file information for each image. Clicking the Thumbnails button opens up a Thumbnail preview dialog box, shown in Figure 15-2. As you select each thumbnail, you'll be rewarded with the full details on each image.

Figure 15-1: Pick your poison. Alaras Apertura lets you browse by filename or image thumbnails.

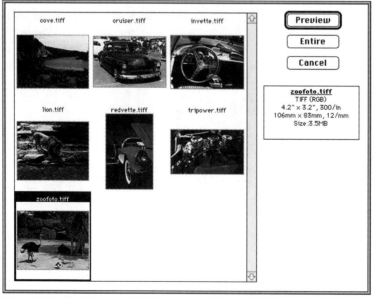

Figure 15-2: The Thumbnail dialog box provides comprehensive information about each image.

Once you've decided which image you want to open, you must decide how you want to work on the image. Clicking Entire will open up the whole image. Clicking Preview (or Open on the first dialog box) will allow you to select a portion—also known as a *crop*—of the image to open. We've decided to open up just the giraffe section of the image, as shown in Figure 15-3. After you've dragged out a selection around the portion of the image you wish to open, the Preview dialog box will report on the size and location of the selection. Click Open to open the cropped portion of the image.

The cropped portion of the image opens up like any other file in Photoshop (although the demo version will include an Alaras Demo banner through the middle). You can even open up multiple chunks (up to ten) of an image at once by Command+dragging a number of selections. The crops will appear in one file, as demonstrated by Figure 15-4.

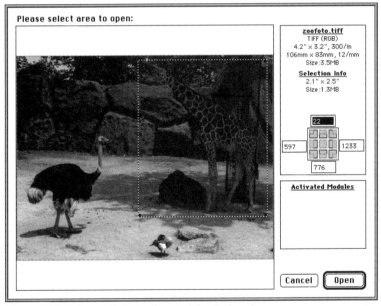

Figure 15-3: Let's get that giraffe out of the shadows!

Figure 15-4: OK, so you don't usually have to retouch a giraffe, an ostrich, and a little bird at once. In the real world, multiple selections are perfect for grabbing all the fleshtones in an image.

TIP *You might want to open up only a half or a quarter of a really large image. Alaras Apertura lets you do this easily. Just double-click on the relevant section of the Marquee Quadrant tool. You'll find this handy feature just below the Selection Info, at the right side of the Preview dialog box.*

Exporting Images With Alaras Apertura

Alaras Apertura allows you to save the cropped image in one of three ways. You can save it back to the original file, you can save it into a duplicate of the original, or you can save just the cropped portion as a new file. When you go to save the image, choose File | Export | Alaras Apertura. A little dialog box will appear with Insert (original), Insert As (duplicate), Save As (just the crop), and Cancel options. Alaras Apertura can remember where to place up to 20 cropped portions per image.

Opening Files From Scitex Disks

To open a file from a Scitex disk or shuttle, choose File | Acquire | Alaras Apertura and click the Prefs button. This will scan the SCSI bus for recognizable media. (Of course, you'll have to have the appropriate drive hooked up to your Mac.) Once Alaras Apertura finds the files, you can open them as you would any other image, assuming you have the file format module loaded.

chapter 16

Alaras Mixxer 2.0

Creator

Alaras Corporation

Purpose

Transforms CMYK images with special effects, including
ghosts, 4/C halftones, and sepia tones

Platforms

Macintosh

Hardware/Software requirements

Same as Photoshop

URL/Contact info for creator of plug-in

http://www.alarascorp.com
Alaras Corporation
1910 Sedwick Road
Suite 300-D
Post Office Box 14562
Research Triangle Park, NC 27709-4562
919/544-1228 voice
919/544-7772 fax

Products that the plug-in works with

Adobe Photoshop

W ant to perform complex process color transformations—such as process color halftones and sepia tones—at the push of a button? Alaras Mixxer delivers high-end capabilities for Mac-based operations.

Who Should Use Alaras Mixxer?

Alaras Mixxer is ideal for graphic designers, printers, and prepress shops who work with four-color (4/C) CMYK images. This PowerPC-native plug-in is used by some of the biggest names in the printing and prepress business, including Quad Graphics, RR Donnelly & Sons, WACE, and World Color.

What Alaras Mixxer Does

Alaras Mixxer applies complex color table transformations to CMYK files. It provides point-and-shoot simplicity with built-in transformation templates in addition to allowing you to create your own custom templates. The built-in templates include:

- 280 Under Color Removal
- 4/C to 1/C Halftone (Light, Autodark, or Dark)
- 4/C to 4/C Black & White
- 4/C to 4/C Sepia Tones
- Shape Enhance in Dark File
- Unwanted Color Reduction—10%
- Contaminated Clean-up (Light, Medium, or Heavy)
- Uncontaminate—10% (Red, Green, or Blue)
- Ghosting (20%, 80%, or Holding Color)

Why Use Alaras Mixxer?

Have you ever had a process color job that called for sepia tone or four-color halftone images? How about ghosted areas? Did you tear your hair out as you struggled to formulate a recipe to create those files? Alaras Mixxer makes these and other complex color transformations, such as color swapping and undercolor removal, a snap. It's also invaluable when creating duotones and tritones.

How Alaras Mixxer Does It

Alaras Mixxer uses a color transformation matrix to convert CMYK values. Thankfully, you don't have to be a color god to make the plug-in pay for itself! Figure 16-1 shows the Alaras Mixxer dialog box configured to use the built-in Unwanted Color Reduction template.

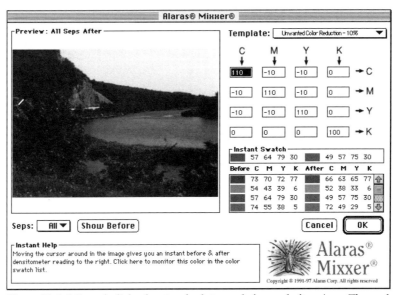

Figure 16-1: Mixxer's dialog box toggles between before and after views. The eyedropper allows you to perform densitometer readings while keeping track of individual colors.

To choose a template, just click on the Template drop-down menu and select the template you want to apply. The preview area lets you get a good look at how the image will appear once the settings are applied. You have the option of viewing either individual CMYK separations or the composite image. When you select a color with the eyedropper, it adds the color to the swatch list. This lets you watch the before and after percentages for critical colors.

Once you've grown comfortable with Alaras Mixxer (and especially if you have experience on high-end Scitex color prepress workstations), you'll probably start creating your own color transformation templates. You can save or delete templates by selecting the Save option from the Template drop-down menu. Templates are created by dialing figures into the matrix. Fine-tuning is simplified through the use of Up and Down cursor keys, which allow you to adjust the figures by 1 or 5 percent increments.

chapter 17

Altamira Group's Genuine Fractals

Creator

Altamira Group, Inc.

Purpose

Works in smaller original files, saves images as compressed FIF files, and opens the same FIF file at various sizes for multiple output requirements

Platforms

Windows 95/NT, Macintosh PowerPC

Hardware/Software requirements

Same as Photoshop

URL/Contact info for creator of plug-in

http://www.altamira-group.com
Altamira Group, Inc.
1827 W. Verdugo Avenue
2nd Floor, Suite C
Burbank, CA 91506
818/556-6099 voice
818/556-3365 fax

Products that the plug-in works with

Any application that is Photoshop 3.0 or later Import/Export plug-in compliant, including Equilibrium DeBabelizer Pro and Adobe PhotoDeluxe

Tired of working in huge original files for large format output? Wish you could send high-resolution color graphics files over a network? Or maybe you'd like to display a full screen of full color on the Web. Take a look at Altamira Group's Genuine Fractals. This import/export plug-in compresses RGB images into scalable fractal image format (FIF) files that can be rendered at resolutions from thumbnail to poster with visually lossless results.

The FIF file format is also supported by other applications, such as Aimtech's Icon Author and CBT Express, Digiflyer's Digiflyer Designer and Digiflyer Player, Image FX's FractalFX 4.0, Iterated Systems's Fractal Viewer plug-in for Netscape Navigator and ActiveX control for Internet Explorer, and Macromedia's Authorware and Director/Shockwave.

Who Should Use Genuine Fractals?

Print designers, artists, and photographers who want to save time by working in medium-sized files for large format output, Web designers who want to quickly display full-screen, full-color images on their Web pages, and game developers who need to maintain color consistency across images can all benefit from using Genuine Fractals.

What Genuine Fractals Does

Genuine Fractals opens resolution-independent FIF files from the Photoshop File Import or Acquire menu and saves files in the compressed FIF format from the Photoshop File Export menu.

FIF files compress RGB image shapes and colors into scalable equations that can be rendered at any resolution from 64 X 64 pixels to the limits of computer memory and resources. In testing, a 450 MB image was rendered from a 1.8 MB FIF with excellent results.

FIF files achieve compression ratios of 4:1 to 125:1, depending on original image detail and Genuine Fractals Export options, and can be displayed in RGB or indexed color with an optimal, system, or custom palette.

Why Use Genuine Fractals?

Genuine Fractals saves time by letting you work in medium-sized original files for high-resolution output. With Genuine Fractals and FIF files, it's no longer necessary to scan at the output resolution size. Since FIF is a resolution-independent file format, you need only between 10 and 25 MB of original data to capture an image for large format output.

How Genuine Fractals Does It

Genuine Fractals uses Photoshop's Import/Acquire and Export File functions to open existing FIF files and create FIFs from RGB images, respectively.

During the export process, patented fractal algorithms repeatedly look over the image, record its details in equations, and then, unlike other compression techniques, discard the actual pixel information. The more detailed equations result in larger compressed files and take longer to encode, but they produce superb images when rendered at any size from screen to print resolutions during the import/acquire process.

Creating Images for the FIF Format

With one compact original file, the FIF format conserves space on your hard drive and shaves hours from your online time. For example, if you need to have the same image at 450MB and 60MB, you can scan or create a 20MB original and do all your image editing at that size. When you have the image looking the way you want it, export it with the Genuine Fractals Pro Graphics option. This results in a file size between 2 and 5MB that can easily be transmitted and stored. At output time, use the Genuine Fractals Import/Acquire feature to render both the 450MB and 60MB image from the same FIF file.

For screen-resolution output, start even smaller. Using Genuine Fractals's 50 Web Graphics options, a 640 X 480 original compresses to between 10K and 150K and renders up nicely for quick display on the Web in the color depth of the viewer's desktop.

For game developers and Web designers, the ability of FIF files to open in either 24-bit or 8-bit color with an optimal color palette means images with 16 million colors are guaranteed to look their best on a computer that displays only 256 colors. When Genuine Fractals opens a FIF with the Indexed Color option, the Optimal Palette setting dynamically picks the best 256 colors in which to render the image in 8-bit color space. Optionally, Genuine Fractals can also display images using the Windows or Mac System palette or a Custom palette for color consistency across images. On the Web, the browser determines the proper color depth of the user's desktop, and FIF files automatically display in either 8- or 24-bit color accordingly.

FIF files allow user interaction on the Web. Once a FIF is downloaded, the image can be flipped, rotated, stretched, scaled, zoomed, cut, pasted, saved, protected, and displayed in grayscale, 8-bit, 24-bit, or inverted color by the user.

Exporting & Importing FIF Files

To export an image, open an RGB image in Photoshop and choose File | Export | Genuine Fractals Export from Photoshop's menu bar. The Genuine Fractals Export dialog box will appear, as shown in Figure 17-1. Then, you can select one of the following options for encoding FIF files from RGB images.

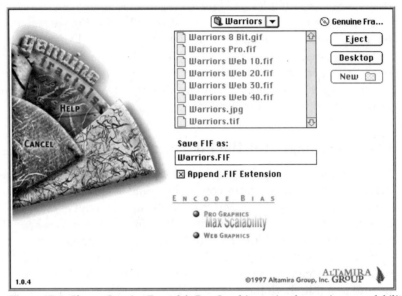

Figure 17-1: Choose Genuine Fractals's Pro Graphics option for maximum scalability.

- **Pro Graphics.** Creates the greatest detail and produces the biggest compressed file but allows images to be scaled to extremely large sizes while maintaining picture and color integrity.

- **Web Graphics.** Creates smaller compressed files that display very quickly on the Web. Web designers can choose from among 50 settings from Small Photographic to Tiny Impressionistic, depending on the desired picture quality and speed of delivery.

To import an image, choose File | Import (or Acquire) | Genuine Fractals Import from Photoshop's menu bar. Enter the desired resolution by specifying the width and height in pixels or the file size in bytes. Turn Constrain Proportions on to maintain the original aspect ratio or off to distort dimensions, and then choose RGB or Indexed Color. Indexed Color mode allows you to choose an Optimal palette, System palette, or Custom palette. You have the option of displaying a thumbnail Preview of the image. Image Info displays the original bitmap file size, width, and height along with the fractally encoded stored file size.

chapter 18

Chroma Graphics's Chromatica

Creator
Chroma Graphics

Purpose
Advanced masking and color editing tools

Platforms
Macintosh, Windows 95/NT

Hardware/Software requirements
Same as Photoshop

URL/Contact info for creator of plug-in
http://www.chromagraphics.com
Chroma Graphics, Inc.
577 Airport Blvd.
Suite 730
Burlingame, CA 94010-2020
415/375-1100 voice
415/375-1118 fax

Products that the plug-in works with
Mac: Adobe Photoshop 2.5 or later, other programs that
support Photoshop 2.5's (or later) plug-in standard
Windows 95 or NT: Adobe Photoshop 3.0.5 or later,
other programs that support Photoshop 3.0's (or later)
plug-in standard

Looking for advanced object-selection, recoloring, and edge-blending tools? Chromatica's two plug-ins—ChromaColor and ChromaPalette—allow you to recolor images with ease.

Who Should Use Chroma Graphics's Chromatica?

Chroma Graphics's Chromatica is well suited for the needs of a broad audience. This pair of plug-ins will find a welcome home with digital artists, graphic designers, photo retouchers, printers, prepress operators, and Web developers, among others.

What Chroma Graphics's Chromatica Does

Chroma Graphics's Chromatica not only addresses masking, it addresses color swapping as well. Using patented technology culled from genetic research and fractal mathematics, Chromatica allows you to create selections and edit colors in the same manner as the human eye perceives them. This provides for realistic color adjustments and superior edge blending.

Why Use Chroma Graphics's Chromatica?

Need to alter the color of a dress to match the exact hue of the fabric? Chromatica's advanced color technology makes it a natural choice for folks who need to perform precise color transformations. The plug-in lets you quickly recolor objects while maintaining integrity and detail. Chromatica is unique in that it allows you to create exciting artwork by applying the palette of one image to another image. It comes with 1,000 palettes, including many from famous works of art. Of course, you can create your own custom palettes as well.

How ChromaColor Does It

ChromaColor allows you to select an area by color attributes and apply a new color to it. The masking tool, ChromaMask, can be used as a stand-alone selection tool or in conjunction with Photoshop's Magic Wand, Lasso, and other selection apparatus. To launch ChromaColor, select the portion of the image you want to recolor and choose Filter | Chromatica | ChromaPalette from the Photoshop menu bar. Figure 18-1 shows the ChromaColor window, where all the masking action takes place. The large work area dominates the window. Below the window, you'll find ChromaColor's toolset, which consists of the CromaMask tool, an Eraser tool, a Pan tool, and a Zoom tool.

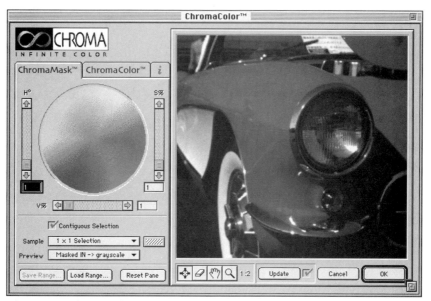

Figure 18-1: ChromaColor's interface can be displayed as a floating window or in full-screen mode.

To build a ChromaMask, you begin by selecting a chunk of the image with the ChromaMask tool. You can choose to mask a specific color by clicking on it, or you can click and drag the tool to draw a marquee around an area of the image. This allows you to select a range of color. To add more colors to the selected area, hold down the Shift key and click on the image. You can also choose whether or not to make your mask a contiguous selection.

ChromaMask provides a number of ways to preview your mask. You can view the masked-in or masked-out areas as white, black, grayscale, or in a color of your choice, as shown in Figure 18-2. On a slower computer, you'll probably want to turn the preview update off. If you've turned the automatic preview off, the Update button will wink at you when the new preview is ready for your viewing pleasure.

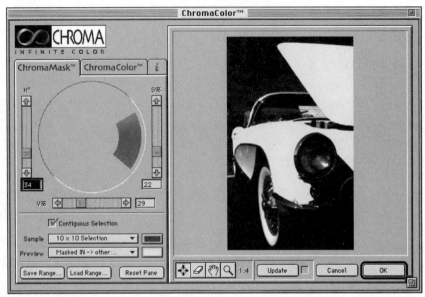

Figure 18-2: Like to look at yellow masked-in areas? No problem! You can change the mask color to suit your fancy.

While the masking tools are powerful, ChromaMask is best used in situations where there's only a handful of overall colors. Take a look at the HSV wheel in Figure 18-2; it shows the currently selected color range. You can tweak the masks with the HSV sliders and fine-tune them by clicking on unmasked areas within the image. The Sample pop-up menu allows you to choose from 1 x 1, 3 x 3, 5 x 5, and 10 x 10 pixel sample areas. Once you've created a color range mask, you can save the settings to use on subsequent images. This can be very useful in situations where you're working with many similar photographs, such as studio product shots that have been set up with the same background.

Once you've built a ChromaMask, you flip to ChromaColor mode by clicking on the ChromaColor tab. This window allows you to recolor your masked areas. Colors can be chosen from the system Color Picker, or they can be loaded from another image. The latter is extremely useful when attempting to perform color matching for color-sensitive items such as clothing. Figure 18-3 shows our classic red Corvette in the process of being recolored in a frightening aqua. Target colors can be specified in RGB, HSV, or CMYK terms. They may also be set to PANTONE colors. In addition to being affected by the target color, the recolored areas are affected by the Value and Tolerance sliders.

Figure 18-3: While you may be more likely to have to change the color of a sweater for a fashion client, it's always fun to play automotive paint "what-ifs."

The EdgeWizard is one of Chromatica's coolest features. This device takes a close look at the edge of your recolored areas and figures out how to blend the recolored area into the background image. The EdgeWizard dialog box, shown in Figure 18-4, lets you choose to have no edge or a calculated edge between 0.1 and 30 pixels, with or without a variable edge width.

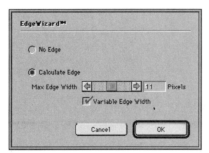

Figure 18-4: The EdgeWizard ensures that your recolored areas don't appear as if they've been recolored.

How ChromaPalette Does It

Swapping color palettes with ChromaPalette can be tons of fun. In just a few clicks, you can take your vacation pictures and recolor them with palettes from the stars or of your own creation. Chromatica comes with 1,000 palettes culled from a wide variety of sources. You'll find color palettes from artists—including Caravaggio, Cézanne, Gauguin, O'Keeffe, Matisse, Monet, Picasso, Renoir, and van Gogh—as well as from food, gemstones, landmarks, people, sports, and nature.

To launch ChromaPalette, choose Filter | Chromatica | ChromaPalette from Photoshop's menu bar. The ChromaPalette window appears with no palettes loaded. Click the Create Palette button to build a palette from your image. You can adjust the palette size slider if you wish, or you can simply leave it set on Automatic and click OK. Once ChromaPalette has built a custom color palette, click the Load Palette button to bring in a palette from Chromatica's collection (or one of your own design). Try fiddling with the different palettes while toggling between the overlay settings (color or color and texture) for some great effects. Figure 18-5 shows a tropic island photograph that's been ChromaPalletized with an O'Keeffe palette.

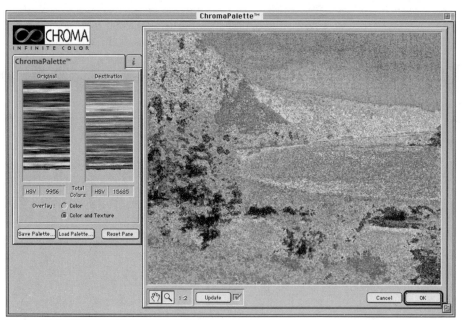

Figure 18-5: What would Andy Warhol's screen prints have looked like if he had had ChromaPalette?

chapter 19

Extensis Mask Pro

Creator

Extensis

Purpose

Generates image masks

Platforms

Macintosh, Windows version expected in Fall '97

Hardware/Software requirements

System 7.5 or higher, Power PC processor

URL/Contact info for creator of plug-in

http://www.extensis.com
Extensis Corporation
1800 SW First Ave, Ste. 500
Portland, Oregon 97201
503-274-2020 voice
503-274-0530 fax

Products that the plug-in works with

Adobe Photoshop 3.0.5 or later

D o you have to perform intricate silhouettes and create complex image compositions? If you've been stuck using the standard Photoshop tools, you're in for a big productivity boost. Extensis Mask Pro allows you to quickly create image masks for use in print and on the Web. Whether you're cutting out images for a trendy fashion catalog or for gritty news graphics, you'll find that this plug-in will save you tons of time.

Who Should Use Extensis Mask Pro?

Extensis Mask Pro should appeal to photo retouchers, graphic artists, designers, printers, prepress operators, Web developers, broadcast designers, advertising agencies, and anyone else who needs to create masks quickly and accurately.

What Extensis Mask Pro Does

Extensis Mask Pro provides a unique methodology that makes the arduous task of creating masks a cinch. The plug-in's toolbox provides color matching technology that allows you to choose the colors you want to keep as well as the colors you want to drop. It also provides familiar brush, fill, and path tools to allow you to complete your mask with the most appropriate mechanism for each situation. Masks can be dropped into separate channels, allowing you to mask multiple elements.

Once you've specified the masked areas, Mask Pro builds smooth vector-based paths that have been optimized for imagesetter output. Complex curved paths often choke imagesetter RIPs (raster image processors) and the curves themselves are often the culprits. Mask Pro avoids problems at the RIP by creating paths that consist of only straight lines. It uses a multitude of little straight line segments to simulate curves. Using lots of little straight lines makes complex curved areas far easier for the RIP to crunch.

Why Use Extensis Mask Pro?

Need to silhouette half a dozen fashion shots before noon? Have a wicked news deadline to meet and a handful of images that need to be cut out and composited? Extensis Mask Pro takes those formerly tedious masking chores and turns them into a swift, pleasurable affair.

How Mask Pro Does It

Extensis Mask Pro works its magic by allowing you to quickly specify the colors you want to keep and the colors you want to drop. To begin, click and drag the Keep eyedropper over the colors you want to remain unmasked, and then click and drag the Drop eyedropper over the colors you want to mask. Once you've specified the keep and drop colors in the image, you use the Magic Brush to paint along the edge of the silhouette. Since you've specified those colors, the plug-in knows where to draw the line, so to speak, as it masks out the drop colors while leaving the keep colors untouched.

Let's go through a typical masking scenario. Perhaps you're preparing a catalog and Web site for a small craft business. They've done their photography themselves, using a bed sheet for a background. Of course, they want to drop all of the backgrounds out in their print version and in their Web site as well. Once you've scanned, cleaned, and cropped the images, you can start masking them out. You can choose to apply the mask to the Background layer once you've added an opacity channel by double-clicking on the icon in the Layers palette (if it's a single layer image), or you can create a layer mask. Using a layer mask provides more flexibility.

TIP *To create a layer mask, double-click on the Background layer and rename it. Then choose Layer | Add Layer | Reveal All.*

To open Mask Pro, choose Filters | Extensis | Mask Pro from Photoshop's menu bar. The Mask Pro window, as shown in Figure 19-1, uses a roomy workspace along with six floating palettes.

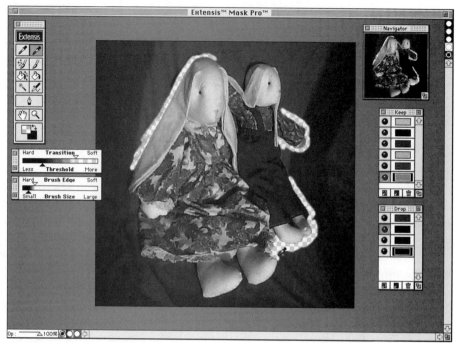

Figure 19-1: Extensis Mask Pro lets you create masks like a pro. The intuitive interface is easy to grasp.

At the top right, you'll see the color channel selectors, while at the bottom left, you'll see a slider for mask opacity and mode (color, grayscale, and holefinder). Clockwise, from the top left, the palettes are:

■ **The Toolbox**. This palette provides access to all of Mask Pro's goodies: Keep Color, Drop Color, Magic Brush, Brush, Magic Fill, Bucket, Magic Wand, Airbrush, Pen, Hand, Zoom, and Mask Mode. We'll cover the tools in depth in a moment.

■ **Navigator**. This palette lets you get the big picture when you're zoomed up on an image. You can use it to zoom and pan around, and you can even run multiple Navigator palettes by choosing Window | New Navigator.

■ **Keep and Drop**. These two little palettes let you control which colors to keep and which to drop. To choose a color set, just click on it. The bright green light lets you know which color set is active on the Keep palette, while the bright red light lets you know which color set is active on the Drop palette. The three icons at the bottom allow you to create new color sets, add a color to a set, or delete a set.

■ **Brush Size**. This palette houses two sliders that control the size and edge effect of all of Mask Pro's painting tools.

■ **Threshold**. The two sliders on this palette control the Magic Brush's Keep and Drop transition and threshold levels.

Time to mask out the bunnies! In an image such as this, where the background isn't too varied, you'll only need to create a couple of Drop color sets. To create a Drop color set, click and drag the red eyedropper through the colors in the image that you want to drop out. These bunnies contain roughly four keep colors overall, so we created four Keep color sets. As we worked the image over with the Magic Brush, it was easy to switch between color sets by selecting them in the Drop and Keep palettes.

The manner in which you work with Mask Pro depends on the image at hand. Sometimes you can take big bites, while other times you'll find yourself nibbling away. Masking areas of clearly delineated and consistent color is an expeditious affair. Just select the drop and keep colors, click the Magic Brush tool, and drag it along the area that you want to mask. When the color changes are more subtle, however, you'll want to fiddle with the transition and threshold levels. And when things get a little tight, you'll switch to a smaller brush size. Generally, you'll want to begin by painting a masked area around your subject, as shown back in Figure 19-1, as you zoom and pan your way around the file.

If the Magic Brush doesn't lend itself to this approach on part of your image, don't fret. Mask Pro's Brush, Magic Wand, Airbrush, and Pen tools are there at your service. If you're familiar with Photoshop's implementation of these apparatus, you'll feel right at home with Mask Pro. All of these tools can be used in both Mask mode and Restore mode; you can flip between Mask mode and Restore mode by clicking on the Mask Mode icon or by pressing the D (default mask), E (erase mask), or X (exchange mode) key:

■ **Brush**. Paint masks (or unmask) as you would with a standard paintbrush.

■ **Magic Wand**. This little puppy crosses Photoshop's Magic Wand with Mask Pro's color Keep/Drop color matching technology.

■ **Airbrush**. Allows you to paint masks with transparency by adjusting the Threshold slider.

■ **Pen**. Love drawing object-oriented paths? This tool lets you click, click, click your way to masking nirvana. It's just the ticket for drawing long, smooth curves.

Once you've drawn a clear area around the area you want to mask, as shown in Figure 19-2, it's time to switch into Hole Finder view; you can do so by clicking on the rightmost of the three circles at the bottom of the Mask Pro window.

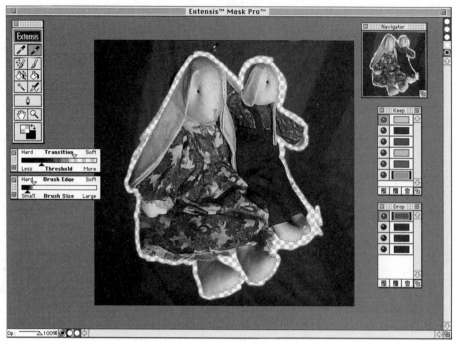

Figure 19-2: With the bunnies cut out, it's time to finish off the mask.

As you can see in Figure 19-3, Hole Finder view shows the masked areas in black, the open areas in white, and the transitional areas in gray. You'll use the Magic Fill tool to patch up holes in the mask and the Bucket tool to fill in the large open areas. The Magic Fill works best in Grayscale view (the middle of the three circles at the bottom of the Mask Pro window), while the Bucket tool works best in the Hole Finder view. The Hole Finder view is the best place to catch overspray as well as stray holes. It's imperative that the ribbon around the cutout be contiguous, with nary a break, lest the bucket fill the entire image.

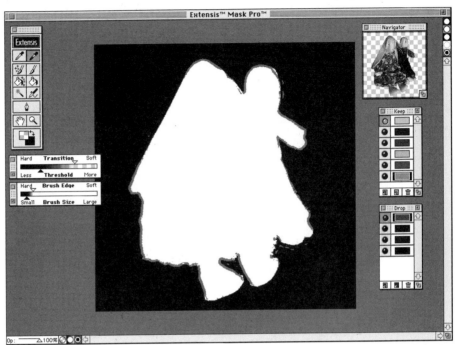

Figure 19-3: Hole Finder view allows you to quickly fill in all the open areas and stray holes in the mask.

TIP *With the mask complete, you may want to save the workspace by choosing File | Save Workspace. This lets you file away all of your keep and drop colors so that you can revisit the image if necessary. Saving your workspace also allows you to use the colors on subsequent images that may be similar in nature.*

After you have finished creating a mask, you can either create a clipping path or you can apply the mask to the image. When you click File | Save/ Apply, the Clipping Path dialog box will appear, as shown in Figure 19-4. The Threshold setting governs the amount of transparency inside the clipping path. The higher the number, the less chance you'll have of getting the dreaded halo effect. The Tolerance setting influences the number of control points in the path. Higher Tolerance settings will result in fewer control points. Click the Path button if you want to create a clipping path. Click the No Path button if you want to apply the mask to the image. Click the Cancel button to go back to Mask Pro. When you click the Path button, Mask Pro places the clipping path into the clipboard. Double-click on Photoshop's Hand tool to revert to Fit-in-Window view. Then paste the path into your image. Figure 19-5 shows the finished product.

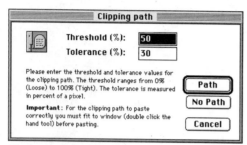

Figure 19-4: The Clipping Path dialog box lets you fine-tune the mask for imagesetting.

Figure 19-5: Who are those masked bunnies?

chapter 20

Extensis PhotoTools

Creator

Extensis

Purpose

Sets highly formatted type. Creates special effects—bevels, embosses, glows, and shadows. Enhances productivity with tool palettes, instant image optimization, and online tips.

Platforms

Windows 95/NT 4.0, Macintosh 68K and PowerPC

Hardware/Software requirements

Mac: System 7.1.1 (or later)

URL/Contact info for creator of plug-in

http://www.extensis.com
Extensis Corporation
1800 SW First Ave, Ste. 500
Portland, Oregon 97201
503/274-2020 voice
503/274-0530 fax

Products that the plug-in works with

Adobe Photoshop 3.0.4 or later

Want to take the drudgery out of your image-editing day? Extensis PhotoTools, a no-nonsense suite of eight productivity and special-effects gadgets, will have you working faster and smarter in no time flat. And your artwork will look better, to boot!

Who Should Use Extensis PhotoTools?

Print designers, Web designers, desktop publishers, and basically any user who wants to take a high degree of control over their typesetting and special effects within Photoshop. Due to its range of options and features, PhotoTools has wide appeal.

TIP *The Extensis PhotoTools demo that you'll find on* The Photoshop Plug-ins Book *Companion CD-ROM is a fully functional program. The demo allows you to put PhotoTools through the paces for a 30-day period.*

What Extensis PhotoTools Does

Extensis PhotoTools adds eight powerful plug-ins to your war chest that allow you to breeze through text and graphic work in Photoshop. PhotoTools consists of:

- **Intellihance Lite.** Little brother of the full Intellihance plug-in (reviewed in Chapter 4). Provides one-click RGB image enhancement, including brightness, contrast, despeckle, saturation, and sharpness.

- **PhotoBars.** Creates customized toolbars as floating palettes or as a static addition to Photoshop UI. Provides instant access to your most frequently used commands.

- **PhotoBevel.** Gives you "the edge" by performing inner and outer bevels in your choice of four different shapes (flat, round, double, and slope).

- **PhotoEmboss.** Creates advanced embossed effects with a range of variations (blur, cutout, edge, and raise).

- **PhotoGlow.** Renders glow effects with precision.

- **PhotoShadow.** Creates professional-quality drop shadows with total control.

- **PhotoText.** Delivers serious typesetting controls, including leading, tracking, kerning, and character widths.
- **PhotoTips.** Provides scores of Photoshop tips and tricks.

Why Use Extensis PhotoTools?

Even though PhotoTools contains some wonderful creative filters, we've chosen to include the collection in "Streamlining Your Work Flow," the third section of this book. There's good reason for this. PhotoTools plug-ins are workhorses. They concentrate on providing day-in-day-out usefulness. By delivering utility rather than just gee-whiz special effects, they'll be the tools that you'll go back to, time and time again.

Let's take a look at PhotoTools, plug-in by plug-in.

How Intellihance Lite Does It

Intellihance Lite makes image optimization a snap. Because it works on RGB images, this plug-in is a natural for Web designers who need to fine-tune their images before saving them in JPEG format. Got an itchy trigger finger? Figure 20-1 demonstrates how Intellihance Lite works with just a single click. We took a mediocre scan of a little red Corvette and applied the default Intellihance Light settings (Normal Contrast, Balanced Tone Brightness, Medium Saturation, Medium Sharpness, and No Despeckle). In moments, the plug-in optimized the image according to those settings. While the result was not perfect, it was a huge improvement over the original scan.

So how do you fine-tune your image optimization without tearing your hair out? All you need to do is to take the time to set five basic controls. Clicking the Preferences button summons the Preferences dialog box, shown in Figure 20-2. This is where you'll tweak the Contrast, Brightness, Saturation, Sharpness, and Despeckle controls to perfection. The default settings will only get you so far. It's important to choose the appropriate settings for each image.

The settings are fairly self-explanatory. Here are the choices for each control:

- **Contrast.** Off, Soft, Normal, Snappy, Flatten Shadow, and Flatten Highlights.
- **Brightness.** Off, Deeper Shadows, Shadow Emphasis, Balanced Tone, Midtone Emphasis, and Highlight Emphasis.
- **Saturation.** Off, Low, Medium Low, Medium, Medium High, and High.

- **Sharpness.** Off, Soft, Medium Sharpness, Hard Sharpness, and Extra Hard.

- **Despeckle.** Off, Overall, Dark Tones Only, and Light Tones Only.

Figure 20-1: With a quick click of the Enhance Image button, we brightened and sharpened this vintage Corvette. Details such as the individual bleachers and the pattern in the headlight glass became evident.

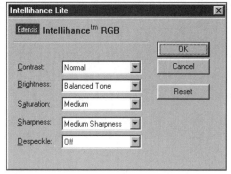

Figure 20-2: Intellihance Lite's image enhancement specifications can be easily modified.

TIP Print designers will want to look at Extensis's full-featured Intellihance 3.0, which is covered in Chapter 4, for optimizing CMYK images.

How PhotoBars Does It

Do you find yourself digging through Photoshop's menus to perform repetitive procedures? PhotoBars moves your most often used commands up to the desktop and allows you to place the commands into floating palettes, as shown in Figure 20-3, or docked toolbars. With the commands just one click away, you'll save time and become more productive—without having to remember any arcane keyboard shortcuts. Each button conveniently provides a pop-up definition, just in case you can't remember what the heck the icon stands for.

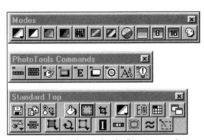

Figure 20-3: The default floating palettes provide access to color modes, PhotoTools operations, and everyday Photoshop functions.

If you're working on a Macintosh, you don't even have to take the time to build your own palettes to gain the productivity boost. The SmartBar feature automatically keeps track of your most frequently accessed commands and builds the palette for you. PhotoBars are easy to work with. They can be resized to a horizontal or vertical orientation merely by tugging on a corner of the palette. To dock a PhotoBar, all you need to do is drag it to the side of the Photoshop window that you wish to dock it to. When you want to make a docked PhotoBar float again, just click and drag it toward the center of the window. Figure 20-4 shows the default PhotoBars docked to the left, right, and top of the Photoshop window.

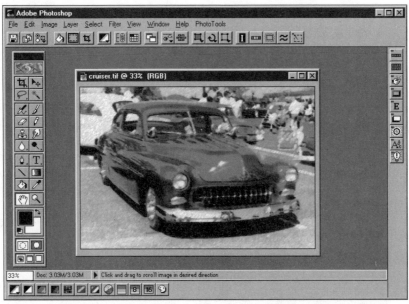

Figure 20-4: Docking the PhotoBars keeps your most frequently used functions close at hand while uncluttering the image workspace.

Building custom PhotoBars is a cinch. Choose PhotoTools | PhotoBars | Customize Toolbars from Photoshop's menu bar to summon the Customize Toolbars dialog box, shown in Figure 20-5. This dialog box allows you to quickly find and drag your favorite functions onto an existing toolbar, no matter whether it's docked or floating. To add a new toolbar, or to delete a toolbar, choose PhotoTools | PhotoBars | Edit Toolbars from Photoshop's menu bar. This dialog box also lets you duplicate and rename your toolbars in addition to turning them on or off.

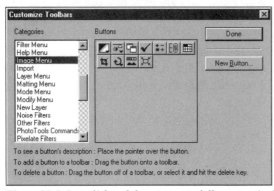

Figure 20-5: Just click and drag to create fully customized toolbars.

The customization feature allows you to create toolbars that are grouped by function or project. If you find yourself doing the same procedures over and over on a particular job, you can quickly create a toolbar that will save plenty of clicks (and time).

How PhotoBevel Does It

Need to add bevels to your images? Whether you're creating buttons for a Web site or three-dimensional effects for a photographic print design, PhotoBevel makes quick work of beveling procedures and provides a range of flexibility. After drop shadows, bevels are among the most frequently used graphic treatments. PhotoBevel provides full control over four basic types of bevels: flat, round, slope, and double, in both inner and outer permutations. Figures 20-6 and 20-7 show examples of each design.

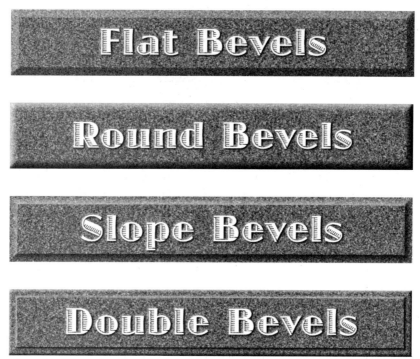

Figure 20-6: Inner bevels work on the image within the currently selected area.

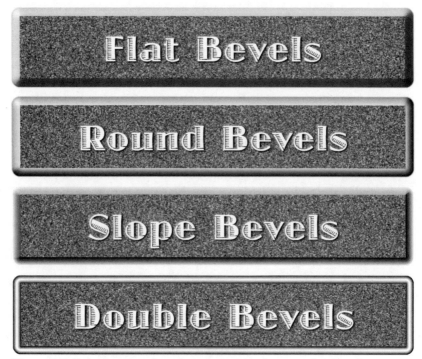

Figure 20-7: Outer bevels work on the image outside the currently selected area.

The inner bevels, especially the slope and double bevels, can create a carved appearance, as if they were chiseled out of stone. Outer bevels, on the other hand, can easily provide the appearance of chrome (round bevel) or neon (double bevel). Choose PhotoTools | PhotoBevel | PhotoBevel (yes, you have to click it twice) from Photoshop's menu bar, to bring up the PhotoBevel dialog box, as shown in Figure 20-8. The PhotoBevel dialog box is chock full of controls, which enable you to render the slickest bevel effects.

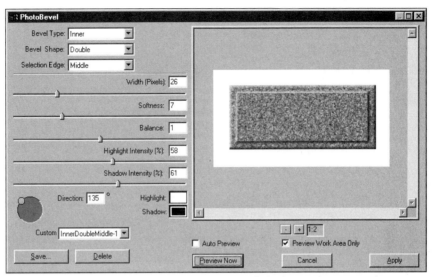

Figure 20-8: The PhotoBevel dialog box lets you do all the fine-tuning you need to create killer bevels.

Working with the PhotoBevel dialog box is a blast. The large image preview area lets you get a good look at your project, and the window is resizable, to boot. Use the scroll bars to pan around the image and the zoom buttons to zoom in and out. Let's take a look at the PhotoBevel controls:

- **Bevel Type.** Inner or Outer bevels affect the area inside or outside the selection area. While you can apply an Inner bevel to an entire image, you can only apply an Outer bevel if you've made a selection that is smaller than the image area.

- **Bevel Shape.** The choices are Flat, Round, Slope, or Double.

- **Selection Edge.** This option is useful when working with feathered selections. Minimum ignores the feathered pixels. Medium works upon the middle of the feathered area. Maximum works on the entire feathered area.

- **Width.** How many pixels wide do you want the bevel to be?

- **Softness.** With this option, you can smooth the highlights and shadows.
- **Balance.** This option controls the balance between the highlight and shadows.
- **Highlight and Shadow Intensity.** How bright do you want the highlights to be? How dark do you want the shadows to be? You can also control the highlight and shadow colors with the pop-up color palettes.
- **Direction.** Spin the little circle around the larger circle to control the direction of light.
- **Custom.** Once you've created the ultimate bevel, you'll probably want to save it to use again. Click the Save button to name and save your custom bevel to the Custom drop-down menu. To delete a custom bevel button, select it from the Custom drop-down menu and click Delete.
- **Auto Preview.** This option will automatically update the image preview area. Leave this button selected if you have a fast computer. If your computer is speed-challenged, leave it unselected.
- **Preview Work Area.** This option will help speed up the preview display by showing only the currently selected area.
- **Preview Now.** This option is useful when you have Auto Preview turned off.

You might think that PhotoBevel is only useful for rectangular selections— think again! The plug-in creates great bevels on a wide range of objects and does a really nice job of beveling text. Figure 20-9 shows some examples of beveled text created using flat, round, slope, and double bevels, respectively. Other PhotoTools effects were also used on this example, with PhotoGlow on the first graphic and PhotoShadow on the second. While PhotoBevel won't replace a real three-dimensional type rendering plug-in, like Xaos Tools's TypeCaster, it can definitely create some cool effects.

TIP *The procedure for beveling text is computationally intensive. By nature, letterforms contain a multitude of curves and can take a while to render. If you have a slow computer, be prepared to wait.*

Figure 20-9: Careful use of PhotoBevel can lead to a number of excellent text effects.

How PhotoEmboss Does It

Looking to emulate embossed paper, wood, leather, or other textures? The PhotoEmboss plug-in provides you with the tools you need to quickly create a wide variety of effects. Figure 20-10 shows the four basic embosses—Cutout, Raised, Edge, and Blur—used as text treatments. The Cutout effect delivers the illusion of a printer's die cut, allowing you to see cleanly through the texture, while the Edge effect makes the text appear as if it has been ripped away (using a coarse-edged typeface helps to enhance the illusion). The exact same Edge emboss was used on a selection just within the edges of Figure 20-10 with strikingly different results.

Figure 20-10: PhotoEmboss works great on text as well as graphic shapes.

The Raised emboss effect makes the text appear as if it has been pressed into the texture. This effect can be applied as a blind emboss (with no "ink" on the letters) or with ink, depending on your needs. The Blur effect would feel at home in a trendy magazine or advertisement (until the trend went out of style, of course).

As you might expect, the PhotoEmboss dialog box, shown in Figure 20-11, follows the same general layout and functionality as the PhotoBevel and other special effect dialog boxes in PhotoTools. The Highlight, Shadow, and Light Direction controls are shared between the two, as are the Softness, Custom, and image preview controls. Emboss width is controlled by the Amount slider, while the overall balance is controlled by the Contrast slider. The Invert check box allows you to directionally toggle the Cutout, Raised, Edge, and Blur effects back and forth.

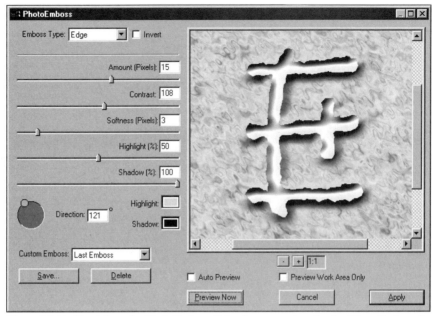

Figure 20-11: Here's how the PhotoEmboss dialog box was set up for the Edge effect, as shown in Figure 20-10.

How PhotoGlow Does It

Want to add an eerie, glowing effect to your text and graphics? There's no need to cut and paste and fiddle with Gaussian Blur anymore! The PhotoGlow plug-in allows you to knock out glowing type that will have less fortunate designers green with envy. Figure 20-12 demonstrates three different glow effects that were created with PhotoGlow. Use this one for the ever-popular neon effect as well as when you want to emulate the appearance of back-lit lettering or signage.

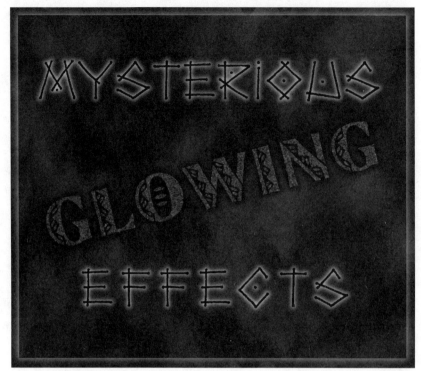

Figure 20-12: Wow, that's some glow you have there. Check out the subtle reversed-out glow on the word GLOWING.

The PhotoGlow dialog box is fairly light on controls, but it is fast to render when compared to its PhotoBevel and PhotoEmboss brethren. With only four settings to adjust—Stroke Width, Radiance, Opacity, and Color—creating good-looking glows is a simple yet pleasurable task.

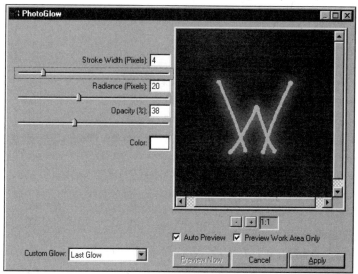

Figure 20-13: Dial it in! The PhotoGlow dialog box makes it easy to create cool glowing effects.

How PhotoShadow Does It

Ah, the drop shadow. As much a staple of the graphic designer's diet as is rice for half the world. Some folks love drop shadows; some folks hate 'em. Nonetheless, PhotoShadow makes them easy to love, as it makes them easy to create. One of the most appealing aspects of PhotoTools is that it makes it easy to combine effects, as shown in the "Add Sizzle" example back in Figure 20-9. Combining beveled type with a drop shadow allows you to quickly create an illusion of three-dimensionality. The bevel makes the type appear to have substance, while the shadow provides the floating effect. Figure 2-14 demonstrates some additional examples of drop-shadowed text.

Figure 20-14: Soft drop shadows are a snap with PhotoShadow.

Creating nice soft drop caps used to be difficult. PhotoShadow's high degree of control, however, makes it a piece of cake. The PhotoShadow dialog box, shown in Figure 20-14, provides all the precision you need. You'll find controls over X/Y Offset, Blur, Opacity, and Shadow color. The higher the Blur setting, the softer and fatter the shadow will appear. The Opacity slider provides the crowning touch, as it allows you to definitively fade shadows into the background.

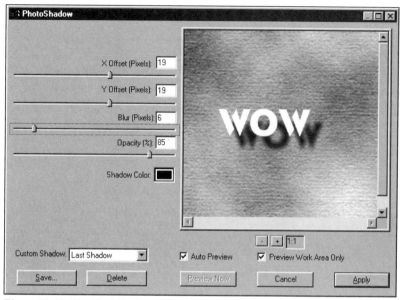

Figure 20-15: The PhotoShadow dialog box lets you get soft and fuzzy or hard edged. It's your call.

How PhotoText Does It

Have you ever been frustrated by the lack of typesetting controls in Photoshop? Until PhotoText, the best solution for finely tuned typography in Photoshop was to first set the type in Adobe Illustrator and then import it into Photoshop. Now, you have an option. PhotoText offers controls that will bring a twinkle to the typemaven's eye (see Figure 20-16). This plug-in allows you to track ranges of text, affecting overall spacing, in addition to letting you kern individual letter pairs. And while type purists may scoff at the idea, PhotoText allows you to set to fit by adjusting character widths. Having the ability to squish or extend a chunk of text can be a huge convenience.

Figure 20-16: The PhotoText dialog box provides real typographic control.

The plug-in contains a number of additional niceties. Have you ever wanted to set type in small caps with Photoshop? With PhotoText, it's as easy as clicking a button. Do you flip back and forth between Photoshop's Type Tool window and final image, while undoing your type a thousand times? PhotoText's large preview window makes that a thing of the past, as it allows you to see how the type looks on the image. It even lets you use the eyedropper tool to pull a color out of the image to use as the text color! If you work with text in Photoshop, PhotoText is well worth the price of admission.

How PhotoTips Does It

With Extensis PhotoTools, each time you launch Photoshop, you can pick up some handy tips and tricks courtesy of the Tips and Tricks dialog box. PhotoTips were written by Deke McClelland, author of scores of books on Photoshop and other graphics applications. The dialog box provides the option of displaying the tips at start-up in addition to allowing you to scroll through over 200 helpful hints and reminders.

chapter 21

Human Software's AutoMask

Creator

The Human Software Company

Purpose

Image masking and color conversion

Platforms

Macintosh

Hardware/software requirements

7 to 12MB of RAM in addition to the minimum Photoshop requirement

URL/contact info for creator of plug-in

http://www.humansoftware.com
The Human Software Co.
14407 Big Basin Way
P.O. Box 2280 Saratoga, CA 95070-0280
408/399-0057 voice
408/399-0157 fax

Products that the plug-in works with

Adobe Photoshop 3.0.5 (or later), Adobe Illustrator, Macromedia
FreeHand, and other programs that support Photoshop 3.0's (or later)
plug-in standard, as well as QuarkXPress.

Want to supplement Adobe Photoshop's built-in masking tools? Human Software's AutoMask filter lets you create both clipping paths and alpha channel masks while also performing RGB to CMYK conversions.

Who Should Use Human Software's AutoMask?

If you're called upon to prepare masked images for print, Human Software's AutoMask may fit the bill. The plug-in should appeal to desktop publishers, graphic artists, designers, commercial printers, prepress operators, and color trade shops. AutoMask's Stencil mode may also be appropriate for Web designers (and others) who need to create alpha channel masks for transparency.

What Human Software's AutoMask Does

AutoMask is an acquire filter that allows you to perform three separate functions. It performs RGB-CMYK conversions and provides advanced tools to create clipping paths and alpha masks. The filter can open and convert PICT RGB, TIFF RGB, Photoshop-native RGB, and PostScript EPS/DCS RGB raster format files to CMYK.

Why Use Human Software's AutoMask?

Photoshop's built-in masking tools are a good start, but they can certainly use some assistance. Human Software's AutoMask provides two additional means to a masked end. ClipPath delivers Bezier drawing tools that surpass the capability of Photoshop's Path tool, while Stencil creates alpha channel masks.

How Human Software's AutoMask Does It

Human Software's AutoMask is an acquire filter. To launch AutoMask, choose File | Import | AutoMask from the Photoshop menu bar. The AutoMask splash dialog box, shown in Figure 21-1, allows you to choose from the Convert, ClipPath, or Stencil modes. In addition, it allows you to set the dialog box size to 640 X 480, 860 X 720, or 1024 X 768 pixels and lets you set AutoMask's scratch disk, as well.

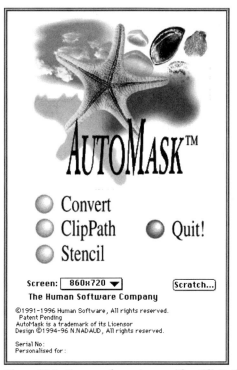

Figure 21-1: You can choose to use either ClipPath or Stencil masking tools to create clipping paths or alpha channel masks, respectively.

Convert

Let's take a look at how AutoMask converts RGB images to CMYK. Click the Convert button to summon the Load an Image dialog box. Locate the image you want to convert, and click the Open button to open the file in RGB Preview, as shown in Figure 21-2. This dialog box allows you to set the undercolor removal (UCR), gray component replacement (GCR), and overall black levels. It also provides access to the Black Creation and Gradation CMYK dialog boxes.

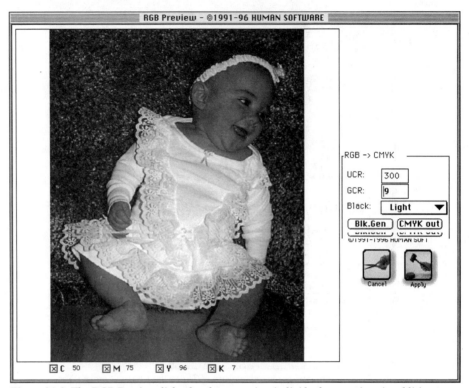

Figure 21-2: The RGB Preview dialog box lets you view individual separations in addition to composite CMYK.

The Black Creation dialog box (hidden under the Blk.Gen button and shown in Figure 21-3), delivers more control than the Black drop-down menu. The dialog box lets you fine-tune the level of black generated at 16 different settings between 0 and 100 percent black. It also lets you save your current settings to use on subsequent images and recalls previous saved settings, as well.

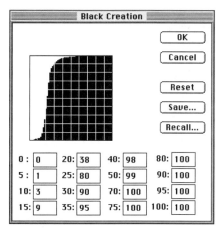

Figure 21-3: Need to boost up the black? Use the
Black Creation dialog box to pump it up.

The Gradation CMYK dialog box (hidden under the CMYK Out button and shown in Figure 21-4), lets you adjust the individual CMYK channels. You have the option of adjusting one channel or multiple channels simultaneously by turning the check boxes (next to the color curve boxes) on or off. The eyedroppers let you quickly set levels by clicking on different highlight, midtone, and shadow areas. As you're working, the densitometer at the bottom of the dialog box keeps track of before and after color percentages. You can quickly switch back and forth between before and after modes by clicking the Image Before/Image After button. To accept the color correction and return to the RGB Preview dialog box, click OK.

Click the Apply button to convert the image and open it into a new file. If the CMYK image is good, save the file. If not, you'll have to reopen the original file with AutoMask and fiddle with the Convert settings.

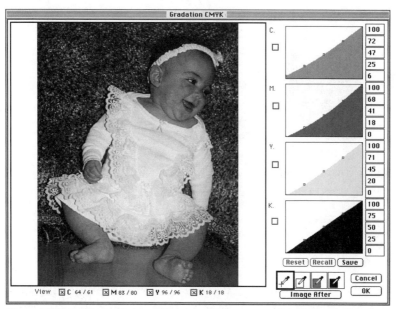

Figure 21-4: Are those cheeks a tad too rosy? You can tweak individual color channels with the Gradation CMYK dialog box.

ClipPath

Need to create a clipping path for artwork that you'll be placing into Illustrator, FreeHand, PageMaker, or QuarkXPress? Check out ClipPath! This mode can accept a range of file formats, including PICT, TIFF, ScitexCT, Photoshop, and raster EPS. The ClipPath dialog box is summoned from AutoMask's splash dialog box. Once you've loaded an image, it will appear in the ClipPath dialog box, shown in Figure 21-5. AutoMask's Panning window provides the means to navigate and zoom the image up (or down). To move around in the image, click and drag the rectangle to the area you want to view. To zoom up on the image, resize the rectangle—the smaller the rectangle, the higher the zoom level. To view the entire image, click the Full Page button.

ClipPath's path editing tools surpass Photoshop's built-in tools. The plug-in provides a dozen path editing implements:

- **Select**. This tool allows you to select and move existing points, as well as adjust curves.

- **Bezier**. Want to draw with a familiar Bezier drawing tool? The Bezier tool will make you feel right at home. Holding down the Option key lets you draw straight lines.

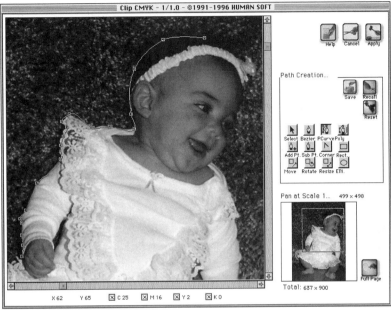

Figure 21-5: AutoMask's ClipPath delivers more functionality than Photoshop's built-in clipping path tools.

■ **PolyCurve**. This tool provides an additional way of drawing curves—by automatically calculating tangent points.

■ **Polygon**. This tool creates polygon objects composed of straight lines.

■ **Add Point**. Need to add an extra control point to a path? Just choose this tool, and click on the path at the location where you want to add the new point.

■ **Subtract Point**. Want to delete an existing control point from a path? Select this tool, and click on the point you want to remove.

■ **Corner**. This tool lets you convert a control point from the default linked tangent mode, thus allowing two independent tangents.

■ **Rectangle**. Choose this tool, and then click and drag to draw a rectangle.

■ **Move**. You can move an entire path with this tool. Just click and drag.

■ **Rotate**. To rotate a path, click a pivot point and then drag around the pivot point to spin the path.

■ **Resize**. To resize a path, click a pivot point and then drag away or toward the pivot point to make the path larger or smaller.

■ **Ellipse**. Choose this tool and then click and drag to draw an ellipse.

The Save, Recall, and Reset buttons allow you to save a path, recall an existing path, or wipe out the path at hand, respectively. Clicking the Apply button will let you save the path and image as a new EPS file. When you open up the new file in Photoshop, you'll have the ability to edit the path if necessary.

Stencil

Want to create a nifty alpha channel mask? AutoMask's Stencil mode works with either RGB or CMYK images and provides three types of tools to create bitmapped masks: Density, Vector Fill, and Brush Stencil. The combination of these three tools enables to you handle a wide range of masking chores. The Stencil dialog box, shown in Figure 21-6, keeps all the tools close at hand. Here, we've been able to mask most of the image with the Density tools and are in the process of masking a big rectangular chunk of the image with the Vector tools.

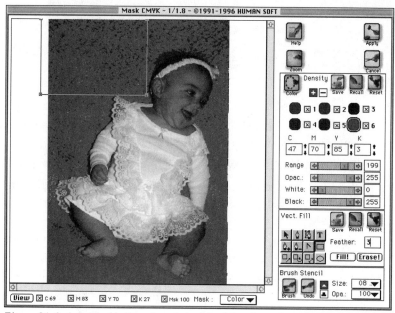

Figure 21-6: AutoMask's Stencil mode builds alpha channel masks using both density- and vector-based tools.

TIP *If you're thinking about using Medley with Illustrator, FreeHand, or XPress, it's important to note that the Stencil masking mode only works within Photoshop.*

Take a quick look at the bottom of the dialog box. You'll see the ever-handy densitometer along with a little drop-down menu that lets you change the mask preview. You can view a mask in black and white or in color. You can use the Mac's color picker to change the color of the mask by clicking the View button and then double-clicking on the stencil color. The opacity of the mask preview can be altered, as well.

Density

You'll want to start out your mask creation in Density mode. This set of tools enables you to select the colors that you want to mask (and not mask) by density. It provides six density color boxes that are set by using the eyedropper to select different sections of the image. Start by clicking the Color button, click the + button, and then click the first of the six density color squares. Select a predominant color with the Eyedropper tool, and then click the #1 check box. To protect a color density from being masked, click the - button, then click a density color box, select the color with the eyedropper, and click the corresponding check box.

Notice that the CMYK percentages for each selection can be adjusted. You may want to tweak the Density sliders, as well:

- **Range**. Adjust this slider to select the widest range of color you can without having the mask slop over into the part of the image that you want to remain unmasked.

- **Opacity**. If you want a full strength mask, keep this slider all the way to the right. But if you want to create a transparent effect, fiddle around with the setting.

- **White** and **Black**. These sliders can be used to tweak the mask threshold. To invert the mask, move the White slider all the way to the right and the Black slider all the way to the left.

Once you've built a density mask, you can use the Save button to store it for later use. The Recall button allows you to summon previously built density masks. The Reset button clears a density mask.

Vector Fill

The Stencil Vector Fill toolset echoes the tools found in AutoMask's ClipMask mode. But instead of building clipping paths, the Stencil Vector Fill tools are used to create objects to be filled with varying degrees of opacity. Create a vector path, select a feather amount and opacity, and then click the Fill button. Click the Erase button to remove the mask from a selected vector path.

After constructing an intricate vector mask, you'll probably want to squirrel it away for safekeeping. Use the Save button to store it for later use. The Recall button allows you to summon previously built vector masks. The Reset button clears all vector mask objects.

Brush Stencil

You'll often use the Brush Stencil tools to touch up masked areas that have been created with the Density and Vector Fill tools. The regular brush lays down the mask in 12 different sizes and a range of opacities (5%, 10%, 20%, 30%, 40%, 50%, 60%, 70%, 80%, 90%, and 100%). The undo brush is available in the same 12 sizes and does more than just remove masked areas. It protects the image by preventing "overspray." Once a section of an image has been touched by the undo brush, you cannot apply a mask to that section.

Click the Apply button to bring the mask into Photoshop as a fourth or fifth channel (depending on whether you're working with an RGB or CMYK image, respectively).

chapter 22

Human Software's CD-Q

Creator
The Human Software Company

Purpose
PhotoCD image acquisition and optimization

Platforms
Macintosh

Hardware/software requirements
7 to 8MB of RAM in addition to the minimum Photoshop requirement

URL/contact info for creator of plug-in
http://www.humansoftware.com
The Human Software Co.
14407 Big Basin Way
P.O. Box 2280 Saratoga, CA 95070-0280
408/399-0057 voice
408/399-0157 fax

Products that the plug-in works with
Adobe Photoshop 3.0.5 (or later), Adobe Illustrator, Macromedia
FreeHand, and other programs that support Photoshop 3.0's (or later)
plug-in standard, as well as QuarkXPress

Do you work with PhotoCD images? Need a faster, more accurate work flow? Human Software's CD-Q automates the process of PhotoCD image acquisition, making PhotoCD a viable means of image acquisition.

Who Should Use Human Software's CD-Q?

Anyone who works with a good number of PhotoCD images—from folks preparing real estate advertisements through high-end graphic designers—can benefit from CD-Q's convenient features. The plug-in is appropriate for print, online, and multimedia applications.

What Human Software's CD-Q Does

Human Software's CD-Q allows you to open PhotoCD photographs in Adobe Photoshop as RGB, CMYK, or grayscale images. In addition to providing the convenience of file format conversion, CD-Q allows you to crop, rotate, color-correct, and vignette as part of the import process.

Why Use Human Software's CD-Q?

With CD-Q, you can perform a number of important procedures on your PhotoCD images before they're opened up in Photoshop. This allows for significant savings in time. Your images come into Photoshop ready to go.

How Human Software's CD-Q Does It _____

Human Software's CD-Q is an acquire filter. To launch CD-Q, click File | Import | CD-Q. The CD-Q splash dialog box, shown in Figure 22-1, allows you to choose the selection method that you'll use to bring images into Adobe Photoshop. While CD-Q allows you to select from the Overview, Image, and Name browsing methods, you may find that some PhotoCD collections (such as those from Corel) do not support the Overview and Image methods.

Figure 22-1: The splash dialog lets you choose an image selection method and lets you quit CD-Q, as well.

Once you've selected and loaded your image using one of these methods, the main CD-Q dialog box will appear, as shown in Figure 22-2.

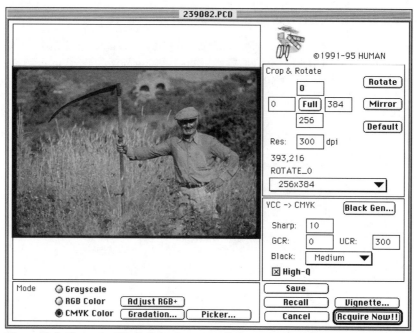

Figure 22-2: The main CD-Q dialog box puts all the controls in your hands with a dynamic preview area.

Let's take a look at the image we opened (from Corel's People of the World PhotoCD), and check out the options that the main dialog box affords:

■ **Crop**. To crop an image, click and drag to create a marquee and then fine-tune your settings by manually entering the left, right, top, and bottom cropping pixel coordinates.

■ **Resolution**. You can choose a target resolution in dpi in addition to selecting the resolution of the PhotoCD image from which you want to sample.

■ **Rotate**. Each time you click the Rotate button, the image will be rotated 90 degrees in a counterclockwise manner.

- **Mode**. Select from Grayscale, RGB, or CMYK Color. When you select RGB mode, the Adjust RGB+ button will become active. When you select CMYK mode, the Gradation and Picker buttons and the YCC to CMYK portion of the dialog box will become active in addition to the Adjust RGB+ button.

- **YCC to CMYK**. Once you're in CMYK mode, you can specify the sharpness, Gray Component Replacement (GCR), Undercolor Removal (UCR), and global Black (None, Light, Medium, or Heavy) settings. Clicking the Black Gen... button summons the Black Generation dialog box for fine-tuning.

TIP *Still running an old non-PowerPC Mac? Try selecting the High-Q check box to speed things up.*

If you're working in RGB mode, you'll probably want to adjust the color levels. Clicking the Adjust RGB+ button summons the Adjust in RGB dialog box. This dialog box allows you to create a custom color lookup table (LUT) by using the Red, Green, and Blue color sliders along with the Brightness and Saturation sliders. You can also choose Remove the Scene Balance Adjustment and Show Out-of-Gamut color. Once you've created a custom LUT, you can save it for later use.

If you're creating CMYK separations for print, the color controls become even more critical. In addition to the Adjust in RGB dialog box, you gain access to two more important dialogs. The Gradation CMYK dialog box, as shown in Figure 22-3, lets you adjust the individual color curves and provides an onscreen densitometer with before and after readouts. The eyedropper allows you to set highlight, midtone, and shadow points, while the Image Before/After button previews the image with and without changes.

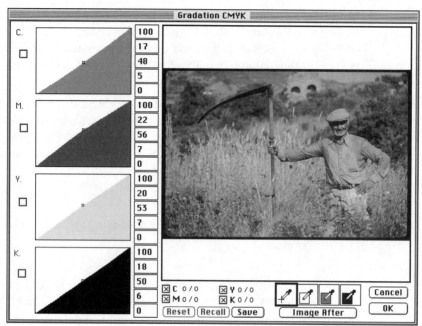

Figure 22-3: The Gradation CMYK dialog box lets you tweak the color curves with a healthy preview.

Want to fine-tune your CMYK color a bit more? Click on the Picker button! CD-Q's Image Picker dialog box, shown in Figure 22-4, feels more than a bit like Photoshop's Variations feature. The Image Picker lets you visually add and subtract cyan, magenta, yellow, and black, with individual control over the highlights, midtones, and shadows. Just choose a Step (3, 6, 9, 12, or 15) strength, and click in the respective preview image to improve the color balance. The grid at the bottom center of the dialog box keeps a running tally of the color correction, while the before and after previews deliver direct feedback through the densitometer readouts. CMYK check boxes let you preview individual color plates as well as composites.

CD-Q even lets you add a vignette to images upon import. Clicking the Vignette button in the main CD-Q dialog box summons the Vignette Box, shown in Figure 22-5. You can choose from Bottom-Up, Left-Corner, 4 Corners, Uniform, Elliptical, Cross, Square, and Diamond-shaped vignettes. The dialog box provides complete control over the vignettes' color, opacity, and blend noise. You can even use the spray can to create free-form vignettes.

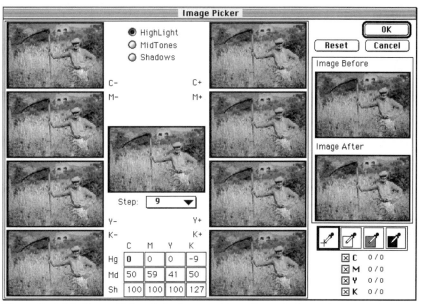

Figure 22-4: The Image Picker dialog box provides point-and-shoot color correction.

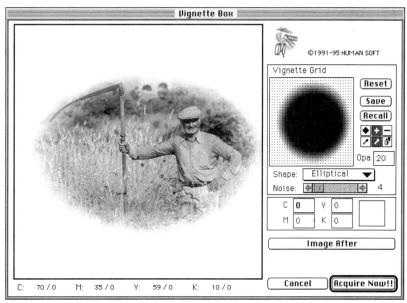

Figure 22-5: Want that old-time look? The Vignette dialog box makes quick work out of vignettes.

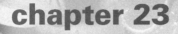

chapter 23

Human Software's Medley

Creator

The Human Software Company

Purpose

Builds huge composite images

Platforms

Macintosh

Hardware/software requirements

9MB of RAM in addition to that which has been allocated to Photoshop, Piggy Plug-In Patch

URL/contact info for creator of plug-in

http://www.humansoftware.com
The Human Software Co.
14407 Big Basin Way
P.O. Box 2280 Saratoga, CA 95070-0280
408/399-0057 voice
408/399-0157 fax

Products that the plug-in works with

Adobe Photoshop 3.0.5 (or later), Adobe Illustrator, Macromedia FreeHand, and QuarkXPress

Do you build large composite images on a regular basis? Looking for an alternative to the standard Photoshop work flow? Take a gander at Human Software's Medley. In addition to creating high-resolution composite images, Medley also provides the tools to handle RGB-to-CMYK conversion, pixel editing, clipping path, and alpha channel creation.

Who Should Use Human Software's Medley?

Human Software's Medley is intended for print professionals who need to assemble large, high-resolution images. The audience includes designers, desktop publishers, graphic artists, quick printers, commercial printers, service bureaus, prepress shops, newspapers, magazines, and other publications.

What Human Software's Medley Does

Medley positions itself as more than just a plug-in. To some folks, it might even be considered a competitor to Live Picture, Macromedia xRes, and Photoshop itself. Medley consists of five modules:

- **Montage**. Here's the meat and potatoes. This is the module used to create the composite image.
- **Convert**. Need a different route from RGB to CMYK? The Convert module provides a few bells and whistles.
- **Brush**. Looking for an alternate method to retouch images? The Brush module allows for quick pixel-level edits on large files.
- **ClipPath**. Need to create vector-based clipping paths for images that will be placed into your page layout program? ClipPath delivers additional functionality.
- **Stencil**. You want alpha channels? Stencil's got 'em.

Why Use Human Software's Medley?

If you're called upon to create large, intricate composites, Human Software's Medley presents an interesting alternative. The plug-in allows up to 64 layers that can be independently moved, resized, color-corrected, masked, blended, or tinted. And best of all, it allows you to build huge images without having insane amounts of RAM.

How Human Software's Medley Does It _____

Medley is an acquire filter. To launch AutoMask, choose File | Import | Medley from the Photoshop menu bar. The Medley splash dialog box, shown in Figure 23-1, provides access to the Montage, Convert, Brushes, ClipPath, and Stencil modes. You can also set the main dialog box size to 640 X 480, 860 X 720, or 1024 X 768 pixels in addition to setting Medley's scratch disk.

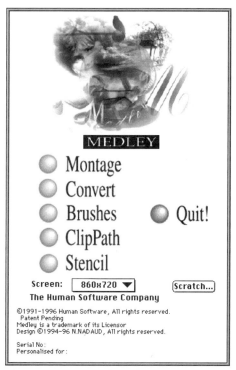

Figure 23-1: The Medley splash dialog box provides your first opportunity to choose between the plug-in's five different modes.

You may recognize the Convert, ClipPath, and Stencil modules from Human Software's AutoMask plug-in, which is covered earlier in this book. In fact, AutoMask and Medley share these three modules, so we'll forgo any redundancy by skipping them in this chapter. Instead, we'll focus on the Montage and Brushes modes.

Montage

 Montage proved to be a worthy companion as we assembled 300 dpi composite color images on our underpowered yet trusty Power Macintosh 7200/90. The following is a quick rundown on how we used Montage for creating some of the color images found on this book's Online Updates Web page (www.vmedia.com/updates.html).

Clicking on the Montage button in Medley's splash dialog box summons the New Background dialog box, shown in Figure 23-2. Here, you are asked for the dimensions, resolution, and mode of the Medley image. You can start with a blank page, or you can choose to build a composite upon an existing image.

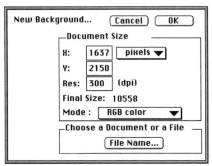

Figure 23-2: The New Background dialog box lets you set up the parameters of your Montage file.

Once you click the OK button in New Background dialog box, the Montage dialog box, shown in Figure 23-3, appears. Many of the controls, such as Zoom, Apply, and Cancel, will be immediately obvious. You'll notice a number of interface elements that persist throughout Human Software's various plug-ins, such as the X-, Y-coordinates and color percentages at the bottom of the dialog box.

Let's get to work and load an image. Click the Image Load button to summon the Load an Image dialog box, shown in Figure 23-4. Medley can open TIFF, Scitex CT, Photoshop, EPS, and PICT format files. You can select an image by filename or visually with the optional Preview feature.

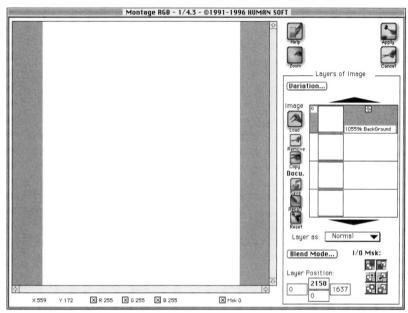

Figure 23-3: The Montage dialog box provides the control and precision you'll need when creating large composite images.

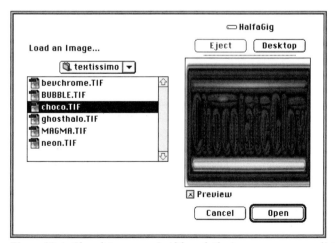

Figure 23-4: Chocolate, anyone? Although the image may appear distorted, the Load an Image dialog box's optional preview comes in handy.

When you click the Open button, the image will be loaded into the scrolling Layers menu. Figure 23-5 shows a loaded Layers menu. You can remove or copy a layer by selecting it from the menu and then clicking the Remove or Copy button, respectively.

Figure 23-5: With all the images loaded, we can rearrange them at will.

The scrolling Layer menu provides XY scaling, file size, and filename details on each layer. You can also quickly access the color correction, masking, and brush modes for each layer. To reposition an image, select its layer and then click and drag it to where you want it to appear in the preview area. You can also fine-tune image placement with to-the-pixel precision. Keep your calculator close at hand, as you have to be careful not to distort an image by changing its height and width. Layers can also be linked together.

Let's take a quick look at some of the other goodies afforded by Medley's Montage mode:

- **Layering**. There are a host of Layering options. Images can be layered using Normal, Additive, Subtractive, Darker, Lighter, Difference, Multiply, or Screen modes.

- **Blend mode**. To really get tricky, try clicking the Blend Mode button. This summons the Blend Following Two Curves dialog box, shown in Figure 23-6. Blend mode lets you build intricate blending effects from top to bottom and from side to side.

- **Masking**. The six I/O Mask buttons at the lower right corner of the Medley dialog box let you apply different treatments to each layer's mask, as well as to the mask on the background layer. You have the option of displaying the area within a mask, the area outside of a mask, or the entire image.

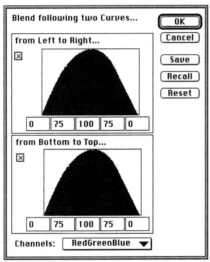

Figure 23-6: You can create some interesting effects by tweaking the Blend mode curves.

The Save button allows you to store a Medley document for safekeeping. You can use the Recall button to load a complete Medley document at a later date. The Reset button wipes out all the layers in the current document.

TIP *All of the images in a Medley document must be of the same type; that is, they must be either uniformly RGB or CMYK images.*

When you're finished creating your Montage masterpiece, you'll render the final image into a single layer. You have the option of creating a smaller render for proofing. Medley will complete all the calculations for you. When the client comes back with a big "yes," you can recall the stored Medley document and re-render at full size. Note that the render dialog box includes a friendly reminder, as shown in Figure 23-7, to save your Medley document so that you can go back in and tweak if necessary.

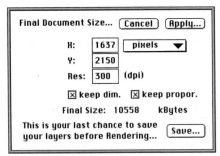

Figure 23-7: Rendering can take some time. Of course, it all depends on the speed of your machine and the size of the images involved.

Brushes

Medley's Brush mode lets you get down to the pixel level to touch up individual layers without having to leave the Medley environment. While it's hard to say why you'd want to do this while using Medley as a Photoshop plug-in, it certainly makes sense when using Medley with your other favorite graphic applications. When Medley is being used as an Illustrator plug-in, a FreeHand Xtra, or a QuarkXTension, pixel editing may become quite handy indeed.

There is one interesting advantage, however. Medley provides a means to edit just a portion of a large file through the use of a panning mechanism. This trick pulls only the current working (visible) chunk of image from the file. When you pan to a different location in the file, Medley stores the previous portion. The brushes are available in varying sizes and opacities and offer some useful effects:

- **Clone**. We're not talking sheep. Use this brush to lose those dust marks.
- **Aerosol**. Spray, spray, spray away.
- **Etch**. This brush provides dodging and burning capabilities. It even lets you get crazy in the color channels to create your own effects.
- **Color**. Be sure to check out the nifty duotone and ghost effects buried in this brush.

- **Effect**. While this one comes standard with such stalwarts as Blur, Sharpen, and Emboss, you can create your own custom effects here, as well.

- **Noise**. Have you ever wanted to paint with noise? Here's your chance!

chapter 24

MEAC SmartMove

Creator

M. E. Aslett Corporation

Purpose

EPS JPEG image compression

Platforms

Macintosh

Hardware/software requirements

Same as Photoshop, Adobe PostScript Level 2 RIP

Contact info for creator of plug-in

M. E. Aslett Corporation
95 Campus Plaza
Edison, NJ 08837
732/225-1922 voice
732/225-1733 fax

Products that the plug-in works with

Adobe Photoshop 3.0.5 or later

D_o you work with large CMYK images? Is your network clogged and are your storage devices stuffed full? MEAC SmartMove presents an alternative to conventional Open Prepress Interface (OPI) servers through the innovative use of visually lossless compression.

Who Should Use MEAC SmartMove?

MEAC SmartMove may fit into the production work flow of publishers, pre-press shops, and catalog houses as well as commercial and publication printers.

What MEAC SmartMove Does

MEAC SmartMove is a combination of an Adobe Photoshop Import/Export plug-in and a stand-alone application. The plug-in allows Photoshop to open and save files in most Photoshop formats, including TIFF, EPS, DCS, and Scitex CT. The application supports the batch processing of files into compressed formats through the use of hot folders.

Why Use MEAC SmartMove?

The two primary reasons to use MEAC SmartMove are decreased file sizes and higher-quality preview files. The JPEG format allows you to compress images at ratios up to 10:1 and beyond. This has obvious benefits in file storage and network file transfer times. The smaller the files, the more you can store on any given storage device, and the faster you can move those images across your network. JPEG proxy files provide the utmost in high-quality onscreen previews when working in QuarkXPress or Adobe PageMaker.

How MEAC SmartMove Does It

Since MEAC SmartMove encompasses both an Adobe Photoshop plug-in and a batch application, it fits into your workflow in two basic ways. If you want to batch convert a bunch of previously scanned images into compressed format files, just drag (or save) them into a hot folder. If you're working in Photoshop and want to save individual images as compressed format files as you go along, you can use the SmartMove export filter. Either method allows you to set the JPEG compression/quality level on a scale of 0-10. MEAC states that their compression is reversible, so images can be compressed, uncompressed, edited, and recompressed without visible degradation to the image.

With an interface that is basically transparent to the average user, SmartMove intelligently compresses graphics so that each image is compressed based upon the composition of the image itself. A blue sky with very little detail would be compressed at a higher level than a green plaid shirt. Thus, the quality of the image to the eye is not compromised.

For folks who don't have the MEAC SmartMove plug-in loaded on their Macintosh, the package ships with a shareware application that converts SmartMove compressed images into Photoshop files. This makes it convenient to send SmartMove images to clients anywhere in the world via modem, ISDN lines, or the Internet. The compressed files will transfer in a fraction of the time that it would take to send conventional TIFF or EPS images.

chapter 25

MetaCreations KPT Convolver

Creator

MetaCreations

Purpose

Interactive image manipulation and effects

Platforms

Windows 95/NT, Macintosh

Hardware/software requirements

Macintosh: System 7 (or later), 68040 processor with FPU or PowerPC
processor, an additional 2.5MB of RAM (on top of what's already
assigned to Photoshop), Windows: an additional 3MB of RAM (on
top of what's already assigned to Photoshop)

URL/contact info for creator of plug-in

http://www.metacreations.com
MetaCreations
6303 Carpinteria Avenue
Carpinteria, CA 93013
805/566-6200 voice
805/566-6385 fax

Products that the plug-in works with

Any application that is Photoshop 3.0 plug-in compliant

Tired of the apply, undo, apply, undo, apply filter cycle? Looking for a fun and interactive way to enhance your Photoshop images? MetaCreations KPT Convolver lets you preview multiple effects before applying them, thus allowing you to save time while exploring new possibilities.

Who Should Use KPT Convolver?

While KPT Convolver will find the happiest homes within the creative community, the plug-in appeals to a gamut of Photoshop users, including advertising agencies, designers, desktop publishers, graphic artists, hobbyists, multimedia and Web developers, newspaper publishers, and photographers, as well as quick and commercial printers.

What KPT Convolver Does

KPT Convolver lets you see what's going to happen before it happens. The plug-in provides real-time previews while applying multiple effects, including a range of blurs, color contrasts, embosses, and sharpens. Convolver's interface is centered around three modes: Explore, Design, and Tweak.

Why Use KPT Convolver?

With KPT Convolver, you'll answer all at once the question, "Hey, what would this image look like with a blur, an emboss, and some color tweaks?"

If you're a fan of Kai's Power Tools, you'll feel right at home with KPT Convolver. Kai Krause's unmistakable interface follows many KPT cues, although Convolver is more production oriented than its predecessor. You'll get real-world functionality in addition to those wild effects.

How KPT Convolver Does It

Let's fire up KPT Convolver and take a quick counterclockwise peek at its interface, as shown in Figure 25-1. Choose Filter | KPT Convolver | KPT Convolver from Photoshop's menu bar. At the top left of the dialog box, you'll see buttons for Convolver's Explore, Design, and Tweak modes. Choosing each one of these modes will cause the dialog box to configure itself accord-

ingly. There's a preset menu hidden beneath the arrow at the bottom center of
the dialog box. At the bottom right, you'll see the familiar Cancel and OK
buttons. And there's no question about the Options menu being at the top
right-hand corner of the Convolver interface.

Preview Modes

Before we dive into the effects, lets see how Convolver's preview options
operate. Figure 25-1 shows the filter's dialog box with a single preview. The
top preview diamond allows you to navigate around the image at hand. Click
and drag in the top diamond to pan. Click in the diamond to toggle between
single and multiple preview tiles. You'll see how the multiple previews function momentarily. To use a split-screen preview, as shown in Figure 25-2, click
the button that's just above the Cancel and OK buttons, at the lower right
corner of the KPT Convolver dialog box.

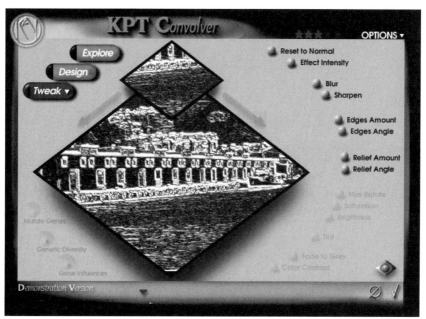

*Figure 25-1: Convolver lets you get a good look at how the multiple effects will appear before
you click the OK button.*

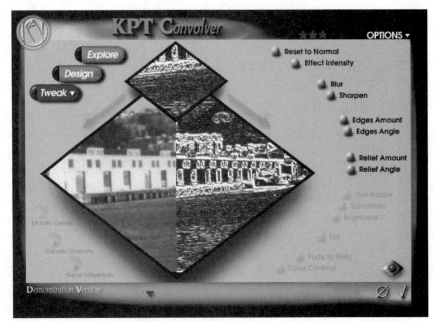

Figure 25-2: Convolver's convenient split-screen preview mode lets you compare the original image with your tweaked image.

Using KPT Convolver to Explore

KPT Convolver's Explore mode, shown in Figure 25-3, is a boon for texture hounds. There are three basic controls here: Mutate Genes, Genetic Diversity, and Gene Influences. Just click the Mutate Genes button or the preview image to roll the gene pool dice. Each time you do, you will be rewarded with a new mix of choices based upon the options specified on the Genetic Diversity and Gene Influences menus.

The Genetic Diversity menu provides Minimum, Minor, Medium, Major, and Maximum choices. The Gene Influences menu allows you to choose Mutate All, Mutate None, Mutate Texture Only, or Mutate Color Only. This lets you achieve complete control over the Blur/Sharpen, Embossing, and Edge Detection options in addition to the Hue, Saturation, Brightness, Contrast, and Tint options.

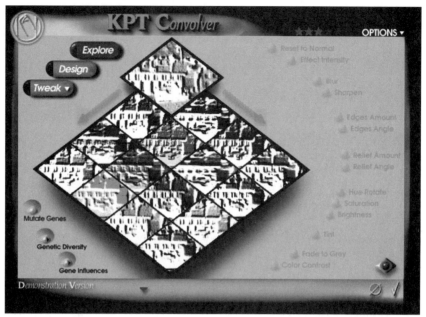

Figure 25-3: With multiple preview areas and just a handful of clicks, you'll quickly explore your way to texture nirvana.

Using KPT Convolver to Design

The Design mode, shown in Figure 25-4, is the simplest of KPT Convolver's three modes. The preview grid lets you see a range of image brightness options. When you click one of the preview images, Convolver will redisplay the image as the midpoint option, thus allowing you to further fine-tune the brightness.

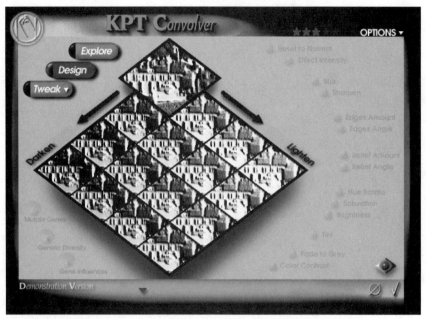

Figure 25-4: Design mode lets you lighten or darken the image interactively.

Using KPT Convolver to Tweak

Looking to spend some time with KPT Convolver? The Tweak mode offers a multitude of possibilities. Tweak is broken down into three submodes: Linear Convolution, Unsharp/Gaussian, and Difference Mask. The Reset to Normal and Effect Intensity options are present in all three submodes. While you're in Tweak mode, you can only preview the image in either full- or split-screen modes, as shown by Figure 25-5. Note that as you look at the interface, there's nothing that specifically tells you which of the three submodes you're in. You'll have to rely on the active options for your first clue.

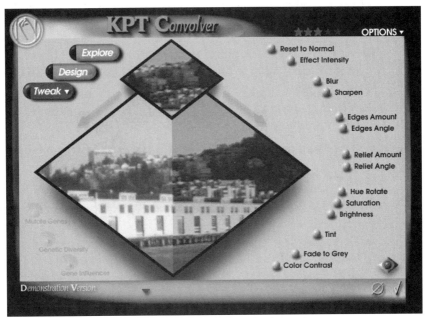

Figure 25-5: KPT Convolver in Tweak/Linear Convolution mode.

Linear Convolution

You can apply a vast range of effects on your image with the Linear Convolution controls. Let's take a look at the options:

- **Blur.** Need some more blur, or less? Click on this button and drag to the right to increase the amount of the Blur effect. Drag to the left to decrease the amount of blur.

- **Sharpen.** Click on this button and drag to the right to intensify the Sharpen effect. Drag to the left to decrease the amount of sharpening.

- **Edges Amount.** Click on this button and drag to the right to increase the Edges Amount effect. Drag to the left to decrease the edges amount.

- **Edges Angle.** Click and drag around this button to set within a full 360-degree range.

- **Relief Amount.** Click on this button and drag to the right to increase the Relief Amount effect. Drag to the left to decrease the relief amount.

- **Relief Angle.** Want to change the lighting angle? Click and drag around this button to set within a full 360-degree range.

- **Hue Rotate**. Click and drag around this button to push the hue settings through a 360-degree range.

- **Saturation.** Click on this button and drag to the right to increase the level of saturation. Drag to the left to decrease the level of saturation.

- **Brightness.** Click on this button and drag to the right to increase the amount of brightness. Drag to the left to decrease the amount of brightness.

- **Tint.** Want to apply a tint color to your image? Click and drag around this button to select a tint color.

- **Fade to Grey.** Need to flatten out the color in your image? Click on this button and drag to the right to increase the Fade to Grey effect. Drag to the left to pump the image full of bright, electric color.

- **Color Contrast.** Click on this button and drag to the right to increase the amount of color contrast. Drag to the left to decrease the amount of color contrast.

Unsharp/Gaussian

As its name implies, the Unsharp/Gaussian submode provides interactive control over Gaussian Blur and Unsharp Masking effects. It also picks up the Hue Rotate, Saturation, Brightness, Tint, Fade to Grey, and Color Contrast controls found in Linear Convolution. Here's a rundown of the specific Unsharp/Gaussian controls:

- **Gaussian.** Click on this button and drag to the right to increase the amount of gaussian blur. Drag to the left to decrease the amount of gaussian blur (and sharpen the image).

- **Unsharp.** Click on this button and drag to the right to increase the amount of unsharp masking. Drag to the left to decrease the amount of unsharp masking (and blur the image).

- **Radius.** Click on this button and drag to the right to increase the Radius amount. Drag to the left to decrease the Radius amount.

- **Threshold.** Click on this button and drag to the right to increase the Threshold amount. Drag to the left to decrease the Threshold amount.

Difference Mask

Difference Mask picks up the Blur, Sharpen, Edges Amount, Edges Angle, Relief Amount, and Relief Angle found in Linear Convolution. It's lots of fun when converting a daytime photograph into an eerily dark neon-like scene, as shown in Figure 25-6.

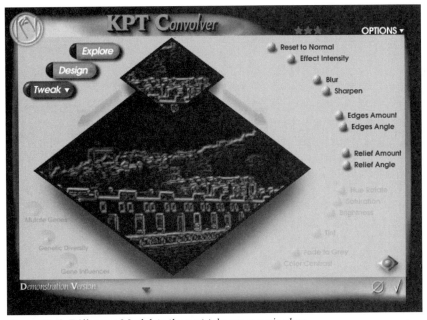

Figure 25-6: Difference Mask lets the port take on an eerie glow.

chapter 26

Digital Dominion's Cinematte

Creator

Digital Dominion

Purpose

Blue screen compositing

Platforms

Windows 95/NT

Hardware/software requirements

Pentium processor

URL/contact info for creator of plug-in

http://users.aol.com/dgdominion
Digital Dominion
1910 Byrd Avenue, Suite 204
Richmond, VA 23230
804/282-3768 fax

Products that the plug-in works with

Adobe Photoshop 3.0.4 or later, other programs that support the
Photoshop 3.0 plug-in standard

Looking for a better way to build composite images from your original photographs? Try blue screening! Digital Dominion's Cinematte brings this traditional Hollywood technique to Adobe Photoshop.

Who Should Use Digital Dominion's Cinematte? _____

Folks who need to composite studio shot photographs will find Digital Dominion's Cinematte a boon to production. The audience includes photographers, graphic designers, magazine publishers, catalog houses, advertising agencies, videographers, multimedia designers, and desktop publishers.

What Digital Dominion's Cinematte Does _____

Digital Dominion's Cinematte works within the RGB colorspace to let you quickly create transparencies around people, animals, minerals, and objects that have been photographed against an evenly lit blue or green screen background. When you build a composite image with Cinematte, the plug-in looks for all levels of the blue (or green) background of your subject image and replaces it with the new background image using identical intensity levels. In addition to creating composites, Cinematte allows you to quickly create drop shadows and glow effects.

Why Use Digital Dominion's Cinematte? _____

Building realistic composite images can be a daunting task. Unlike other techniques, blue screening provides a high level of edge detail and transparency control with tough subjects like glass, smoke, and hair. If you're shooting subjects within a controlled studio environment, you'll find that it's hard to beat the degree of manipulation that Cinematte affords.

How Digital Dominion's Cinematte Does It _____

To work with Cinematte, you'll have to set your photo studio up to capture images with blue or green screen backgrounds. If you're an experienced photographer, this is really not all that tricky. The Cinematte documentation thoroughly explains the concepts behind blue screening, as well as the actual operation of the plug-in itself. In addition, it provides tips for setting up your studio—complete with sources and ideas for the blue paint, screens, and lighting.

Blue-screened images can be brought into your computer from digital cameras, PhotoCD, video grabs, and scanned images. Once you've photographed your subject on a blue (or green) screen background and brought the image into Adobe Photoshop, you'll need to fire up Cinematte. Let's take a run through the plug-in's dialog box, as shown in Figure 26-1:

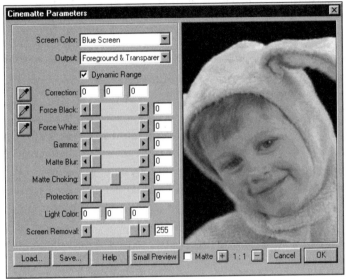

Figure 26-1: The Cinematte Parameters dialog box puts you in the director's chair.

- **Screen Color.** You can specify a blue or green screen.

- **Output.** Select from Foreground and Transparency, Foreground, Matte Only, Matte and Transparency, Transparency Only, and Background from Clipboard (you'll want to use this choice when working with image-editing software that does not support Photoshop layers).

- **Dynamic Range.** Use this option only with poorly lit blue screens as a last resort. While it can improve edge blending, it may also lose detail as a result.

- **Correction.** Click and drag the eyedropper around the worst section of blue screen to create an RGB correction value. This value is used to purify the blue screen while maintaining detail.

■ **Force Black** and **Force White.** These two controls operate in a similar manner but provide opposite results. The Force Black control lets you push dark grays to pure black. As you raise the level, more of the background will show through at full intensity. The Force White control lets you push light grays to pure white. As you raise the level and push to full white, none of the background will show through.

To use these controls, click and drag a marquee with the appropriate eyedropper tool in the most contaminated black or white areas of the image, respectively.

■ **Gamma.** Use this slider to govern the matte's contrast and brightness.

■ **Matte Blur.** Use this control to soften the edges of the matte with a Gaussian blur. You'll want to stick with low levels to avoid obscuring the image.

■ **Matte Choking.** This control lets you eliminate blue spill by choking the matte into the image. You can also spread the matte to create halo effects.

■ **Protection.** While this one might sound like Doctor Ruth's favorite feature, it's really just there to maintain the color integrity of the subject image. With Protection turned on, you'll prevent blue components from being removed from your subject.

■ **Light Color.** You can use this control to tweak the spill lighting on your subject image.

■ **Screen Removal.** This control lets you govern the threshold of blue that is taken out of the subject image.

When using Cinematte to process a number of images from the same shoot, you'll probably want to save your settings once they've been established. The Save button allows you to save the settings, while the Load button lets you use previously stored settings.

Now let's take a look at how easy it is to build a composite image with Cinematte. We'll start by opening up two sample JPEG images (canfalls.jpg and bunny.jpg) from the Cinematte installation disk. Since we want the kid in the bunny costume to be layered over the gorgeous outdoor shot, we've dragged the bunny.jpg background layer from its Layers palette onto the canfalls.jpg image, as shown in Figure 26-2, thus creating a new layer. With Layer 1 (the kid in the bunny costume) selected, choose Filter | Dominion | Cinematte from Photoshop's menu bar. The Cinematte Parameters dialog box will appear, as shown back in Figure 26-1.

Click the Correction eyedropper, and then drag a marquee in the blue screen. You'll want to grab the noisiest part. Click the Matte option in the Cinematte Parameters dialog box to display only the matte in the preview area. Now, you'll want to get a closer look at the matte. Use the + button to zoom up on the preview and pan around the image by clicking and dragging. If there are gray areas that need to be pushed to black, click the Force Black eyedropper and then click and drag a marquee around the gray area. (You may also want to fiddle with the Correction settings.) There will probably be some light gray in areas that should be completely open. Raise the Force White slider until these areas are eliminated. Set the Protection slider to one. Click the OK button to create the matte, shown in Figure 26-3.

Figure 26-2: Cinematte's controls will make fast work of this fuzzy little dude.

Figure 26-3: From the studio to the wild in just a handful of clicks!

Once you've created the matte, you can move the transparency into a Layer Mask. Choose Layer | Add Layer Mask from Photoshop's menu bar. Then choose Selection | Load Selection. In the Load Selection dialog box, select Transparency and Invert. You can then edit the layer mask. After you're done tweaking, choose Filter | Dominion | Kill Transparency to remove the original transparency.

Part IV

Bust Loose With Creative Filters

chapter 27

Alien Skin Eye Candy

Creator

Alien Skin Software, LLC

Purpose

Image processing filters

Platforms

Windows 95/NT, Macintosh

Hardware/software requirements

Same as Photoshop

URL/contact info for creator of plug-in

http://www.alienskin.com
Alien Skin Software, LLC
1100 Wake Forest Rd.
Suite 101
Raleigh, NC 27604
919/832-4124 voice
919/832-4065 fax

Products that the plug-in works with

Photoshop 3.0.4 and later and programs that say they use Photoshop plug-ins, but compatibility with other graphics programs is not guaranteed. Alien Skin states that the following programs pass muster: JASC Paint Shop Pro 4.12, Corel Photo-Paint 7 Plus (build 7.663), Corel Photo-Paint 7 (Revision B, build 7.467).

Want to create super groovy special effects with just a few clicks? Alien Skin Eye Candy—the successor to the ever popular Black Box—is fun and easy to use. This set of 21 filters features a great interface and provides endless possibilities.

Who Should Use Alien Skin Eye Candy?

Alien Skin Eye Candy is great for artists, graphic designers, desktop publishers, photo retouchers, and basically anyone who wants to manipulate images and text with wild special effects.

What Alien Skin Eye Candy Does

Alien Skin Eye Candy adds extensive functionality to Photoshop's existing filter library. Eye Candy greatly expands the properties of existing filters through a custom interface. Eye Candy saves you the trouble of remembering sequences of commands or filter settings through its aptly named filters, such as Glow, Fur, Cutout, Drop Shadow, and Smoke, among others. You can use it in conjunction with Photoshop's Actions dialog interface to further expand your library of effects.

Most of Eye Candy's filters have preset options—with over 200 preset options overall! This is nirvana for folks who like to just point and shoot. Of course, you can save your own custom presets, as well. Eye Candy's interface will default to the last settings you chose for that filter.

Why Use Alien Skin Eye Candy?

Eye Candy is both easy and fun to use. With 21 customizable filters, the array of possibilities is so limitless that you're sure to find the perfect treatment. Be sure to spend plenty of time playing with it before those critical production deadlines or you could fall into the addictive abyss of endless experimentation and lose all sense of time!

How Eye Candy Does It

Eye Candy lets you manipulate entire images or selections through a simple interface. The filters feature fully customizable settings. Eye Candy's interface is invisibly tied to Photoshop's own filters through Photoshop's channels. This allows you to transparently and interactively manipulate a wide variety of options as opposed to Photoshop's constraints of a single dialog per filter at a time. The Eye Candy interface, as shown in Figure 27-1, allows you to preview the results and view the effects dynamically.

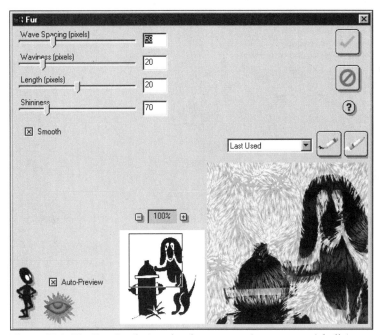

Figure 27-1: The Eye Candy interface lets you preview your special effects.

The interface is extraordinary, offering the user a variety of controls and options. Every filter that uses an interface has a Preview window, Zoom options, a Navigator window, and Presets and Saving/Restoring settings. Click the funky alien in the lower left corner of any filter to change the interface from Fancy to Plain or to access online support. You can even get a whimsical rundown of who's who and who does what at Alien Skin, as shown in Figure 27-2.

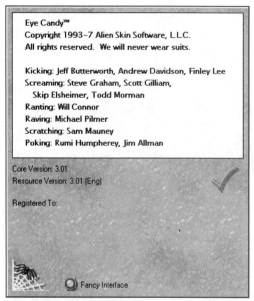

Figure 27-2: The spider web is a hot spot that will launch your Web browser.
You can also choose between a fancy or plain interface.

Let's take a look at the 21 filters in Eye Candy's library:

■ Antimatter

■ Carve

■ Chrome

■ Cutout

■ Drop Shadow

■ Fire

■ Fur

■ Glass

■ Glow

■ HSB Noise

■ Inner Bevel

■ Jiggle

■ Motion Trail

■ Outer Bevel

■ Perspective Shadow

- Smoke
- Squint
- Star
- Swirl
- Water Drops
- Weave

How Antimatter Does It

Antimatter inverts a selection's brightness without affecting the selection's hue and saturation values, as shown in Figure 27-3. With Photoshop's Invert filter, negative is made positive, which affects the color. Magenta becomes cyan, for example. Unlike with the Invert filter, with Antimatter, a dark green becomes a light green, maintaining hue and saturation values. There are no controls or presets available with this filter.

Figure 27-3: Applying Antimatter to the lizard makes it a contrast reverse without changing the hue or saturation.

How Carve Does It

Carve makes selections appear carved or chiseled into the image. This filter uses shadows and highlights similar to the two Bevel filters, but it also darkens the deeper areas of the selection, as shown in Figure 27-4. If you find that this effect looks too much like Inner Bevel, try moving the light source to the top of the image and increasing the Darken Depths slider.

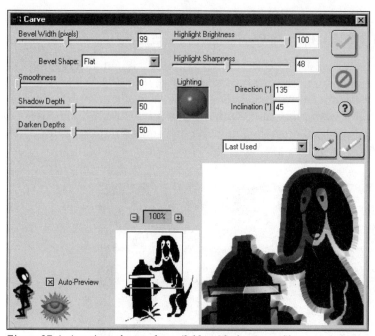

Figure 27-4: A variety of controls available with the Carve filter can make your image look raised or chiseled.

The controls available for Carve are:

■ **Bevel Width.** Controls the distance from the edge of your selection to the bottom of the carve.

- **Shadow Depth.** Higher values darken shadows, which makes the chiseled effect more pronounced.

- **Smoothness.** Lower values give the beveled edges of your selection a rougher appearance by leaving little ridges; higher values remove the ridges and make the carve smoother.

- **Bevel Shape.** See Inner Bevel.

- **Darken Depths.** Larger values help strengthen the illusion of depth.

- **Highlight Brightness** and **Highlight Sharpness.** As with other filters, Brightness and Sharpness affect the white highlights that appear on the parts of your selection that face the light. Brightness controls the intensity of these highlights, while Sharpness affects their diffusion. Higher values give a glossier effect.

- **Direction.** Controls the direction from which the light falls on your selection. You have a full 360-degree range from which to choose. A value of 0 degrees yields light directly from the right, 90 degrees yields light from the top, 180 degrees yields light directly from the left, and 270 degrees yields light from the bottom.

- **Inclination.** Controls the angle formed by the light and the page. This gives the effect of more depth. If the light originates from directly overhead, the light angle will be at 90 degrees. As the light comes more directly from the side, the value will approach 0 degrees.

How Chrome Does It

It's time for some heavy metal! The Chrome filter produces a cool metallic effect that can be used to simulate chrome, gold, and other metals, as shown in Figure 27-5. The best way to learn about Chrome is to use it; the description of the controls barely indicates its amazing potential. This filter works especially well on fat objects and text. It needs some substance to really see the dynamic effects it produces.

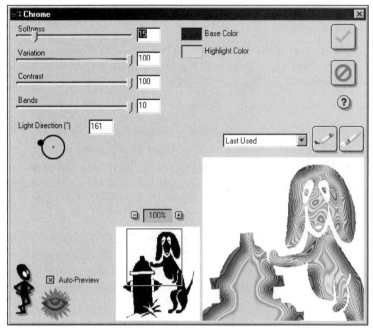

Figure 27-5: Chrome doggies!

Manipulate these controls to see the effects:

- **Bands.** Controls the number of dark bands between the edge of your selection and the middle.

- **Softness.** Controls the softness of the metallic effect. Higher values generally produce wider bands.

- **Variation.** Controls the placement of the bands; higher values generally move the bands more toward the middle of the selection.

- **Contrast.** Controls the amount of contrast between the lightest and darkest areas of the affected area; higher values increase the contrast.

- **Light Direction.** Controls the direction from which the light falls on your selection. You have a full 360-degree range from which to choose. A value of 0 degrees yields light directly from the right, 90 degrees yields light from the top, 180 degrees yields light directly from the left, and 270 degrees yields light from the bottom.

- **Base Color** and **Highlight Color**. Choose any color for your metallic effects; these two controls produce a huge range of possible color combos. Clicking in either of these boxes will bring up the color picker you have previously selected in Photoshop.

How Cutout Does It

Cutout makes your selection appear as if there is a hole in the image. It does this by adding a shadow and optional fill color inside the selection so that they appear recessed behind the rest of the image, as shown by Figure 27-6.

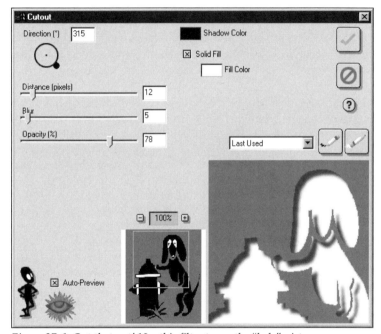

Figure 27-6: Cut that out! Use this filter to see the "hole" picture.

Here's what each control does:

- **Direction.** Controls the direction in which the shadow of your selection is offset. You have a full 360-degree range from which to choose. A value of 0 degrees offsets the shadow directly to the right, 90 degrees offsets it toward the top, 180 degrees offsets it to the left, and 270 degrees offsets it toward the bottom.

- **Distance.** Controls how far your shadow is offset inside of the cutout. Following the axis set by the direction slider, the value measures the number of pixels from the selection to the shadow.

- **Blur.** Controls the sharpness of the shadow inside the cutout. Higher values make the shadow more blurry, giving the effect of a dim or far-away light source.

- **Opacity.** Adjusts the overall transparency of the shadow inside your cutout. Higher values darken the shadow so that the fill color or layer behind the shadow is less visible.

- **Shadow Color.** The shadow can be any color you like. Clicking in this box brings up the color picker you have previously selected in Photoshop.

- **Fill Color.** The fill color can also be any color. Choosing a fill color increases the effect of the cutout by making it appear that there is a different image behind the hole. To choose a fill color, click in the color box and the color picker you have previously selected in Photoshop will appear.

TIP *You can disable Solid Fill. This has two possible effects. If your selection is on the background layer, Cutout leaves the original image at the bottom of your new hole. However, if your selection is on a layer other than the background and Preserve Transparency is disabled, you will be able to see through your cutout to the layers behind it.*

How Drop Shadow Does It

This is the classic drop shadow, the most used and abused effect of all time. You can make your text or objects appear to float by creating a soft-edged shadow beneath them, as shown by Figure 27-7. Drop shadows easily add a 3D quality to any document and are particularly useful for making an object spring to the foreground of a composition.

TIP *This filter requires a selection to do its job unless you are applying Drop Shadow to an object in a layer by itself. The shadow shape will be roughly the same as your selection.*

Remember that this filter draws outside of your selection. If you are using a program other than Photoshop 4.0, this will cause you to lose your selection if you have not saved it before applying the filter. Don't forget to save the selection if you will need to use it after this operation!

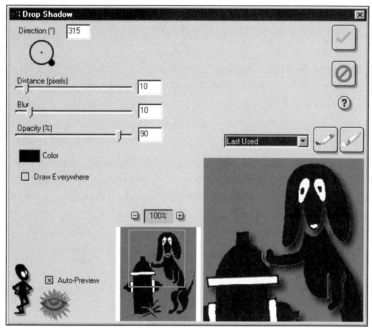

Figure 27-7: Drop shadows are a staple for any graphic designer and a quick way to add pseudo-three-dimensionality to a composition.

To ensure that Drop Shadow works correctly in a layer, make sure that the Preserve Transparency check box is not checked. This is important for Photoshop users since this filter cannot perform properly with Preserve Transparency enabled. Note that Photoshop 4.0 automatically enables Preserve Transparency when it creates type and when it places an image in a layer. Disable it and you will be able to use this filter without a problem.

Here's a rundown on the Drop Shadow controls:

■ **Direction.** Controls the direction in which the shadow is offset from your selection. You have a full 360-degree range from which to choose. A value of 0 degrees offsets the shadow directly to the right, 90 degrees offsets it toward the top, 180 degrees offsets it to the left, and 270 degrees offsets it to the bottom.

■ **Distance.** Controls how far from your selection the shadow will appear. Higher values increase the distance, which makes the selection appear to be floating farther from the background.

- **Blur.** Controls how blurred the edges of your shadow will be. Higher values make the shadow more blurry, giving the effect of a dim or far-away light source.

- **Opacity.** Adjusts the overall transparency of the shadow. Higher values darken the shadow so that the background or layer behind the shadow is less visible.

- **Color.** The drop shadow can be any color you like. Clicking in this box brings up whatever color picker you have selected in Photoshop.

- **Draw Everywhere.** When this control is enabled, the filter will draw the entire shadow (not just outside the selection). This feature is very useful when applying a shadow to its own layer. Just make a selection, make a new layer, and apply the Drop Shadow with Draw Everywhere enabled. You may not want this box checked if you are applying the filter to the same layer as the selected image since it could draw over your selection.

How Fire Does It

You want a hot-looking image? Turn on the blow torch. The Fire filter produces a realistic flame effect rising from your selection, as shown by Figure 27-8. Once again, this is a filter that requires a selection to do its job unless you are applying Fire to an object in a layer by itself.

TIP
Remember that this filter draws outside of your selection. If you are using a program other than Photoshop 4.0, this will cause you to lose your selection if you have not saved it before applying the filter. Don't forget to save the selection if you will need to use it after this operation!

Pay attention to the Preserve Transparency option in the Layers window. If you want this filter to work right, make sure that the Preserve Transparency check box is not checked. This filter cannot perform properly with Preserve Transparency enabled. Note that Photoshop 4.0 automatically enables Preserve Transparency when it creates type and when it places an image in a layer. Disable it and you will be able to use this filter without a problem. Use these controls to direct the flame:

- **Flame Width.** Controls how wide the wisps of fire will be. Higher values yield wider (and thus fewer) wisps.

- **Flame Height.** Controls the height of the wisps of fire. Higher values yield longer flames.

Figure 27-8: Flame on! This filter is alight! Create a visual inferno and watch your image catch fire.

■ **Movement.** Controls the amount of movement in the flames. Higher values yield a more turbulent fire effect.

■ **Random Seed.** The placement of the wisps of fire has a random element. This slider allows you to control the random element, producing a wide variety of changes to the fire. Have fun experimenting!

■ **Inside Masking.** Controls how much the fire covers the inside of your selection. Lower values allow the fire to cover the selection more completely, while higher values produce a very diffuse fire effect.

■ **Edge Softness.** Controls the sharpness of the flame wisps. Lower values yield sharper wisps, while higher values produce a very diffuse fire effect.

■ **Color.** The fire effect is made up of an inner and outer color, both of which can be any color you like. The Natural setting in the drop-down menu yields a realistic bright orange and yellow flame. Choose User Defined from the pop-up menu to enable the inner and outer color boxes. Clicking in either box brings up the color picker you have previously selected in Photoshop.

How Fur Does It

Load your fur gun and fire at will! You've blasted your image with random furry clumps, as demonstrated by Figure 27-9. The spacing and shape of these clumps can be controlled to achieve a hair-raising fur ball of effects.

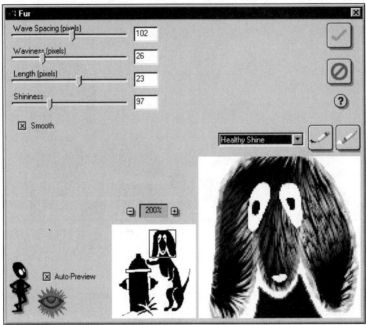

Figure 27-9: If your image is limp and lifeless, adding Fur to it will bring it back to life.

No animals were harmed while testing this filter, which puts a nice warm winter coat on your selection. Fabulous Fur can be yours with these controls:

■ **Wave Spacing.** While the fur clumps are randomly spaced, this slider controls the average distance between their centers. Lower values create many closely spaced, tiny clumps. Higher values create bigger, chunkier clumps. Note that Wave Spacing is a pixel-based setting. This means that settings generated for a 72-dpi image will look different when applied to a 300-dpi image.

- **Waviness.** Controls how much the direction of the hair strands will vary in a clump. A value of 0 will create straight strands of fur. Beats using an iron to straighten hair. A value of 100 will create erratic clumpings like hair strewn on a barbershop floor.

- **Hair length.** Controls the length of the hair strands in each clump. Long hair is always fashionable here. Since each strand also smears the graphic information below it, the higher the value, the more the image will be smeared. Note that Hair Length is a pixel-based setting. This means that settings generated for a 72-dpi image will look different when applied to a 300-dpi image.

- **Shininess.** Adds white highlights to fur that are at a right angle to the reflected light. Higher values create more white highlighted strands. Go for the silver fox look.

- **Smooth.** When checked, this eliminates graininess, otherwise known as greasy buildup. Sleek is chic, baby.

How Glass Does It

Go ahead, look at the world through rose-colored glasses (or any color in the spectrum). The Glass filter puts a sheet of tinted glass on top of your selection, as shown in Figure 27-10. The edges of the glass effect are smooth and beveled, while the middle can be as lumpy, bumpy, gritty, and grungy as you like. Eye Candy's Glass effect is achieved by simulating three physical effects: refraction, light filtering, and specular reflection. The Refraction and Flaw sliders give you control of image warping. The glass color control and Opacity slider govern light filtering. Specular reflection, the reflection of the light source on the glass, is controlled by the highlight sliders and light directions sliders.

TIP *This filter works best on large, simple selections that are not filled in with a solid color, like those made with the rectangle and ellipse selection tools.*

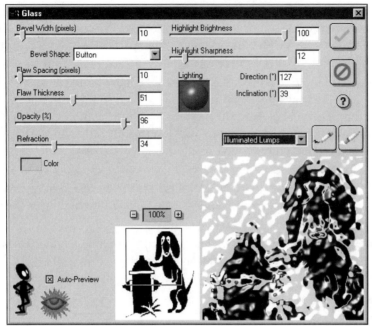

Figure 27-10: In case of emergencies, break out the Glass.

These controls will bring you through the looking glass:

■ **Bevel Width.** Controls the width of the smooth outer edge of the glass. Larger values will make your glass appear thicker (when used with high refraction) or the slope of the beveled edge more gradual (when used with low refraction). Similarly, smaller values make the glass seem thinner (with low refraction) or the bevel steeper (with high refraction).

As with Inner Bevel, widening the bevel shrinks the area of your selection that appears to be raised and flat. When your bevel width is greater than half the width of the selection, no area will be left flat.

■ **Flaw Spacing** and **Flaw Thickness.** Flaws are simulated ripples in your glass. They mimic the defects you find in older glass. Larger spacing makes these defects cover a larger area, while smaller spacing increases their frequency. Higher thickness values make these defects more pronounced.

■ **Color.** Click in this box to select the color that tints the glass.

■ **Opacity.** Adjusts the overall transparency of the effect. In this case, the slider affects the tint of the glass. A higher value tints your glass more toward the color selected in the color picker. With a lower value, the glass is more transparent and allows the image underneath to show through more clearly.

■ **Refraction.** Refraction controls the amount your selection is warped by the glass above it. At lower values, the effect is subtle. With higher values, straight lines curve noticeably and rigid geometric shapes skew. At very high values, the image beneath the glass is extremely distorted.

■ **Highlight Brightness** and **Highlight Sharpness.** As with other filters, Brightness and Sharpness affect the white highlights that appear on the parts of your selection facing the light. Brightness controls the intensity of these highlights, while Sharpness affects their diffusion. Higher values give a glossier effect.

■ **Direction.** Controls the direction from which the light falls on your selection. You have a full 360-degree range from which to choose. A value of 0 degrees yields the light directly from the right, 90 degrees yields light from the top, 180 degrees yields light directly from the left, and 270 degrees yields light from the bottom.

■ **Inclination.** Controls the angle formed by the light and the page. This gives the effect of more depth. If the light originates from directly overhead, the light angle will be at 90 degrees. As the light comes more directly from the side, the value will approach 0 degrees.

How Glow Does It

Light up the night with neon! The Glow filter draws a semitransparent glow around the outside edge of the selection, as shown in Figure 27-11. Besides the usual neon effect, creative use of color and opacity will give you effects subtle enough for many purposes. For instance, a very thin and transparent dark glow can be used to enhance contrast around an object and help free it from a busy background.

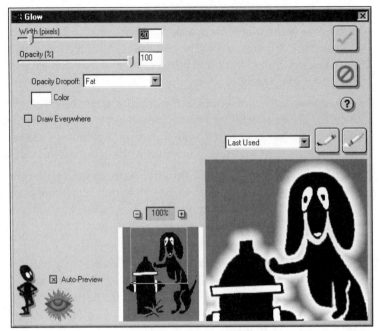

Figure 27-11: From neon to subtle contrasts, use this filter for glowing results.

TIP │ *This filter requires a selection to do its job unless you are applying Glow to an object in a layer by itself.*

Once again, the usual warning: Remember that this filter draws outside of your selection. If you are using a program other than Photoshop 4.0, this will cause you to lose your selection if you have not saved it before applying the filter. Don't forget to save the selection if you will need to use it after this operation!

To be sure that Glow works correctly in a layer, make sure that the Preserve Transparency check box is not checked. This is important for Photoshop users since this filter cannot perform properly with Preserve Transparency enabled. Note that Photoshop 4.0 automatically enables Preserve Transparency when it creates type and when it places an image in a layer. Disable it and you will be able to use this filter without a problem.

Glow and the world glows with you. Tweak these controls:

■ **Width.** Controls the distance from the edge of your selection to the point where the opacity of the glow drops to zero. Higher values yield a wider glow.

■ **Opacity.** Adjusts the overall transparency of the glow. Higher values make the glow more opaque so that the background or layer behind the glow is less visible.

■ **Opacity Dropoff.** Controls how rapidly the opacity drops to zero. The thinner the drop-off, the more quickly the opacity is reduced. The Diffuse setting simulates the type of glow achievable through channel operations.

■ **Color.** The glow can be any color you like. Clicking in this box brings up the color picker you have previously selected in Photoshop.

■ **Draw Everywhere.** When this control is enabled, the filter will fill the selection as well as draw the glow. This feature is very useful when applying a glow in its own layer. Just make a selection, make a new layer, and apply the glow with Draw Everywhere enabled. You may not want this box checked if you are applying the filter to the same layer as the selected image since it could draw over your selection.

How HSB Noise Does It

HSB Noise lets you add noise to a selection by varying the hue, saturation, brightness, and transparency of the selection. Adding noise to computer-generated artwork can help it appear more natural, as demonstrated by Figure 27-12. Transparent noise can be applied to a selection in a layer, creating random semitransparent spots. This filter only works in RGB mode.

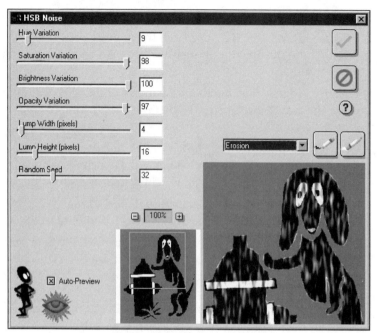

Figure 27-12: HSB Noise gives a natural look to computer-generated artwork.

Play with these controls to turn up the volume on HSB Noise:

- **Hue Variation.** Higher values increase the range of hue variation for the selection.

- **Saturation Variation.** Higher values increase the range of variation in how colorful or washed out the color of the selection appears.

- **Brightness Variation.** Higher values increase the amount of light emitted by each pixel.

- **Opacity Variation.** In a layer, this slider determines the range of transparency for a given pixel—from zero up to the slider value. A low value will have little to no transparency. A high value will have many transparent holes. A high-opacity setting can generate interesting fog or ghostly images when applied to a layer. To ensure that the opacity parameter of HSB Noise works correctly in layers, make sure that the Preserve Transparency check box is not checked. This is important for Photoshop users; the Opacity control cannot perform properly with Preserve Transparency enabled. Note that Photoshop 4.0 automatically enables Preserve Transparency when it creates type and when it places images in layers. Disable it and you can use the Opacity slider without a problem. This slider will have no effect when the filtering is applied to a selection in the background layer.

■ **Lump Width** and **Height.** These sliders determine the size of the noise and allow you to create a wide variety of textures. The higher the values, the more amorphous the noise will appear. A higher width value will create horizontal streaks; a higher height will create vertical streaks. Note that Lump Width and Height are pixel-based settings. This means that settings generated for a 72-dpi image will look different when applied to a 300-dpi image.

How Inner Bevel Does It

Inner Bevel will give your selection an embossed look or the appearance of being raised up from the rest of the image, as shown in Figure 27-13. This filter is an excellent way to quickly and easily create buttons of any shape. The bevel is created by adding highlights and shadows around the inside edge of your selection. Since the effect appears inside your selections, this filter has a tendency to make objects look smaller; the bevel width is essentially subtracted from the selection. If you would like to maintain the size of your selections, try Outer Bevel.

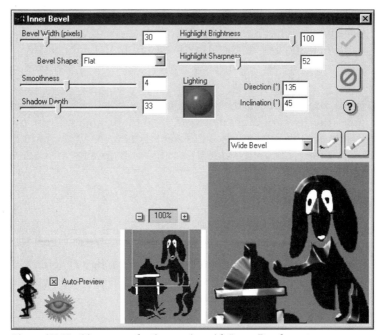

Figure 27-13: Give your selection a raise with Inner Bevel.

The Inner Bevel filter allows you to manipulate these controls:

- **Bevel Width.** Controls the distance from the selection edge to the highest part of the bevel. Higher values will shrink the raised area of your selection. Once your bevel width is equal to half the width of the selection, no area is left flat. Higher values only decrease the steepness of the bevel.

- **Shadow Depth.** Higher values darken shadows, making the effect more pronounced. Darker shadows may also make the bevel appear steeper.

- **Smoothness.** Lower values give the beveled edges of your selection a rougher appearance by leaving little ridges. Higher values remove these ridges and make the bevel smoother.

- **Bevel Shape.** You have four choices, from full height to zero, for the shape of the bevel's drop-off. Each results in a slightly different look to your filter effect.

- **Highlight Brightness** and **Highlight Sharpness.** As with other filters, Brightness and Sharpness affect the white highlights that appear on the parts of your selection that face the light. Brightness controls the intensity of these highlights, while Sharpness affects their diffusion. Higher values can give a glossier effect.

- **Direction.** Controls the direction from which the light falls on your selection. You have a full 360-degree range from which to choose. A value of 0 degrees yields light directly from the right, 90 degrees yields light from the top, 180 degrees yields light directly from the left, and 270 degrees yields light from the bottom.

- **Inclination.** Controls the angle formed by the light and the page. This gives the effect of more depth. If the light originates from directly overhead, the light angle will be at 90 degrees. As the light comes more directly from the side, the value will approach 0 degrees.

How Jiggle Does It

Jiggle produces a new kind of distortion based on randomly placed bubbling. Unlike the standard Photoshop distortion filters, the Jiggle filter is not based on a wave pattern or around a single axis. Instead, Jiggle yields a more organic distortion, as shown in Figure 27-14, resulting in a selection that appears as if it is bubbling, gelatinous, or even shattered.

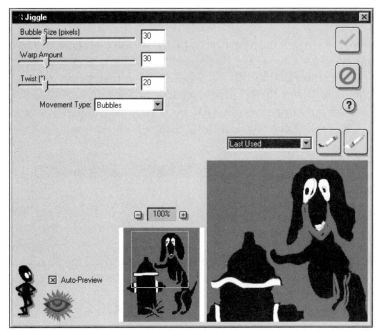

Figure 27-14: Shake it up and add a new kind of distortion with Jiggle.

The Jiggle filter lets you try your hand at these controls:

■ **Bubble Size.** This slider controls the spacing or frequency of the defects. It works like whirlpool spacing in Swirl; the lower the value, the more closely spaced the distortion.

■ **Warp Amount.** This slider controls how much your selection is stretched. It is analogous to the Smear Length slider in Swirl.

■ **Twist.** Like Swirl, Jiggle can also twist your selection. This slider controls the amount of twisting that occurs. The movement is measured in degrees.

■ **Movement Type.** This menu selects the way you want the image jiggled. There are three types of warping: Bubbles, Brownian Motion, and Turbulence. Bubbles produces a fairly smooth and evenly spaced distortion. Brownian Motion simulates random movement to create a more ragged effect. If you want still a more shattered effect, choose Turbulence, which creates sharper breaks in the image.

How Motion Trail Does It

Motion Trail smears the selection outward in one direction, producing the illusion of motion, as shown by Figure 27-15. This filter is different from the Motion Blur filter that's built into Photoshop in that it smears in one clear direction and leaves the original selection more recognizable. If the effect appears too faint or seems nonexistent, try turning on Just Smear Edges and/or increasing the value of the Opacity slider.

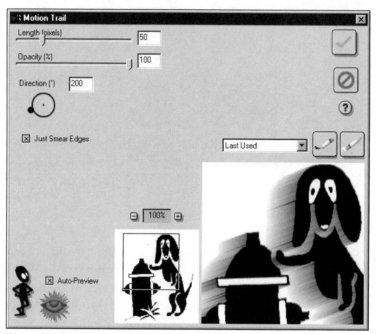

Figure 27-15: Motion Trail puts cool streaky effects simulating motion into your selection.

Remember that this filter draws outside of your selection. If you are using a program other than Photoshop 4.0, this will cause you to lose your selection if you have not saved it before applying the filter. Don't forget to save the selection if you will need to use it after this operation!

Also, to ensure that Motion Trail works correctly in a layer, make sure that the Preserve Transparency check box is not checked. This is important for Photoshop users since this filter cannot perform properly with Preserve Transparency enabled. Note that Photoshop 4.0 automatically enables Preserve Transparency when it creates type and when it places an image in a layer. Disable it and you will be able to use this filter without a problem.

The Motion Trail filter allows you to alter these settings:

- **Length.** Controls the distance the trail extends from the selection. Higher values yield a longer motion trail.

- **Opacity.** Adjusts the overall transparency of the motion trail. Higher values darken the effect so that the background or layer behind the motion trail is less visible.

- **Direction.** Controls the direction from which the light falls on your selection. You have a full 360-degree range from which to choose the placement of your motion trail. A value of 0 degrees places it directly to the right, 90 degrees places it at the top, 180 degrees places it to the left, and 270 degrees places it at the bottom.

- **Just Smear Edges.** When this box is checked, the motion trail is created by copying color only from the edges of the selection and smoothly decreasing in opacity as it moves away. When this box is not checked, the effect may appear very faint for large Length settings.

How Outer Bevel Does It

Outer Bevel makes your selection appear embossed or raised up from the rest of the image, as shown in Figure 27-16. As with Inner Bevel, this effect is achieved by adding highlights and shadows. However, with Outer Bevel, they appear around the outside of the selection. Since the bevel is created around the outside edge of the selection, the selected object may seem bigger after the effect is applied. If you think the bevel is crowding other parts of your composition, then try Inner Bevel.

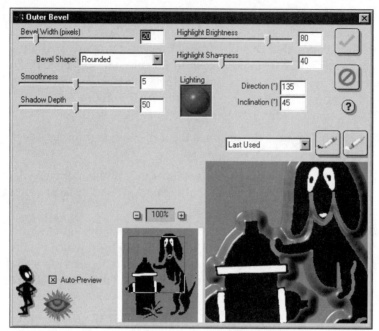

Figure 27-16: It's easy to create an embossed or raised effect with Outer Bevel.

This filter requires a selection to do its job. Unlike some of the other filters that require a selection, Outer Bevel will not work when applied to an object in a layer without a selection. Remember that this filter draws outside of your selection. If you are using a program other than Photoshop 4.0, this will cause you to lose your selection if you have not saved it before applying the filter. Don't forget to save the selection if you will need to use it after this operation!

Also, to ensure that Outer Bevel works correctly in a layer, make sure that the Preserve Transparency check box is not checked. This is important for Photoshop users since this filter cannot perform properly with Preserve Transparency enabled. Note that Photoshop 4.0 automatically enables Preserve Transparency when it creates type and when it places an image in a layer. Disable it and you will be able to use this filter without a problem.

The Outer Bevel filter allows you to adjust these controls:

■ **Bevel Width.** Controls the distance from your selection edge to the outer edge of the bevel. Higher values yield a wider bevel.

- ■ **Shadow Depth.** Higher values darken shadows, making the effect more pronounced. Darker shadows may also make the bevel appear steeper.

- ■ **Smoothness.** Lower values give the beveled edges of your selection a rougher appearance by leaving little ridges. Higher values remove these ridges and make the bevel smoother.

- ■ **Bevel Shape.** See Inner Bevel.

- ■ **Highlight Brightness** and **Highlight Sharpness.** As with other filters, Brightness and Sharpness affect the white highlights that appear on the parts of your selection that face the light. Brightness controls the intensity of these highlights, while Sharpness affects their diffusion. Higher values can give a glossier effect.

- ■ **Direction.** Controls the direction from which the light falls on your selection. You have a full 360-degree range from which to choose. A value of 0 degrees yields light directly from the right, 90 degrees yields light from the top, 180 degrees yields light directly from the left, and 270 degrees yields light from the bottom.

- ■ **Inclination.** Controls the angle formed by the light and the page. This gives the effect of more depth. If the light originates from directly overhead, the light angle will be at 90 degrees. As the light comes more directly from the side, the value will approach 0 degrees.

TIP | *Outer Bevel works best when applied to a background layer of a texture or color. Make a selection based on text or an object and then apply Outer Bevel to the background layer.*

How Perspective Shadow Does It

This filter creates a shadow behind your selection that is tilted so that the selection appears to be standing up as the light comes from above and in front, as shown in Figure 27-17. The shadow is attached to the object rather than floating below it, which creates a 3D perspective illusion unlike the one produced by the Drop Shadow filter.

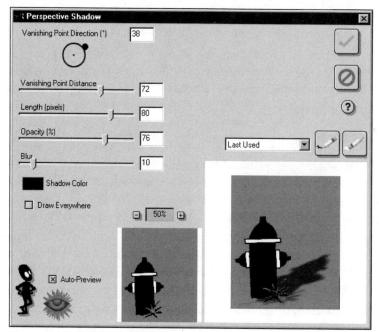

Figure 27-17: Simulating 3D is a cinch with Eye Candy's Perspective Shadow.

This effect requires a selection to do its job unless you are applying Perspective Shadow to an object in a layer by itself. Remember that this filter draws outside of your selection. If you are using a program other than Photoshop 4.0, this will cause you to lose your selection if you have not saved it before applying the filter. Don't forget to save the selection if you will need to use it after this operation!

Also, to ensure that Perspective Shadow works correctly in a layer, make sure that the Preserve Transparency check box is not checked. This is important for Photoshop users since this filter cannot perform properly with Preserve Transparency enabled. Note that Photoshop 4.0 automatically enables Preserve Transparency when it creates type and when it places an image in a layer. Disable it and you will be able to use this filter without a problem.

The Perspective Shadow filter allows you to tweak these controls:

- **Vanishing Point Direction.** Controls the direction from which the shadow falls behind your selection. If you set this value at 0 degrees, the shadow falls to the right; at 90 degrees it falls toward the top of the selection; at 180 degrees it falls to the left. Note that the shadow cannot fall in front of your selection.

- **Vanishing Point Distance.** Controls how far the vanishing point on the horizon is from your selection. Lower values bring the vanishing point closer, which makes the shadow taper more rapidly.

- **Shadow.** Controls the length of the shadow with little effect on the tapering. Lower values produce a shorter shadow. Experiment with Shadow Length and Vanishing Point Distance to produce a range of effects that simulate different angles of light.

- **Blur.** Controls how blurred the edges of your shadow will be. Higher values make the shadow more blurry, giving the effect of a dim or faraway light source.

- **Opacity.** Adjusts the overall transparency of the shadow. Higher values darken the shadow so that the background or layer behind the shadow is less visible.

- **Shadow Color.** The perspective shadow can be any color you like. Clicking in this box brings up the color picker you have previously selected in Photoshop.

How Smoke Does It

This one's more fun than a smokehouse full 'o salmon! The Smoke filter can produce a variety of smoky effects rising from your selection, as demonstrated by Figure 27-18. The Smoke filter requires a selection to do its job unless you are applying Smoke to an object in a layer by itself.

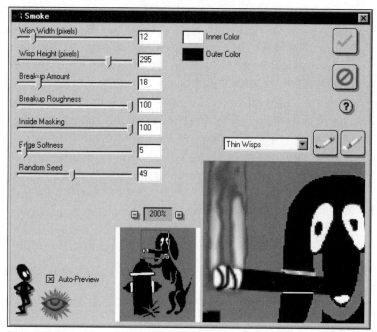

Figure 27-18: Add some atmospheric effects by generating a little Smoke.

Remember that this filter draws outside of your selection. If you are using a program other than Photoshop 4.0, this will cause you to lose your selection if you have not saved it before applying the filter. Don't forget to save the selection if you will need to use it after this operation!

Also, to ensure that Smoke works correctly in a layer, make sure that the Preserve Transparency check box is not checked. This is important for Photoshop users since this filter cannot perform properly with Preserve Transparency enabled. Note that Photoshop 4.0 automatically enables Preserve Transparency when it creates type and when it places an image in a layer. Disable it and you will be able to use this filter without a problem.

TIP *Where there's smoke, there's fire! If you plan on using the Fire and Smoke filters together, try applying the Smoke filter to your selection first and then applying a somewhat smaller Fire to the same selection for a realistic effect.*

The Smoke filter allows you to adjust these controls:

■ **Wisp Width.** Controls how wide the wisps of smoke will be. Higher values yield wider (and thus fewer) wisps.

■ **Wisp Height.** Controls the height of the smoke wisps. Higher values yield longer wisps.

■ **Breakup Amount** and **Breakup Roughness.** These two sliders control how much the smoke is perturbed from a smooth flow and how erratically the smoke behaves. Playing with both controls gives you a variety of turbulent effects.

■ **Random Seed.** The placement of the wisps of smoke has a random element. This slider allows you to control this random element, producing a wide variety of changes to the smoke. Have fun experimenting!

■ **Inside Masking.** Controls how much the smoke covers the inside of your selection. Lower values allow the smoke to cover the selection more completely, while higher values block the smoke from the inside of the selection.

■ **Edge Softness.** Controls the sharpness of the smoke wisps. Lower values yield sharper wisps, while extremely high values produce a very diffuse smoke effect.

■ **Inner** and **Outer Color.** The smoke effect is made up of an inner and outer color, both of which can be any color you like. Clicking in either box brings up the color picker you have previously selected in Photoshop.

Squint

Get a good look at it! The Squint filter is a new kind of blur that basically unfocuses your selection by spreading each pixel around the edge of a circle, as shown in Figure 27-19. The result resembles a reflection in a vibrating mirror or an image projected out of focus. While Photoshop's Gaussian blur creates an extremely smooth blur, Squint more closely duplicates rough poor vision.

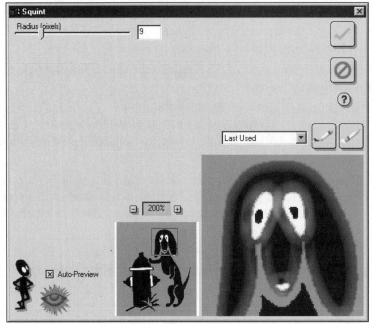

Figure 27-19: Squint unfocuses your selection with a blur effect.

Squint offers one basic control:

■ **Radius.** This slider controls the radius of the circles around which your selection is blurred; another way to think of it is that it changes the vibration of the mirror or the focus on the projector. The larger the radius, the blurrier the image will be. As the radius value increases, the specifics of your selection are spread over a great distance, and the selection becomes more fuzzy. If you increase the radius enough, your selection will probably turn into gray mush.

How Star Does It

The Star filter quickly and easily creates stars and other regular polygonal shapes without the need to import them from another program or use paths to approximate them. Figure 27-20 demonstrates some of these effects. If you use this filter on a selection, your star will initially be placed in the center of that selection. If the star is bigger than your selection, only part of the star will show. The Star filter will also work without a selection, as well as in a completely empty layer. In both of these cases, the star will initially be placed in the center of your image. If you use this filter to place the star in an empty layer, you can then select the star and move it anywhere in that layer.

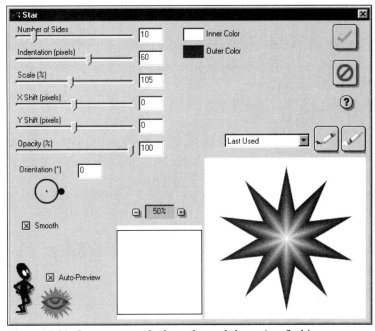

Figure 27-20: Create stars and other polygonal shapes in a flash!

The Star filter allows you to adjust these controls:

- **Number of Sides.** A star can have from three to 50 sides.

- **Indentation.** Controls the distance that the sides of the star are indented from the outer points. Higher values increase the indentation. A value of zero yields a straight-sided polygonal shape.

- **Scale.** Controls the size of the star. Lower values reduce the size of the star; higher values increase it. Note that the scale is at 10 degrees when the star is created. The range is from one-fifth to two times the original size.

- **X Shift** and **Y Shift.** These sliders control the horizontal and vertical distance the star is moved from the center of your selection or from the center of your image if no selection is made. For X Shift, a positive value moves the star to the right, and a negative value moves it to the left. For Y Shift, a positive value moves the star down, and a negative value moves it up.

- **Orientation.** Put your own spin on it with a full 360-degree rotation.

- **Opacity.** Adjusts the overall transparency of the star. Higher values darken the star's colors so that the background or layer behind the star is less visible.

- **Inner** and **Outer Color.** The star is made up of an inner and an outer color, both of which can be any color you like. Clicking in either box brings up the color picker you have previously selected in Photoshop.

- **Smooth.** When checked, this button softens the edges of the star shape.

How Swirl Does It

Swirl smears the image using randomly placed whirlpools, as shown in Figure 27-21. The spacing and shape of these whirlpools can be controlled to achieve an amazing variety of effects. This filter tends to have a striking effect on images containing lots of detail and speckles. Therefore, you will probably find HSB Noise and Swirl (used in that order) to be an effective combination.

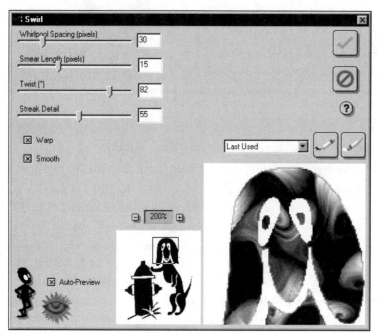

Figure 27-21: Swirl makes an amazing range of dramatic effects.

If you're working in a layer and you're not happy with the effect you're getting, try disabling Preserve Transparency on Photoshop's Layers palette for the layer you are working in. This will let Swirl edit transparency.

The Swirl filter lets you put your own spin on these controls:

- **Whirlpool Spacing.** Although the whirlpools are randomly placed, this slider gives you control over the average spacing between their centers. Lower values will make many closely spaced, tiny whirlpools. Large values create long streamlines with no whirlpool center visible, simulating hair or wood grain. Whirlpool Spacing is a pixel-based setting. This means that settings generated for a 72-dpi image will look different when applied to a 300-dpi image.

- **Smear Length.** Larger values blur the image more. If the Warp setting is on, then this also controls how far the image is stretched along streamlines. This is a very time-intensive graphic effect when the smear length is large. Try experimenting with lower values first. Smear Length is a pixel-based setting. This means that settings generated for a 72-dpi image will look different when applied to a 300-dpi image.

- **Twist.** Values near 0 degrees give a starburst effect. Values near 90 degrees give a spiral effect.

- **Streak Detail.** Larger values create darker streaks.

- **Warp.** When this box is checked, the image will be more significantly stretched along streamlines.

- **Smooth.** When checked, this eliminates graininess.

How Water Drops Does It

The Water Drops filter randomly places water drops on your selection, as shown by Figure 27-22. In some ways, this effect is similar to the Glass filter. The appearance of the drops is achieved by simulating the same three physical effects: refraction, light filtering, and specular reflection. The refraction and thickness sliders give you control of image warping. The color picker, the Opacity slider, and the Edge Darkness slider give you control over light filtering. Specular reflection, or the reflection of the light source, is controlled by the highlight sliders and the light Direction and Inclination.

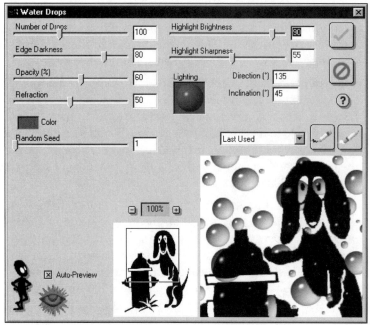

Figure 27-22: Water Drops creates natural-looking water droplets on your selection.

The Water Drops filter lets you immerse yourself in these controls:

■ **Numbers of Drops.** Controls the number and size of the drops that appear on your selection. As the number of drops increases, their size decreases.

■ **Edge Darkness.** Controls the shadows that help to simulate the water drops' hemispherical shape. Different values will make the water drops stand out more against different backgrounds. With a darker background, try a lower value, and with a lighter background, try a higher value.

■ **Opacity.** Adjusts the overall transparency of the effect. This filter adjusts transparency by affecting the color tint of the drops. Higher values tint them more toward the color selected in the picker. A value of zero allows the image underneath the water drops to show through untinted.

■ **Refraction.** As in the Glass filter, refraction controls the amount your selection is warped by the water drops above it. At lower values, this effect is subtle. However, with higher values, straight lines curve noticeably and rigid geometric shapes skew. At very high values, the image beneath your drops becomes indistinct.

■ **Highlight Brightness** and **Highlight Sharpness.** As with other filters, Brightness and Sharpness affect the white highlights that appear on the parts of your drops that face the light. Brightness controls the intensity of these highlights, while Sharpness affects their diffusion. Higher values can give a glossier effect.

■ **Direction.** Controls the direction from which the light falls on your selection. You have a full 360-degree range from which to choose. A value of 0 degrees yields light directly from the right, 90 degrees yields light from the top, 180 degrees yields light directly from the left, and 270 degrees yields light from the bottom.

■ **Inclination.** Controls the angle formed by the light and the page. This gives the effect of more depth. If the light originates from directly overhead, the light angle will be at 90 degrees. As the light comes more directly from the side, the value will approach 0 degrees.

■ **Random Seed.** There is a random element to the placement of the water drops on your selection. This slider allows you to control this random element, producing a wide variety of possible distributions of drops. Have fun experimenting!

■ **Color.** Click in this box to select the color that will tint the drops that appear over the selection. The color picker you have previously selected in Photoshop will appear.

How Weave Does It

The Weave filter gives your selection the appearance of being woven, as shown by Figure 27-23. You may select the width of the strips and gaps that form the weave. You may specify the color, if any, of the gaps. In addition, you can add texture to the woven strips.

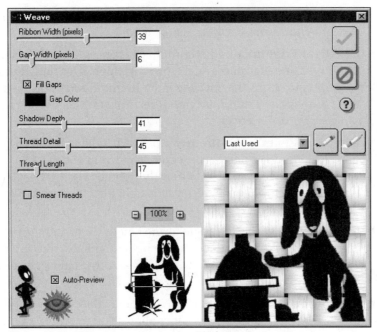

Figure 27-23: Weave your own magic with this texturing effect.

The Weave filter lets you finesse the warp and weave by adjusting these controls:

- **Ribbon Width.** Controls the width of the strips that make up the woven portion of the selection.

- **Gap Width.** Controls the width of the gaps between the woven strips.

- **Shadow Depth.** Controls the darkness of the shadows created by the weave. With a lighter selection, darkening these shadows will make the strips appear thicker. However, with a darker selection, a higher value may be necessary for shadows to be noticeable.

- **Thread Detail** and **Length.** These sliders give the woven strips texture. The thread detail gradually adds a cloth-like effect, and the thread length determines how long the individual strands of thread are. The strands themselves are a kind of noise similar to HSB Noise.

- **Gap Color.** When the Fill Gaps check box is checked, you can click in the color box to select the color that will fill the gaps between the strips of the weave. The color picker you have previously selected in Photoshop will appear. Note that you can disable Fill Gaps. If your selection is on a layer other than the background and Preserve Transparency is disabled, you will be able to see through the gaps in the weave to the layers underneath.

- **Smear Threads.** When this control is enabled, the filter smears the selected image along the threads. A longer thread length causes greater smearing.

chapter 28

Andromeda Series Filters

Creator

Andromeda Software

Purpose

Photographic, screening, texture, and motion special effects

Platforms

Macintosh, Windows

Hardware/software requirements

Same as Photoshop

URL/contact info for creator of plug-in

http://www.andromeda.com
Andromeda Software, Inc.
699 Hampshire Road
Westlake Village, CA 91361
805/379-4109 voice
805/379-5253 fax

Products that the plug-in works with

Mac: Adobe Photoshop 2.5 or later, other programs that support
Photoshop 2.5's (or later) plug-in standard
Windows 95 or NT: Adobe Photoshop 3.0.5 or later, other programs
that support Photoshop 3.0's (or later) plug-in standard

Want to spice up your photographs, create cool mezzotints, build awesome textures, and apply amazing motion blurs? If so, the Andromeda Series Filters deliver a comprehensive collection of special effects that deserve a home on your desktop.

Who Should Use Andromeda Series Filters?

Andromeda Series Filters are perfect for photographers, designers, graphic artists, Web and multimedia developers, desktop publishers, and broadcast designers, among others. These are workhorse filters that you'll use again and again.

What Andromeda Series Filters Do

In this chapter we're going to take a look at four of Andromeda's products:

- **Series 1 - Photography Filters.** This collection consists of ten filters—Circular Multiple Image, Designs, Diffraction, Halo, Prism, Rainbow, Reflection, Star, Straight Multiple Image, and Velocity—which allow you to create classic photographic effects.

- **Series 3 - Screens Filter.** A terrific filter for print designers, the Screens Filter lets you create an awesome range of mezzotint and mezzoblend effects. These are invaluable when designing projects for one-, two-, and three-color print projects such as newsletters and brochures.

- **Series 4 - Techtures Filter.** This plug-in uses 900 seamless high-resolution textures tiles along with a trio of texturing and a pair of special effects engines to enable you to create truly unique images.

- **Velociraptor.** Don't settle for Photoshop's Motion Blur! Velociraptor is the ultimate motion blur filter, with three overall trail styles and an infinitely adjustable number of variations.

These creative filter packages are available individually as well as in bundle form. What about Andromeda's Series 2 - 3D Filter, you ask? Fear not! We'll review it in the 3D section toward the end of this book.

Why Use Andromeda Series Filters?

Have you ever had a photograph that you knew had incredible potential, yet it was missing something? The Andromeda Series Filters let you unlock that potential by allowing you to create tasteful effects that push your image from the "ho-hum" to the "oh, wow!" As we progress through the "how they do it" portion of this chapter, your mind will race with the possibilities that these filters afford.

How Andromeda's Series 1 - Photography Filters Do It

The 10 individual filters in Andromeda's Series 1 - Photography Filters collection provide you with a set of effects that would make an expert photographer jealous. Whether you want to create multiple image effects, add sparkly highlights, or add a little motion, the Photography Filters deliver professional results. Each filter provides fast previews and easy adjustments. You can change the focal point of an effect by merely clicking and dragging it on the preview image. Let's take a run through each of the 10 filters.

Circular Multiple Image

Want to create a bug's-eye view? Bugs see multiple images, as if they are looking through a wall of glass blocks. The Circular Multiple Image filter, shown in Figure 28-1, lets you wheel iterations of an image around itself. You can use a radial, square areas, or a tiled grid to duplicate the image. Depending on which method you choose, the filter provides control over the radius, height, width, intensity, number of areas, and transition effect.

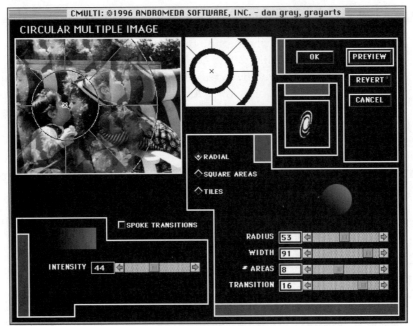

Figure 28-1: The Circular Multiple Image filter lets you create images that a horsefly would love.

Designs

The Designs filter, shown in Figure 28-2, lets you add dimensional texture and mezzotint screens to your images. There are 96 1-bit patterns built into the filter. Depending on the mode you're working in, the patterns can be colored in either RGB or CMYK colors. Mezzo screens can only be applied to grayscale images and come in handy when creating special effects for print.

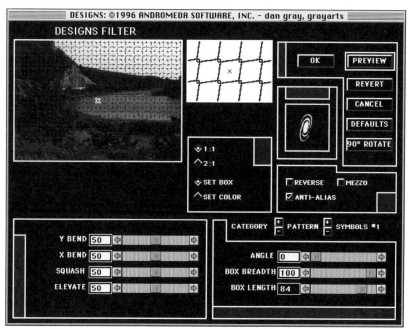

Figure 28-2: The Designs filter packs plenty of wallop for print designers.

The Designs filter provides total control over its patterns, with sliders for X and Y Bend, Squash, Elevate, Angle, Box Breadth, and Box Length. It also allows you to specify ratio, color, and anti-aliasing, among other features. It's interesting to note how the technology in this one module spawned an entirely new package. If you are looking for total control over mezzotinting, check out Andromeda's Series 3 - Screens Filter, which is covered later in this chapter.

Diffraction

Want to add a rainbow sparkle to an image? The Diffraction filter, shown in Figure 28-3, lets you adjust the thickness, intensity, radius, and length of each diffraction. A diffraction can have from one to 50 spokes. You can also alter the diffraction angle to rotate the spokes around their focal point.

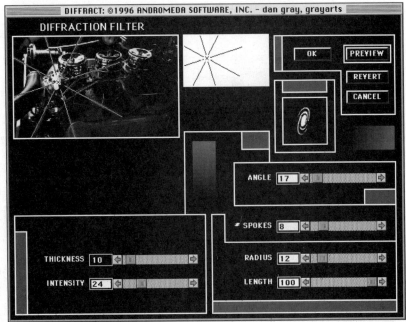

Figure 28-3: You might want to use the Diffraction filter when a single color sparkle just won't do.

Halo

Apart from what you might think, the Halo filter does not merely add a glowing ring around someone's head. The filter, shown in Figure 28-4, is used to add a variable glow to an entire image (or chunk thereof). This filter creates wonderfully soft painterly effects. The dialog box provides sliders to control box breadth and length, along with the intensity, spread, and cutoff of the effect.

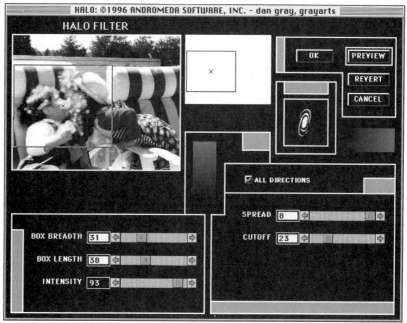

Figure 28-4: The Halo filter can turn a photograph into an impressionist painting in seconds!

Prism

Are you after a jittery, unsettling effect? The Prism filter, shown in Figure 28-5, can make your image appear as if it's being viewed through a prism on Sunday morning, after a raucous Saturday night. The rainbowed multiple images are controlled by Spread, Intensity, Angle, Box Breadth, and Box Length sliders.

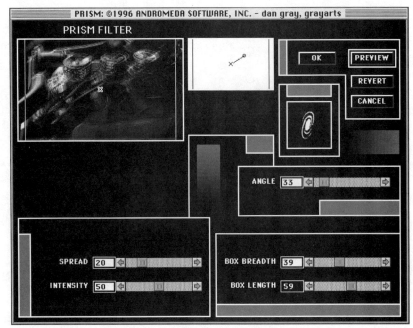

Figure 28-5: The Prism filter will have your audience squinting their eyes and reaching for that bottle of aspirin.

Rainbow

Looking to add an extra touch to that landscape? The Rainbow filter, shown in Figure 28-6, lets you really mess with Mother Nature. You can create your own rainbow, with total control over its origin, intensity, fade, angle, radius, and width. And best of all, you can even add that pot of gold!

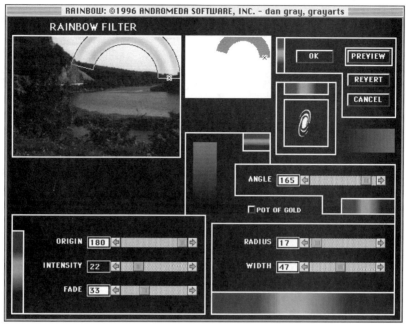

Figure 28-6: The Rainbow filter delivers everything, save the leprechaun.

Reflection

Need to render a professional-quality reflection? Reflection effects are a perfect way to turn a dull water shot into an exciting image. The Reflection filter, shown in Figure 28-7, lets you create expert reflections with ease. The dialog box allows you to control the angle, box breadth and length, gap, transition, and intensity.

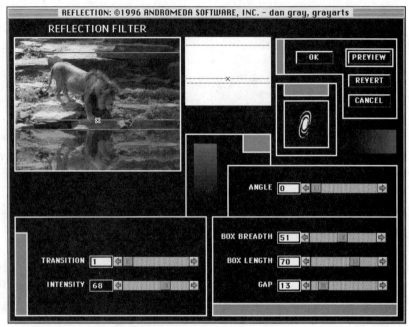

Figure 28-7: The water in this original image was scummy and lifeless. By painting over the surface with a simple blend and creating a fairly realistic reflection, we quickly cleaned up the pond.

Star

Is your chrome shiny enough? The Star filter, shown in Figure 28-8, can awaken that greasy brightwork. You can add multiple stars to an image, with your choice of 4, 8, or 16 points. The Star dialog box lets you adjust each attribute of a star, including its overall size along with the size of its sun, halo, and rays. You can vary a star's thickness, fade, and view angle in addition to changing its color. The dialog box lets you move individual points and also allows you to soften the sun and add a speckle effect to the star.

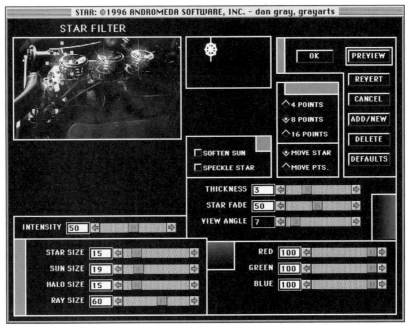

Figure 28-8: The Star filter makes those air filters sparkle, without the elbow grease!

Straight Multiple Image

Need to add some speed? The Straight Multiple Image filter, shown in Figure 28-9, lets you add multiple iterations of an image. The dialog box provides control over spacing, intensity, angle, and the number of areas. You can use parallel lines, square areas, or parallel combined effects, with or without a fade.

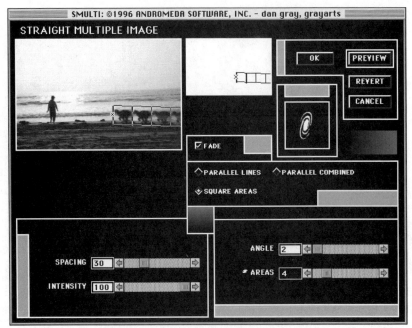

Figure 28-9: Is that a galloping sheep dog on the beach, or is it a thoroughbred?

Velocity

Want even more speed? Velocity filter, shown in Figure 28-10, delivers a high level of control over smear and blur effects. Sliders allow you to fine-tune the angle, intensity, and X and Y stretch as well as the box breadth and length. You can use either a one-way smear or a local area blur with the lightest, darkest, or average color. The motion trail can be flipped along its X- and Y-axis and can follow a straight line or an arc.

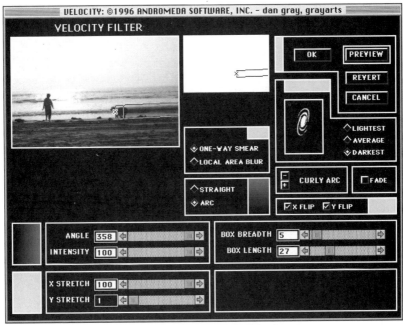

Figure 28-10: That sheep dog isn't galloping; she's flying!

If you're looking for the ultimate in control over velocity effects, you should take a gander at Andromeda's Velociraptor filter, which is covered later in this chapter.

How Andromeda's Series 3 - Screens Filter Does It _____

If you're familiar with the printing process, you know that ink is an all-or-nothing proposition. Ink either prints or it doesn't. While you can alter the transparency of a color on your monitor, you can only simulate transparency in print. Variations in tint and color are made possible by halftone screens. Standard halftone screens are made up of equally spaced rows and columns of spots. While the spots can be round, square, diamond, or other shapes, they are uniform in shape throughout an image. The lightness or darkness of the color is controlled by the size of the halftone dot. Mezzotint screens, on the other hand, are made up of irregular, even wormlike objects. They are not uniform in shape throughout an image. Figures 28-11 and 28-12 demonstrate the difference between a halftone image and a mezzotint image.

Figure 28-11: A standard halftone image tells the story one way...

Figure 28-12: ...While a big fat 45 wpi mezzotint says something all together different—especially when you print it in a different color!

While Photoshop has a built-in Mezzotint filter, it's pretty basic. It's safe to say that the Andromeda Screens Filter blows the standard Photoshop Mezzotint filter to smithereens. If you're designing for print, this plug-in will prove to be indispensable. To apply the Andromeda Screens Filter, choose Filter | Andromeda | Screens from the Photoshop menu bar. The Andromeda Screens dialog box, shown in Figure 28-13, provides you with the tools you need to craft bold mezzo effects, whether you are a novice or an expert.

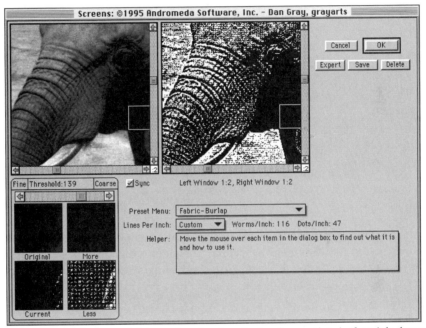

Figure 28-13: Novice mode lets you knock out professional mezzotints in the wink of an eye.

The preview windows at the top of the dialog box display before and after views of your image, and they have zoom and panning controls. Clicking the Sync button will synchronize the two windows. The variations windows at the bottom of the dialog box let you play with the brightness level of your image. You can lighten or darken the image by clicking on the More or Less samples, respectively, or you can use the Threshold slider. When you click on the Expert button, the dialog box will switch to Expert mode, shown in Figure 28-14. While Expert mode offers infinite possibilities, you'll likely find that the Novice mode will meet most of your needs.

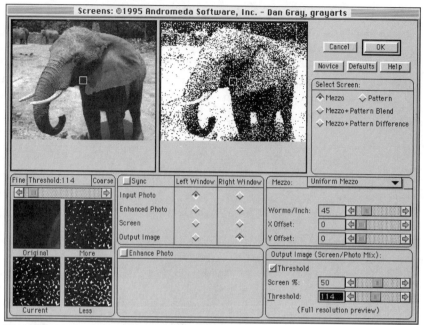

Figure 28-14: Expert mode is a screen tweakers delight!

The Novice mode's Preset Menu provides a host of cool effects. You're just a click away from mezzo-nirvana! The Helper box provides a full rundown on each effect. In Novice mode, the Andromeda Screens Filter dialog box includes preconfigured settings for:

- **Mezzoblends.** Mix it up in your choice of dots, ellipticals, and lines.

- **Mezzograms.** You can create Mezzograms with worm per inch (wpi) rates from 35 through 150.

- **Mezzotints.** Render classic Mezzotints with 35 through 150 wpi rates.

- **Patterns.** Want something a little different? Choose from circles, diamonds, dots, ellipses, lines, spokes, stars, and other tasty patterns.

- ■ **Special Effects.** If you're looking for something really special, check out these effects! You'll find half a dozen Fabric effects, five Intaglio effects, and a bunch of goofily named goodies like Chromosome Damage, DaDa Dominos, Flaming Waffle, and Pinwheel Paradise.

- ■ **Text-Presets.** The Text-Presets are a special treat. We had a hard time resisting these settings! Check out Figures 28-15 through 28-17 for a bevy of cool examples. You can create effects ranging from subtle to edgy.

Figure 28-15: Capital Corrosion, Chisel Text Block, Moovable Type, Rose Vine, and Serrated Chisel text presets applied to a 600 dpi image.

Figure 28-16: Chips African, Moovable Type, Ribbon Stack, Serrated Chisel, and Serrated Swirl text presets applied to a 300 dpi image.

Figure 28-17: Capital Corrosion, Moovable Type, Serrated Chisel, Serrated Swirl, and Soap Suds text presets applied to a 150 dpi image.

Once you've applied a screen effect to an image, you'll need to choose Image | Mode | Bitmap from the Photoshop menu bar. Then apply the 50% Threshold option.

TIP *For optimum results with the Screens Filter, Andromeda recommends a file resolution four times the lpi of the printed screen. So if you're going to be using a 65 lpi screen, you should start with a file resolution of at least 260 dpi. The higher the initial resolution, however, the better the final results.*

How Andromeda's Series 4 - Techtures Filter Does It _____

Any trendy designer will tell you that you can never be too rich, too thin, or have too many textures. If you're having trouble hitting your goals on the first two points, you can always use Andromeda's Series 4 - Techtures Filter to help you to achieve the third. This plug-in is more of a texture application filter, as opposed to a texture creation filter, like Xaos Tools Terrazzo. The Techtures Filter lets you apply existing textures to an image using a variety of methods and controls. The plug-in ships with 900 hand-rendered, 300 dpi seamless textures.

The Blending, Texturing & Deep Pixel Engines _____

Andromeda's Series 4 - Techtures Filter allows total flexibility when applying textures to images. There are three basic texturing engines built into the plug-in: Blending, Texturing, and Deep Pixel. Figure 28-18 illustrates a bit of the difference in the application of the three engines. Let's take a quick look at what each of the three engines does:

- **Blending.** Use this engine to blend a texture with the original image with control over the texture's opacity. You have the option of applying a weave or panel with the blended texture.

- **Texturing.** Use this engine to combine the highlight and shadow of a texture with that of the original image. You can control the highlight and shadow colors.

- **Deep Pixel.** Use this engine to achieve an embossed effect. You'll find that the Deep Pixel engine will come in handy when creating transparent surfaces, such as water and glass.

Figure 28-18: Two examples of the Blending, Texturing, and Deep Pixel treatments. The differences between the effects can be subtle, but as you can see by the pair of stars in the third column, the Deep Pixel effect imparts the highest degree of dimensionality.

The interface for Andromeda's Series 4 - Techtures Filter is both friendly and functional. Choosing the Texture, Environment, or Map mode at the upper left corner of the dialog box configures the filter for each mode. Figure 28-19 shows the dialog box in Texture mode. Buttons at the lower left side of the window let you switch between Blending, Texturing, and Deep Pixel modes. Click on the Light Color button to set the texture's highlight and shadow colors with the system color picker. The textures for the Blending, Texturing, and Deep Pixel engines are divided into the following categories: Bold Color, Bold Embroidery, Bold Pattern, Coarse, Decay, Fabric, Foliage, Masonry, Polished Stone, Subtle Color, Subtle Pattern, Subtle Embroidery, Swirls, Tiles, Black/White, and Wood.

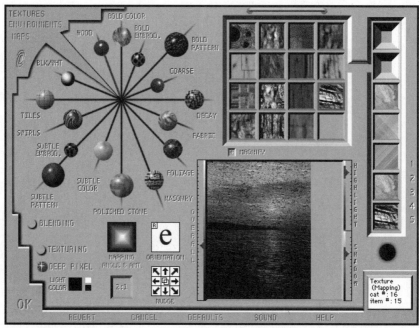

Figure 28-19: Andromeda's Series 4 - Techtures Filter texturing options are infinitely adjustable. Here, the dialog box is shown in Deep Pixel Texturing mode. The Mapping Angle and Amount control lets you adjust pixel displacement.

The Techtures Filter lets you get a good look at how your texture will appear before you apply it to the final image. The marbles allow you to switch between texture categories, while the 16 browser cells let you preview each texture. The window at the bottom right of the dialog box provides a zoomable preview. The Overall, Highlight, and Shadow sliders surrounding the preview window let you fine-tune the application of each texture. The Orientation button lets you rotate the texture in 90 degree increments. Use the Nudge buttons to slide the texture around the image. Once you've tweaked a perfect texture, drag it over to the row of seven preview cells at the right side of the dialog box to save it with all its settings.

Environments

Switching to the Environments engine allows you to apply a single tile to the entire image. Figure 28-20 demonstrates a simple application of the Environment engine. The textures for the Environment engine are divided into the following categories: Light, Shade, Screen, Smoke, Star, Karma, Explosion, and Shatter.

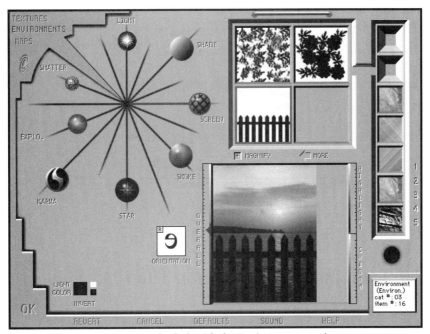

Figure 28-20: Get a view from the deck with the Environments engine.

Maps

Want to push those pixels into the perfect illusion? The Maps engine repeats its tiles across the entire image and actually displaces pixels to simulate diffraction. The textures for the Maps engine are divided into the following categories: Andromeda, Designs, Life, Linear, Patterns, Stained Glass, Surface, Water, and Wavy. Figure 28-21 demonstrates how the Maps engine can be used to create the illusion.

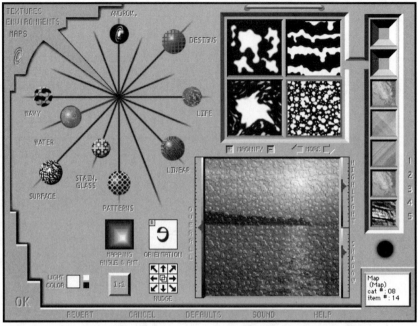

Figure 28-21: Environment Maps let you apply cool dimensional effects, like water on glass.

How Andromeda's Velociraptor Filter Does It _____

Want to create the ultimate motion trail effects? Andromeda's Velociraptor Filter lets you take complete command of your trails. Velociraptor offers even more options than the Velocity filter, which is built into Andromeda's Series 1 - Photography Filters collection. To apply the filter, choose Filter | Andromeda | Velociraptor from Photoshop's menu bar. The Velociraptor dialog box, shown in Figure 28-22, provides a host of controls.

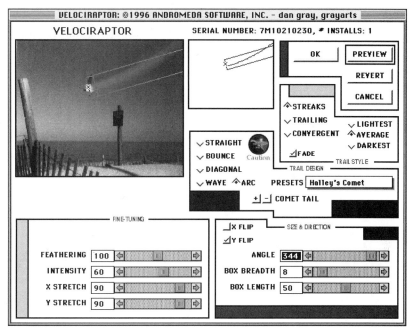

Figure 28-22: Cleared for landing! The Haley's Comet preset has our seagull swooping in with authority.

Velociraptor is infinitely tweakable. The Trail Design choices include Straight, Bounce, Diagonal, Wave, and Arc modes. Furthermore, there are five different types of bounce, two diagonals, three kinds of wave, and two arcs. You can choose from Streaks, Trailing, or Convergent trail styles, using the lightest, average, or darkest colors. Sliders allow you to adjust the angle, box breadth, and box length of your trails. And you can fine-tune the feathering, intensity, and X and Y stretch, as well.

Don't feel like tweaking? The Straight Streak, Descending Bounce, Wavy Tail, Ascending Arc, Descending Arc, From Infinity, Diminishing Bounce, Radio Signal, and Haley's Comet presets let you instantaneously apply professional motion trails.

If you make a selection in your image, invert it, and then summon Velociraptor, the dialog box will appear in a different mode. In this mode, as shown by Figure 28-23, the dialog box allows you to create multiple iterations of the original selection. Depending on the Trail Design, you can adjust the

Angle, the Number of Copies, and the Spacing options, as well as the smoothing and intensity of the effect. This mode includes the following presets: Vanishing Point, Converging Hop, Wonderful Wave, Casual Curve, Spiral Loop, Swoop Down, Springy Path, Super Swell, and Swoop Up.

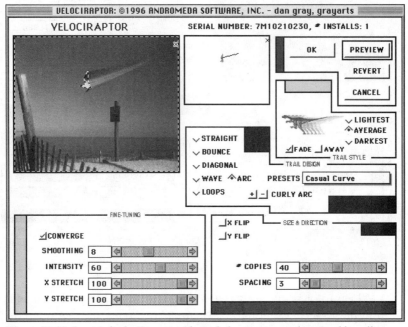

Figure 28-23: Inverted selections provide a whole new range of motion blur effects.

chapter 29

Auto F/X Photo/Graphic & Typo/Graphic Edges

Creator

Auto F/X

Purpose

Edge effects

Platforms

Macintosh, Windows

Hardware/software requirements

Same as Photoshop

URL/contact info for creator of plug-in

http://www.autofx.com
Auto F/X
Black Point Association
HCR-73, Box 689
Alton Bay, NH 03810
603/569-8800 voice
603/569-9702 fax

Products that the plug-in works with

Adobe Photoshop 3.0.5 or later, Adobe Illustrator 6.0 (and later),
Adobe PageMaker 6.0 (and later), Adobe PhotoDeluxe 1.0,
CorelPHOTO-PAINT! 6 (and later), Deneba Canvas 5.0, Fractal Design
Painter 4.0.3, JASC Paintshop Pro 4.0, and Macromedia FreeHand 7

Want to give your artwork a natural edge? The Auto F/X Photo/Graphic & Typo/Graphic Edges filters create cool edge effects for photographs, typography, and line art. You can use them for print, Web, and multimedia projects to lend a hand-rendered or special edge effect.

Who Should Use Auto F/X Photo/Graphic & Typo/Graphic Edges?

The Auto F/X plug-ins are staples of the creative community worldwide. Their tagline pretty much sums it up: "Cool Special Effects for Designers." Among other shops, they're well suited to advertising agencies, designers, desktop publishers, graphic artists, hobbyists, multimedia and Web developers, newspaper publishers, and photographers.

What Auto F/X Photo/Graphic & Typo/Graphic Edges Do

The Auto F/X Photo/Graphic & Typo/Graphic Edges filter collections allow you to apply hand-rendered edges to your artwork. They provide complete control over the size, width, softness, color, and feathering of the edges.

Why Use Auto F/X Photo/Graphic & Typo/Graphic Edges?

Tired of straight-edged artwork? Looking for distinctive typographic treatments? By using the Auto F/X filters and their collection of canned edge effects, you can quickly create distinctive pieces that look as if they took hours to render.

How Auto F/X Photo/Graphic Edges Does It

Auto F/X's Photo/Graphic Edges' offering consists of one plug-in with three volumes of edge effects, which cover Traditional, Geometric, and Artistic categories. The Traditional collection includes darkroom effects, including emulsion transfers, film frames and strips, in addition to decked and ripped designs. The Geometric collection is more synthetic, with abstract and impressionist designs. The Artistic collection features hand-painted edges, including charcoals, splatters, scratchboard, and watercolor effects.

To launch Auto F/X Photo/Graphic Edges plug-in, select an area of your artwork and then choose Filter | Auto F/X | Photo/Graphic Edges from the

Photoshop menu bar. To apply an edge effect with Auto F/X Photo/Graphic Edges, you begin by clicking the Select Outside Effect button. This brings up a dialog box that allows you to choose the edge effect from the thousands of effects that Auto F/X supplies on CD-ROM. Each of the Edge collections comes with a handy, well-illustrated catalog of effects. Once you've selected the Outset Effect, it will be displayed in the preview area, as shown in Figure 29-1.

Figure 29-1: The Auto F/X Photo/Graphic Edges interface is straightforward and easy-to-operate.

With the basic Outset Effect selected, you can adjust the edge to suit your liking. The Auto F/X Photo/Graphic Edges dialog box provides a range of easy-to-use controls:

- **Rotate border.** Clicking the button at the bottom right corner of the preview rotates the border effect. Option- (Mac) or Alt-clicking (PC) rotates only the Outset Effect. Command- (Mac) or Control-clicking (PC) rotates only the Inset Effect.

- **Mirror border.** Clicking the buttons that surround the preview image mirrors the border effect. Option- (Mac) or Alt-clicking (PC) mirrors only the Outset Effect. Command- (Mac) or Control-clicking (PC) mirrors only the Inset Effect.

- **Inset Scale.** This slider resizes the Inset Scale effect. Just move the slider to resize it proportionally. Hold down the Option (Mac) or Alt (PC) key while moving the slider to stretch the effect vertically. Hold down the Command (Mac) or Control (PC) key to stretch the effect horizontally.

■ **Inset Blur/Sharp.** Move the slider to soften the Inset Effect. Hold down the Option (Mac) or Alt (PC) key while moving the slider to sharpen the effect.

■ **Outset Scale.** This slider resizes the Outset Scale effect. Just move the slider to resize it proportionally. Hold down the Option (Mac) or Alt (PC) key while moving the slider to stretch the effect vertically. Hold down the Command (Mac) or Control (PC) key while moving the slider to stretch the effect horizontally.

■ **Outset Blur/Sharp.** Move the slider to soften the Outset Effect. Hold down the Option (Mac) or Alt (PC) key while moving the slider to sharpen the effect.

■ **Select Outset Effect.** Click this button to select the Outset Effect from the Auto F/X CD-ROM. Hold down the Command (Mac) or Control (PC) key while clicking to remove the current Outset Effect.

■ **Select Inset Effect.** Click this button to select the Inset Effect from the Auto F/X CD-ROM. Hold down the Command (Mac) or Control (PC) key while clicking to remove the current Inset Effect.

■ **Background Color.** Click this button to select a color to be used behind your image. Hold down the Option (Mac) or Alt (PC) key while clicking to make the background transparent. Hold down the Command (Mac) or Control (PC) key while clicking to set the background color to white.

■ **Edge Border Color.** Click this button to select an edge color. Hold down the Command (Mac) or Control (PC) key while clicking to set the edge border color to black.

You can apply the effects with a myriad of options. Figure 29-2 shows just an Outset Effect, while Figure 29-3 shows the same photograph with an Inset and an Outset Effect. In the second example, we selected the same file for both the inner and outer effects and applied a touch of blur.

Figure 29-2: This image only uses an Outset Effect.

Figure 29-3: Here, the same effect was used for both the inset and outset.

When you use different Inset and Outset Effects, you can achieve interesting results. And when you combine this with other filters, you can create some really great looks. Figure 29-4 demonstrates an edge effect created with two different edges. After we were done with Auto F/X, the outside border was selected, filled with noise, motion-blurred, and drop-shadowed with the WildRiverSSK MagicMask filter.

Figure 29-4: Yes, you too can turn a so-so sunset shot into an edgy image!

How Auto F/X Typo/Graphic Edges Does It

Need to create a distinctive typographic effect? Auto F/X Typo/Graphic Edges allows you to quickly turn your crisp digital typography into weathered, rough-edged designs. Auto F/X Typo/Graphic Edges installs its own menu into Adobe Photoshop. To use the plug-in, begin by selecting the piece of type that you want to alter. Then choose Typo/Graphic Edges from the Auto F/X menu. The Auto F/X Typo/Graphic Edges dialog box, as shown by Figure 29-5, allows you to specify the Horizontal and Vertical settings as well as the edge size and style of the effect.

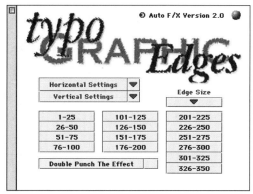

Figure 29-5: The Auto F/X Typo/Graphic Edges dialog box does not provide an interactive preview of the effect. You must rely upon the printed catalog of edges.

The first thing you want to do when the dialog box opens is specify the amount of edge with the Horizontal and Vertical Settings drop-down menus— the higher the number, the more edge you'll receive. Then you'll want to set the edge size to either larger or smaller. (By default, the dialog box is configured to provide Horizontal and Vertical settings of 3, with a small edge.) Selecting Double Punch will apply the effect twice. Once you've taken care of all of those settings, you'll specify an edge effect by clicking on a numbered effect menu button. As soon as you select the effect and release the mouse, the plug-in will go to work. Once it has rendered the effect, a dialog box will appear, asking if you approve of the results. If not, click the Try Again button, dial in your new settings, and give it another whirl. Figure 29-6 demonstrates a handful of effects created with Auto F/X Typo/Graphic Edges.

Figure 29-6: Rough-looking type designs such as these are easy pickings with
Auto F/X Typo/Graphic Edges.

chapter 30

Second Glance Chromassage

Creator
Second Glance

Purpose
Color table and palette manipulation

Platforms
Macintosh

Hardware/Software requirements
System 7.0.1 or later, 1MB of RAM in addition to the Photoshop minimum

URL/Contact info for creator of plug-in
http://www.secondglance.com
Second Glance
7248 Sunset Avenue NE
Bremerton, WA 98311
360/692-3694 voice
360/692-9241 fax

Products that the plug-in works with
Adobe Photoshop 1.07 or later, other programs that support the Photoshop plug-in standard

W ant to create bold and exciting color effects for multimedia projects as well as for silk screen and spot color print jobs? Second Glance Chromassage lets you twiddle color tables and palettes to blast your images into a whole new dimension. Whether you just want to introduce a little extra color or inject a wild exotic look, Chromassage delivers the means to a colorful end. And best of all, it's a whole lot of fun!

Who Should Use Second Glance Chromassage?

Second Glance Chromassage is an entertaining trip for artists, designers, and other graphics professionals who love to create exciting color effects for print, Web, and multimedia projects. It's especially appropriate for multicolor silk screen work, including T-shirts and other attire.

What Second Glance Chromassage Does

Chromassage works its magic in two basic ways. The plug-in uses jog wheel sliders to twist color palettes from its working palette to your image's original palette, while the color injector deftly squirts color into specific areas. The results can range from subtle to psychedelic.

Why Use Second Glance Chromassage?

Have you ever fiddled with Photoshop's rather basic Posterization feature only to give up in frustration? The Posterization dialog box is severely limited in that it only provides the means to specify the number of levels of color. Chromassage, on the other hand, is a complete environment for color palette alteration environment. If you're working with a limited number of colors in a print job or in a Web page color palette, Second Glance Chromassage will prove its worth by being both useful and enjoyable.

How Second Glance Chromassage Does It

To launch Chromassage, choose Filter | Second Glance | Chromassage from Photoshop's menu bar. Chromassage begins by building a histogram of the image. Once the histogram is complete, the Chromassage dialog box displays the image, as shown by Figure 30-1. The 256 most dominant colors in the image are loaded in both the Current and Working palettes in identical order. You can sort the color palettes using a number of color spaces, including RGB,

HSL, and Yiq. When you change the sort method, the colors in the Current palette will be reordered. The color order affects the manner in which color changes take place.

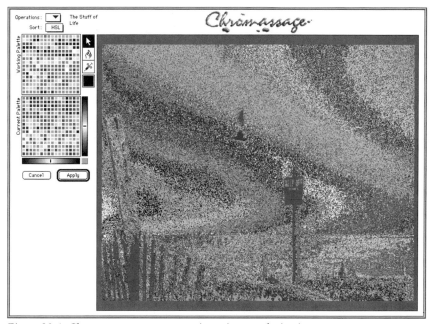

Figure 30-1: Chromassage puts a new spin on image colorization.

TIP *By default, colors are sorted in the Yiq colorspace. Although Yiq may be unfamiliar to print professionals, the color space is often used in the broadcast video world.*

Let's take a look at the methods used to cook up a wild image with Chromassage:

■ **Give it a spin!** The fun begins when you start spinning the jog wheels. When you spin the vertical jog wheel, you affect the hue of the Current palette. When you spin the horizontal jog wheel, the color squares cycle, marching through the Current palette. The button next to the horizontal jog wheel enables you to shift the hue of the Current palette by one degree with every complete cycle.

■ **Moving colors.** It's easy to move colors from the Working palette. To move colors from the Working palette to the Current palette, just click and drag on the color you want to move. To select a range of colors, Shift+click on the starting and ending color. To select a number of specific colors from the Working palette, use Command+click. Use the eyedropper tool if you want to pull colors from the preview image.

■ **Instant effects.** The Operations menu lets you quickly apply a number of color effects to the color lookup table (CLUT). The Randomize CLUT option scatters the color lookup table in the Working palette, while the Negative CLUT option inverts the color values in the Working palette.

■ **Injection tool.** Don't worry, this won't hurt a bit! Just select the Injection tool, choose a color from either palette, and click on the color you wish to infuse in the preview image. The new color will permeate all areas of the image that had the same original color. The Injection tool offers control over both the extent of color depth of the selection and the opacity of the injected color. Low opacity settings can be useful for subtle tinting effects.

chapter 31

Fortune Hill WildRiverSSK

Creator

Fortune Hill

Purpose

Awesome special effects

Platforms

Macintosh, Windows 95/NT

Hardware/software requirements

Mac: Adobe Photoshop 2.5 or greater; Windows: Adobe Photoshop 3.0 or greater; Same as Photoshop

URL/contact info for creator of plug-in

http://www.fortunehill.com
Fortune Hill, Inc. USA
814 Glendover Cove
Lexington, KY 40502
606/259-0933 voice
606/268-2724 fax

Products that the plug-in works with

Any application that is Photoshop 3.0 plug-in compliant

Who Should Use WildRiverSSK?

WildRiverSSK is appropriate for graphic artists, designers, Web developers, photographers, desktop publishers, broadcast designers, and basically anyone—from novices through professionals—who has the desire to create cool effects with type and images in Adobe Photoshop.

What WildRiverSSK Does

WildRiverSSK is an exciting collection of seven effects filters. The seven filters in the package can be divided into three groups based on their application in Photoshop.

Hue Manipulation

- **Chameleon.** Allows you to shift colors from one range to another.

Channel Operations (CHOPS)

- **MagicMask.** Lets you create incredible special effects with text and other selections.
- **MagicCurtain.** Creates exciting gradients and textures with 42 wave patterns.
- **MagicFrame.** Builds unique multicolor frames and borders.

Special Effects

- **DekoBoko**. Infamous beveling tool that creates cool buttons and panels.
- **TileMaker.** Turns an image into a mosaic in a flash.
- **TVSnow.** Adds a bit of bad reception to your image. This plug-in will have you scrambling for the remote control!

▼ **Super Sucking Kobanzame**

Want to know where the name WildRiverSSK comes from? Naoto Arakawa, of Japan, is the author of the set of plug-ins. In Japanese, Arakawa means wild river. The SSK comes from Super Sucking Kobanzame. "What's that?" you ask? The Kobanzame is a Japanese fish that keeps its young nearby. The relationship is such that all the little fish attach around the parent fish, thus making it look larger and more powerful. The analogy is somewhat difficult for westerners to identify with and is one reason that the product was renamed WildRiverSSK.

Why Use WildRiverSSK?

WildRiverSSK lets you create stunning special effects without forcing you to
memorize a list of commands. With just a few clicks, you can build unique
images complete with intricately rendered text and complex gradients. The
interface makes it easy enough to point and shoot while allowing plenty of
room for you to tweak your effects to perfection.

How WildRiverSSK Does It

Before we tackle each of the individual plug-ins, let's take a quick look at
WildRiverSSK's interface as a whole. Although the plug-ins in WildRiverSSK
perform a variety of functions, there is a high degree of continuity in their
interface features. We'll use the Chameleon interface, which is shown in Figure
31-1, as an example. To begin with, each of the filters provides a built-in help
function. The information presented here, though somewhat generalized,
should keep you from having to dust off the reference manual. The help bar is
located on the top right of each filter and is activated by a simple mouse click
on the question mark.

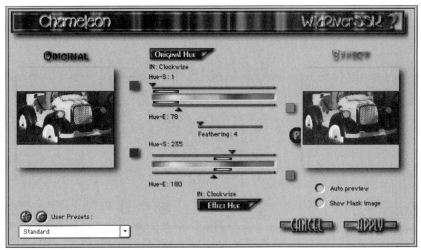

*Figure 31-1: Chameleon shares many of its UI elements with the rest of WildRiverSSK.
Perform the Vulcan mind-meld with the package, and you will be amply rewarded.*

Although the filters have an easy apply approach, there are lots of sliders
and subtle controls. If you wish to repeat an effect with consistency, you can

save the parameters and reuse them at a later date. Once you've created that masterpiece bevel or color change and have applied it, you'll probably want to save the effect for another image. Just click the + button next to User Presets. This launches a dialog box that allows you to name your settings. The presets are stored as part of the resource fork of that filter. Each time you reload a filter, your user presets will be recalled when you select the User Preset drop-down menu.

TIP | *The filters always load the last-used settings by default.*

On the following pages, we'll look at each of WildRiverSSK's seven components.

How Chameleon Does It _____

Although it might seem rather common, the name Chameleon is a great description for this quick-change color assistant. When Fortune Hill demonstrates their plug-in technology to folks in the photography industry, Chameleon is the one that always draws the "oohs and aahs." Photographers love the thought of major color changes with the click of a mouse. When Chameleon is shown to graphic artists, however, they often challenge, "What is the difference between this and the hue command in Photoshop?" Simply put, Chameleon remaps hue elements on a global scale, whereas Photoshop remaps hues on a channel level. If you wish to make a primary color change in an area in Photoshop, you are in for a multistep procedure.

TIP | *Chameleon only works with color images. Black, shades of gray, and white are not hues and cannot be adjusted with Chameleon.*

You can apply Chameleon to an image that is in RGB mode only. The filter can be applied to a selected area or an entire image. If you apply Chameleon to an entire image, however, you may end up making subtle changes to areas of the image that you'd rather not affect. It's always a good idea to use the magic wand or the lasso tool to define the area that you want to adjust.

When you launch Chameleon on an image, you will see a preview of the unadjusted image in the Original window on the left side of the dialog box, as shown in Figure 31-1. The adjusted image will be in the Effect window on the right side of the dialog box. The controls to manipulate the hue elements are located in the center of the dialog box. The top control defines the hue you wish to change. The top slider is the beginning point of the selection, and the bottom slider is the end of that particular range. It is important to note that Chameleon will allow you to replace a single hue with either a different single hue value or a range of hues. Although these controls are sliders, they represent a hue wheel/dial with values from 0 to 360. These numbers are arbitrary, although they correspond to degrees around the wheel. You can also select a range of hues to be replaced by either a single hue or a different range of hues. Change the direction the sliders work by pressing on the original hue area. A pop-up menu provides the option of clockwise or counterclockwise rotation. Selecting the counterclockwise option is very helpful when you wish to replace a wide range of red hues.

Here's a rundown of each of the controls:

- **Spot values.** The two small squares at the end of the sliders are the spot values of the selected hues. If you press and hold the mouse over these squares, you'll activate the eyedropper. This allows you to pick up a hue from anywhere on your screen. Since the previews are comparatively small in the dialog box, you may find this very helpful in selecting the exact hue from the original image window. The hue values are also numbered. To select a single value to replace, set both the top and bottom sliders with the same number.

- **Effect Hue.** The slider set below the input range is the output hues desired, or the effect hue. These sliders and spot color squares behave in the same manner as the input sliders.

- **Auto-Preview.** Chameleon is in Auto Preview mode by default. If you are performing color manipulation on a large image, it may be helpful to define your hue and manipulate it with Auto Preview disabled. When the Auto Preview has been turned off, you'll want to preview your changes by clicking the P button on the left-hand side of the Effect preview.

- **Show Mask Image.** This option is another valuable tool. Selecting this button masks out all but the area that will be changed when the filter is applied. If you are applying Chameleon to an entire image, you will find it worth your while to check your work before you apply the filter.

- **Feathering.** The feathering control works as its counterpart does in Adobe Photoshop. When you are working with a selection and the hue change is dramatic, there may be jaggies at the edges of the image. Adjusting the feathering can help to soften that edge. While Chameleon is often used to adjust the hue in contone/photographic images, it is equally effective on synthetic images, as well.

How Magic Mask Does It

For many folks, MagicMask is the primary reason they purchased WildRiverSSK. This plug-in is the centerpiece of the entire package. MagicMask offers 24 special effects filters bound under one interface. Many of these are bread-and-butter effects. If you are doing multimedia design, you'll find yourself constantly using one or more of these effects. Drop shadows, glows, smoke, metal, bevels and stamps are the order of the day. Magic Mask is a wonder for working with both text and object selections, such as the fish shown in Figure 31-2.

Figure 31-2: Magic Mask is a must-have plug-in for designers who create contemporary graphics for the Web, print, or interactive multimedia.

Putting MagicMask to Work

When you click MagicMask from the Filters menu and view the interface for the first time, you will notice that MagicMask has already gone to work on your selection. To change the effect, press on the script W in the lower left side of the dialog box, and a dialog box of 24 different filter possibilities will appear, as shown in Figure 31-3. This allows you to choose your effect visually. Click on another one of the stylized Ws and watch what happens. Your preview will change to match the effect. As you make these changes, watch as the name to the right of the template changes as well. You can also specify the effect you want to use by selecting it from a drop-down menu. Click on the name drop-down menu, and the list of all 24 effect names will be displayed.

Just to the right of the Ws, there's a check box to force the plug-in into acting only within a selection. Certain filters, such as the Metalize effect, work only within a selection whether the setting is checked or not. Others, like DekoStamp, can be forced to bevel the edge without casting a shadow.

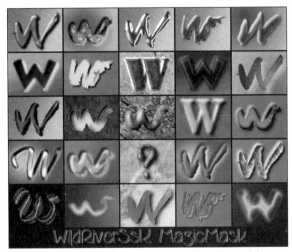

Figure 31-3: Magic Mask's 24 special effect filters deliver incredible results and are just plain fun to use!

The preview area is dynamic. If you click-hold on the preview, the arrow will change to a grabber hand, and you can move the image (provided the selection is larger than the preview area). There are three buttons on the top of the preview. These are the zoom controls:

- **Zoom out.** The - button on the left allows you to zoom out.
- **100% view.** The eye in the center selects 100% view.
- **Zoom in.** The + button allows you to zoom in for a closer view.

There are two controls on the left of the preview:

- **Color picker.** The topmost control is a color picker. Filters such as Colored Drop Shadow use the color picker to select a shadow color. If you click on the color picker and hold the mouse button down, it changes to an eyedropper. You can drag-click anywhere on the screen to pick up your choice of color.

■ **Auto-preview.** This button displays the automatic preview status. It displays a P if auto-preview is disabled. Auto-preview can be toggled on and off from the Options menu at the top right of the dialog box.

There are four elements that you may change in the options menu:

■ **Application Mode.** For pixel efficiency and speed, MagicMask supports two application modes. The resolution variable allows you to work in either a medium- or high-resolution mode. If you are using MagicMask with images (such as Web graphics) that are under 100 dpi, you should use the medium-resolution setting. On images for print, you should consider using the high-resolution setting. When the high-resolution setting is selected, it doubles the effective pixel distance that objects are offset.

■ **Auto Preview.** When you work on large selections with little memory or on a slow computer, the auto preview is a time-saver. With auto preview disabled, you can call a preview anytime by pressing the P on the left side of the preview.

■ **Mask Color.** The mask area is defined by the selection area. The mask color can be set to white, black, or gray. This adjustment can be helpful when you are applying a shadow to a selection that has a dark background.

■ **Preferences.** WildRiver and, in particular, MagicMask support a wide variety of plug-in-savvy applications in addition to Adobe Photoshop. These applications vary in their ability to support the Photoshop SDK (Standard Developers Kit). To accommodate the varying ability of each application, there are two settings. A-type applications, including Adobe Photoshop, let you apply an effect that makes changes outside the selection area. B-type applications do not allow this. If you use MagicMask in applications other than Photoshop, be sure to select the appropriate application type. You can set your preference to display previews upon opening the plug-in. If you disable this setting, MagicMask will open much faster.

As you select various filters in MagicMask, certain color sliders become available. The most important is the one that controls strength. The strength effect governs the strength of the light source on the selection. Let's take a look at some of these controls:

■ **MeltEdgeLevel.** This control may not seem all that obvious. It's only active on certain filters, such as Metalize. As the value increases in MeltEdgeLevel, so does the width and intensity of the edge in both the highlight and shadow areas.

■ **Blur Variable.** This control is essential when creating custom shadows and bevels. The intensity and drop off of the shadow are controlled by the value of the blur variable. The number here is actually the number of pixels from the selection edge to where the effect ends. If you set the option to high-resolution variable, this number is set to 31. When the option is set to middle-resolution variable, the value is 15 pixels.

■ **Lighting.** The Lighting controls are essential for realistic shadows and lighting effects. The shadow or lighting direction buttons fall at 45 degree intervals. The highlighted button indicated on the lighting dial is the direction the shadow will fall. The X-Offset and Y-Offset are alternate lighting controls. The XY level indicates how high you wish to simulate your selection floating above the surface.

TIP *The lower 20 percent of the MagicMask dialog box can be disabled by unchecking the Hints and User Presets box. If you are tight on screen real estate, this could be helpful. Otherwise, there are several useful hints on the application of each individual filter for all of the 24 filters in MagicMask. These are at the bottom left of the dialog.*

MagicMask is very computationally intensive. Here are a few simple rules to follow:

■ Don't apply MagicMask to an entire image. It will work slowly. Use it on a selection instead. And remember, MagicMask is a highlighting tool.

■ MagicMask loves RAM, so make sure you give it room to roam. Image processing pros know that it's futile to try to run Photoshop with a minimum amount of RAM. If you are living right, you will have a minimum of 25 to 30MB for Photoshop to play with. If you don't have much RAM, try allocating about 2MB of RAM above the size of your image for MagicMask to work in.

■ It is a good idea to save your selections before proceeding into the MagicMask plug-in. Many of the routines used in these filters remove the selection as they create the changes you specify. It is probable that your selection will be gone after you apply MagicMask.

TIP *Although WildRiverSSK was written to support Photoshop 2.51, you need to have version 3.0 and above to get the most from it. The reason is that 3.0 was the first version that supported the user affecting an area of the image outside the selection. When you put in a drop shadow, for example, most of the shadow lies outside the type selected. Many of the filter applications inside MagicMask use this technique to create the effect.*

The Photoshop 4.0 Difference

MagicMask was designed to run optimally on Photoshop 3.0. The introduction of layers into Photoshop 4.0 has made creating many effects easier. There is a caveat when using MagicMask on a layer in Photoshop 4.0, however. You may get unexpected results, or the filter won't work if you use a filter that applies a shadow or acts outside the selection area. There are a couple of workarounds here. One is to save the selection, flatten the image, and load the selection. Then call MagicMask and apply the filter. The other applies to text selections. Use the textmask tool instead of the text tool. The text tool creates a new layer each time you select the text, and hence the problem. One of the benefits of using PS this way is that you will get more realistic shadows, especially if you are working on nonwhite backgrounds.

How MagicCurtain & MagicFrame Do It

We are grouping the MagicCurtain and MagicFrame plug-ins into one unit because they are almost identical in function. The difference is in the application. Once you have a handle on MagicCurtain, MagicFrame will be a snap to learn. MagicFrame is a subset plug-in that applies the MagicCurtain gradient in a selection that's defined by a rectangular frame. The main differences between these two filters will be covered at the end of this section.

MagicCurtain

MagicCurtain is one of the most powerful plug-ins in the suite. The name was used in the original Sucking Fish plug-ins and is derived from the gradient effects that resemble the shading seen in a hanging curtain. MagicCurtain is a gradient design engine that uses wave forms to describe the highlight and shadow of the gradient. This plug-in is often used to generate wild backgrounds, transitional effects, or multi-element gradients. You can apply MagicCurtain to images in both RGB and Grayscale mode. It can be applied to an entire image or any type of selection.

People often ask, "What is MagicCurtain's purpose now that Photoshop has gradients?" Well, here's the skinny. Photoshop has a limit of 14 colors or transitions. MagicCurtain, on the other hand, has an unlimited range. It is totally configurable by the user. To the new user, unfortunately, the interface may seem confusing. However, if you concentrate on the wave forms and work with them to generate the effect you wish to achieve, you will not only soon be on your way to creating ingenious effects, but you will also get a better handle on understanding color management.

Let's take a look at MagicCurtain's interface, as shown in Figure 31-4. The large rainbow-colored bar in the center of the interface serves as both the preview and the gradient design window. Probably one of the best/worst-kept interface secrets in MagicCurtain is the small cyan-colored triangle to the left of the preview window. By clicking this triangle, you can access 25 preset curves. They are great to experiment with for your initial forays into the plug-in.

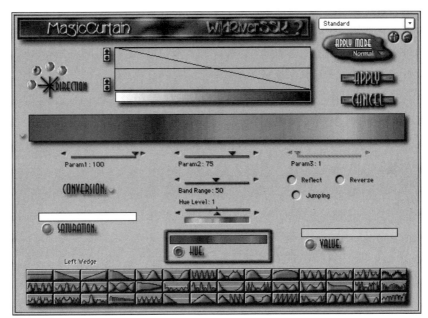

Figure 31-4: Pull back the shades and see the light! MagicCurtain produces complex gradients with ease.

At the bottom of the interface are the wave form selections. There are 42 named waveforms to choose from. The name of the current waveform is displayed above and to the left of the table of waveforms. The selection is displayed in the histogram at the top center of the plug-in interface. If you wish to shorten the menu, you can simply click on the waveform name and the waveforms will disappear. Click on it again and they reappear.

Waveforms can be applied in a variety of directions. By selecting one of the buttons, you can change the orientation of the gradient. Unfortunately, since the preview is static in its direction, you will not see this change until the plug-in is applied. The default button is set to the topmost button. This yields a horizontal gradient on any selection.

The plug-in operates in three color modes: HSV, RGB, and Grayblend. When working with the filter for the first time, you should probably work in the RGB mode—it's the simplest color conversion model to use. When you make changes in the conversion, the interface control elements will be changed. By making changes in these conversion components, you change the appearance of the gradient. Each of these components has a number of associated parameters, and each of the elements has an associated wave form.

There are 10 different Apply modes that can be used to apply the plug-in's action to the selected image. Many of these elements are common to plug-in or filter applications—they are mathematical operators called Boolean operations. Among other things, these operations add, subtract, or multiply the values of the pixels of the filter's application to the underlying image. Let's take a look at the two unique modes that are included in WildRiverSSK exclusively:

- **WR Blend.** When you select the WildRiver Blend mode, the plug-in lays the gradient on as a transparent overlay and preserves the detail of the underlying image. It is applied on the same layer you are modifying.

- **WR Difference.** When you select the WildRiver Difference, the plug-in applies an effect similar to Photoshop's Difference option (although the application of the differencing factor is inverted).

Let's put MagicCurtain to work and create an RGB image in Photoshop. The background should be white. Choose Filters | WildRiverSSK | MagicCurtain from Photoshop's menu bar, and make the following settings:

1. Set the Apply mode to Normal.

2. For the Direction option, click the topmost button.

3. Set the User Preset option to Standard.

4. Set the Secret Presets* option (to left of preview box) to Rainbow Base.

Once you've selected Rainbow Base, the waves and conversion settings will be adjusted for the preset. After you have done this, click on Saturation. A darkened border will appear around that portion of the dialog indicating that you are able to modify that portion of the selection.

Each component of the gradient has its own set of parameters. Saturation has its own wave, which is set to flat line. This means that the saturation of the gradient is consistent throughout its application. If you have trouble seeing the flat line, it is because it is set to 100. The amount of saturation is visually indicated by the white bars below the histogram and above the word Saturation. You can adjust the amount of saturation in two ways. If you click on Saturation and hold down the mouse button, a list of all 42 waveforms will appear. This might be helpful if you have a small screen and don't have the real estate to display the waveforms graphically. Let's take a look at some of the options:

- You can adjust the slider in the bar that is located above the word "Hue." This also indicates the amount of saturation of the gradient.

- You can move the Up and Down arrows to the left of the histogram. While there are four arrows, only the upper two are active on simple line forms. When you wish to modify more complex waves, the lower set becomes active. The other waves act from the midline of the graph. You can compress the lower or top halves of the graph independently by using these sliders.

- Here is where the fun begins! Try selecting some other wave forms and watch what happens to your preview. You will also note that the number of changeable parameters is based on the waveform you select. The more complex the wave form, the greater number of parameters there are available to vary the shape of the curve. On all nonlinear wave forms, you can also adjust the amplitude of the curve. When you finish experimenting, reset the wave to a flat line setting. You can also switch to the Hue and Value selections and vary them as you wish.

TIP *You can apply MagicCurtain to selections in layers, channels, and on paths.*

MagicFrame Specific Features

MagicFrame is a variant of MagicCurtain. We discussed most of the core functionality of this plug-in in the preceding paragraphs. As you can see in Figure 31-5, both plug-ins share a similar interface. MagicFrame applies gradients that are created in the same fashion that they are created in MagicCurtain. The difference is that MagicFrame's gradients are limited to a rectangular area. If no selection is made, the rectangular area is defined by the image border. If you define a rectangular selection, MagicFrame works within that selection. If you use a circular or irregular selection, the frame will be defined by the extent of the selection. The preview in MagicFrame is exactly the width of the frame dimension that will be created when the plug-in is applied.

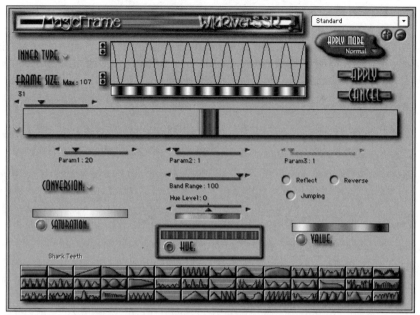

Figure 31-5: With MagicFrame, you'll never have to buy that picture for the frame again. This plug-in lets you quickly create unique framed effects.

The plug-in automatically calculates the widest frame size (width) possible for the image. A slider below the frame size indicator allows you to set the width of the frame in pixels. There are three selections for Inner Type option:

- **Transparent.** This leaves the area inside the frame alone and makes no alterations to the image data on the working layer inside the frame area.

- **Black.** Selecting this fills the area inside the frame with black.

- **White.** Selecting this fills the area inside the frame in white.

How DekoBoko Does It

The DekoBoko plug-in is the one that started it all for Fortune Hill. A primitive version of DekoBoko beveling filter was distributed as freeware/mailware in the original Sucking Fish filters. Web developers love that 3D beveled frame look, and DekoBoko was one of the first tools to automate the process and make this design easy to create for Web designers. The shareware version is still quite popular.

▼ **More Japanese**
The term DekoBoko means concave convex in Japanese.

TIP *DekoBoko works exclusively on rectangular selections. If you wish to bevel irregular areas, you can use MagicMask's Dekostamp or Bokostamp filters.*

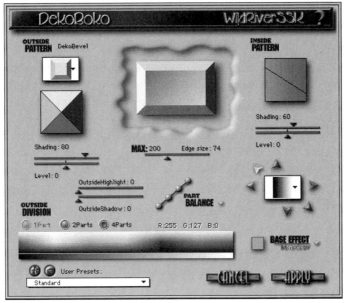

Figure 31-6: It's easy to knock out those Web page buttons with DekoBoko!

The DekoBoko interface, shown in Figure 31-6, makes the creation of cool beveled buttons a snap. A simple preview is located in the center of the DekoBoko dialog box. Just under the preview is a slider that controls the width of the bevel. Primary bevel style changes are made in two areas, the Outside Pattern and the Inside Pattern. There is a variety of different outside and inside bevel shapes to choose from. At the top left of the dialog box, you can access the different patterns. Click-hold on the square button to activate the submenu and select a bevel from one of the eight styles. Use the Shading sliders to modify the highlight and shadows on the bevel. The grayscale preview directly above the sliders helps you adjust the contrast. The Outside Highlight and Outside Shadow sliders are essential when developing beveled frames using light colors. Depending on the colors selected, the highlight may become washed out and the shadow can get too dark. To fix the subsequent lack of detail, use these controls. Additional control can be achieved by selecting the four-part Highlight and Shadow buttons. The Part Balance controls are used to set the lighting distance from near to far. These are active only if you are using four-part highlights.

Take a look at the controls afforded at the right-hand side of the dialog box:

- **Shading.** The inside shading control menu (just above Base Effect) provides five basic effects that are applied to the rectangle inside the bevel. These vary from a flat look to a cubic sheen. In addition, the six arrow buttons that surround the menu change the apparent lighting direction. You can tweak the balance of inside shading by adjusting the Shading sliders.

- **Base Effect.** The Base Effect selection at the lower right corner of the dialog box offers three choices: MonoColor, Grayscale, and Brightness. If you want your beveled image to have a certain color, choose MonoColor. You can pick up that color by selecting it on the color chart. Move the cursor onto the color chart, and then click-hold anywhere on the screen to pick up that color. If you wish to bevel an area, keep the original color of the selection, or give the bevel effect a stamped look, choose Brightness. This setting will preserve the underlying color and change only the shading of the image.

TIP *DekoBoko can be used in less obvious and creative ways. Other interesting effects— such as pyramids and frames—are easy to create, as well.*

How TileMaker Does It

Want to create a mosaic from your image, or posterize a color channel? TileMaker is the perfect plug-in to do it. The interface, shown in Figure 31-7, is quite straightforward and, subsequently, is probably the easiest plug-in in WildRiverSSK to learn. On the left side of the dialog box are two sliders that control the height and width of the tiles, with the numbers indicating the tile size in pixels. You can apply a grid overlay (or grout) to the borders between each of the tiles:

- **LineLevel.** This slider gives you the flexibility to vary the contrast between your grid and the tiles. The lowest value of 1 corresponds to the lowest amount of contrast between the tiles and the grid. Using a value of 100 gives the highest amount of contrast.

■ **Line Width.** This control sets the width of the grid. The width is divided into two pixel increments from 2 to 10 pixels.

Figure 31-7: Creating mosaic tiles has never been as easy as it is with WildRiverSSK's TileMaker.

The preview in the center of the dialog box responds to changes you make in the dialog box. To calculate the color sampling for the tiles, use the Average Method drop-down menu. The main divisions in deciding the tile color are via RGB Average, Brightness Component, and Channels:

■ **RGB Average.** When you select RGB Average, the pixel values in the tile area are averaged and the color of the tile is calculated from all channels.

■ **Brightness.** If you select this component, the tile color is derived from the brightest set of pixel values in the tile area.

■ **Channels.** This tile selection component refers to the RGB channels. You can create color-specific tiles that form from any one of these primary color channels by selecting Red, Green, or Blue Components.

■ **Color Sampling.** The color of the tiles can also be influenced by adjusting the Color Sampling variable. If the value is set to 1, 10 percent of the pixels are averaged to calculate the tile color. The increments are in 10 percent units up to 10 (or 100 percent). The higher the color sampling value, the longer the calculations take. When you use lower sampling numbers, the tiles will yield brighter colors.

How TVSnow Does It

TVSnow is pretty unassuming when compared to some of the other plug-ins in the WildRiverSSK package. While some folks might call it a noise filter, TVSnow is surprising in its usefulness. TVSnow can come in handy when creating granite textures, a burnished metal look, ripples in water, starry skies, and of course, TV Text. Let's take a look at the TVSnow interface, which is shown in Figure 31-8.

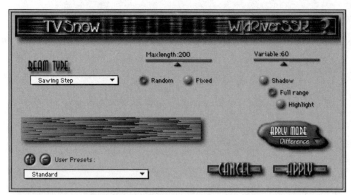

Figure 31-8: Think of TVSnow as a supernoise generator. Of course, you can always emulate that "bad reception on Granny's television set" look.

- ■ **Preview.** The preview provides a grayscale view of the effect.

- ■ **Beam Type.** This is the main control. There are five types of beams in the pull-down menu. Random and slope are the two most common and can be used to create granite or brushed metal textures. Sawing, Sawing2, and 2Bit Digital steps all tend to have a more harsh application.

- ■ **Maxlength.** Use this slider to adjust the size of the beams.

- ■ **Random** and **Fixed.** These buttons control whether the beams will have a uniform or random length/size.

- ■ **Variable.** This control adjusts the levels of brightness in the beam according to the Apply Mode type. As the variable number increases, so do the levels of brightness.

- ■ **Shadow, Full Range,** and **Highlight.** These controls affect how the beams will be applied to the image.

So Where Did TVSnow Come From?

When Fortune Hill started working on the TVSnow plug-in, the developer, Naoto Arakawa, code-named it Mid-nights TV. Which just goes to show what night owls software developers can be. Fortune Hill ran with this theme and came up with TVSnow.

chapter 32

Human Software's Squizz

Creator
The Human Software Company

Purpose
Image distortion effects

Platforms
Macintosh

Hardware/Software requirements
Same as Photoshop

URL/Contact info for creator of plug-in
http://www.humansoftware.com
The Human Software Co.
14407 Big Basin Way
P.O. Box 2280 Saratoga, CA 95070-0280
408/399-0057 voice
408/-399-0157 fax

Products that the plug-in works with
Adobe Photoshop 3.0.5 (or later), Adobe AfterEffects,
Adobe Illustrator, Macromedia Director, Macromedia
FreeHand, and other programs that support Photoshop
3.0's (or later) plug-in standard

Want to perform Kai's-Power-Goo-like image transformations within Adobe Photoshop? Whether you're crafting a wacky caricature of the CEO for your company newsletter or producing a morphing scene for a QuickTime movie, Human Software's Squizz provides you with the tools you need to warp, bend, fold, and mutilate your images into remarkable shapes.

Who Should Use Human Software's Squizz?

Human Software's Squizz is a creative tool that should meet the needs of anyone who wants to twist an image for print, Web, or multimedia projects. The audience includes artists, designers, and hobbyists.

What Human Software's Squizz Does

Squizz provides Brush, Grid, and Envelope distortion tool sets that allow you to push and tug at images as if they were made of clay. The Brush tools afford freehand distortions, while the Grid uses a series of horizontal and vertical lines, and the Envelope tool uses a Bezier framework. Regardless of the tools used, preview images are warped in real-time, providing instant feedback.

Why Use Human Software's Squizz?

The first and foremost reason to use Squizz is because it's just plain fun! There's a simple joy in having the ability to really twist an image, whether it's a picture of your boss or your little brother.

So what's the difference between Squizz and Kai's Power Goo? In general, Goo is targeted at the consumer rather than at the professional market. Since Squizz works with Photoshop, you're able to work in any color mode. With Goo, you're limited to just the RGB color space. While Goo is fun to use, it lacks such niceties as grids and envelopes. The precision built into Squizz makes it possible to correct a smile or perspective with accuracy.

How Human Software's Squizz Does It

Ready to start Squizzing? To fire up Squizz, choose Filters | Human Software | Squizz from Photoshop's menu bar. You'll be greeted by a menu dialog box, as shown in Figure 32-1, which lets you choose from Brush, Grid, or Envelope modes. The dialog box includes a Large Memory check box (it's a good idea to leave this selected, unless your Mac is running lean) and a button to assign a scratch directory. It also features the all-important Quit button—if you've Squizzed yourself into a corner, you'll need to return here to get back to an unSquizzied image. Let's start out by taking a look at Squizz's Brush mode.

Figure 32-1: Get your Squizzies! The splash dialog box 2allows you to select your Squizzy tool of choice.

Squizzing in Brush Mode

If you're familiar with Kai's Power Goo, you'll soon feel at home with Squizz's Brush mode. Just click the Squizz Brush button, choose a strength and size from the drop-down menus, and get to Squizzing! As you move the Squizz brush around the image, pixels are displaced in a sort of super-smudge manner. We quickly chopped the top of the cruiser shown in Figure 32-2, while adding a silly snarl to its front grille.

Let's take a look at the controls in the Distort Brush dialog box:

- **Brush Control.** There are Jitter and Displace brushes in addition to the Squizz brush. These brushes allow for a range of cool effects. The Jitter brush can be used with either a Frost or Storm effect (with full control over the strength and particle size), while the Displace brush allows you to load a displacement file in either stretch-to-fit or tile mode. The Displace brush uses Photoshop's Displace filter to work its magic. Once you've built any brush, you can use the Save button to store it so that it can be used again. To load a stored brush, use the Recall button.

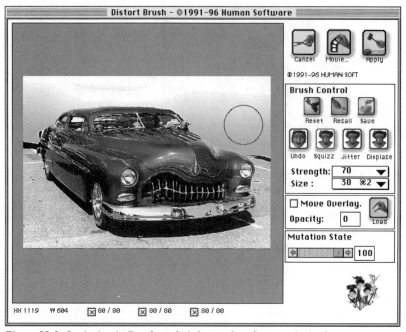

Figure 32-2: Squizzing in Brush mode is better than finger-painting!

■ **Move Overlay**. This option overlays an image onto your Squizzed image. No more Squizzing in the dark! Loading a background image lets you see exactly how your Squizzed image will look. This feature is essential when you are working with layered images. By using the overlaid image as a template, you can perform precise Squizz maneuvers. The Opacity percentage helps you fade the overlay in and out of view as necessary.

■ **Mutation State**. This slider lets you control the overall strength of your changes. By moving the slider, you can preview and apply your changes in a range from 0 (no change) to 100 (full strength). This allows you to temper the overall effect and make subtle adjustments.

If you slip with the brush and apply a little too much Squizz, don't fret. You can switch to the Undo brush and paint over the image. The Undo brush gradually applies the original image (if you want to return to the original image in one fell swoop, click the Reset button). Once you've Squizzed your image to perfection, click the Apply button to apply the changes to the actual image. If you're not happy with your efforts, click the Cancel button to return to the Squizz menu dialog box.

As we take a look at the Grid and Envelope modes, note that Squizz shares much of its interface and many of its features from mode to mode.

TIP *Keep track of where you are. Watch the bottom of the dialog box— you'll see the brush's X-, Y-coordinates, as well as the underlying color info.*

Squizzing in Grid Mode

Want a little more control over your Squizzing efforts? Try using the Grid mode, shown in Figure 32-3. You'll be rewarded with a fully customizable grid, with independent control over the horizontal and vertical lines.

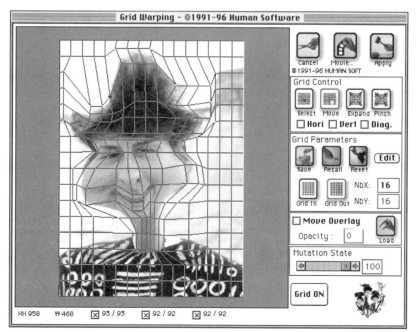

Figure 32-3: Grid mode lets you distort images by clicking and dragging points. Gee, won't Deb be surprised when she sees this shot?

Start by plugging in the number of columns (NbX) and rows (NbY) under Grid Parameters. Then, use the Select tool (under Grid Control) to specify a grid intersection point (or points), and switch to the Move tool to drag the point(s) to a new location. The Horizontal, Vertical, and Diagonal check boxes provide the means to distort the image in a mirrored fashion. You can use the Expand and Pinch buttons to manipulate selected points, as well. Clicking on the Edit button accesses the Edit Grid dialog box, where you can edit individual intersection points with numerical accuracy (in pixels millimeters, inches, or points).

If you think you like what you see, click the Grid On button to preview your Squizzy handiwork sans gridlines. Once you've created a wild and woolly distortion grid, you can save it to use again later. The Recall button lets you call up a previously stored grid.

TIP *Select multiple points by either Shift+clicking or selecting a marquee.*

Squizzing in Envelope Mode

When you're ready to get into some heavy-duty Squizzing, check out Envelope mode for serious vector-based distortions. Envelope mode works with three paths: a From path, a To path, and a Limit path. You create a path that you want to envelope from and then create a path that you want the first path to envelope to. The Limit path sets a border. Only the area within the border will be affected by the envelope. Figure 32-4 demonstrates a simple application of Squizz's Envelope mode on a pensive lion.

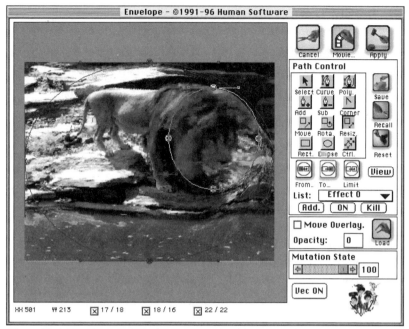

Figure 32-4: Envelope mode is the most complex of Squizz's three modes. While the interface may seem daunting at first, it's not that tough to figure out.

Let's take a look at the Path controls to see how we mutated the lion. First, we clicked the From button (the From button turned red to let us know it was active). Then we clicked the Ellipse button and dragged an ellipse around the lion's face. Since the ellipse didn't encompass his whole face, we clicked the Select button and selected individual points on the ellipse to adjust it. Next, we clicked the To button (which then turned red), then the Ellipse button, and then dragged out another ellipse, above and to the right of the first (From) ellipse. We clicked the View button to preview the mutation and then used the Select tool to adjust the size, shape, and location of the second (To) ellipse. Limit paths are not necessary for some distortions. Since the default Limit path didn't need to be altered in this case, we left it alone.

There are 12 tools that can be used to create or alter a path. If you're comfortable with Photoshop's vector tools, or with Adobe Illustrator, you'll catch on quickly:

- **Select**. This tool allows you to select any node or group of nodes.
- **Curve**. This tool allows you to draw curved line segments. Just click and drag to create a curve, and then click for your next node.

■ **Poly**. This tool allows you to quickly draw closed polygons. All you need to do is click-click-click to create your path.

■ **Add Point**. Need to add a node? Click this tool, and then click on the path in the position where you want to add the new node.

■ **Subtract Point**. Want to delete a node? Click this tool, and then click the offensive node.

■ **Corner**. This tool turns smooth curved nodes into corner points.

■ **Move**. Need to nudge that path a bit? This tool lets you click and drag a path to a new position.

■ **Rotate**. This tool allows you to rotate a path. Click a pivot point, and move the mouse away from the path. Then, click and drag around the pivot point to rotate.

■ **Resize**. Want to make that path larger or smaller? Like the Rotate tool, you'll have to click a pivot point and move the mouse away from the path. Then, click and drag toward or away from the pivot point to resize.

■ **Rectangle**. This tool draws a closed rectangle.

■ **Ellipse**. This tool draws a closed ellipse.

■ **Control**. This tool allows you to map nodes from path to path.

Just below the From, To, and Limit buttons, you'll see the List drop-down menu along with three buttons (Add, On, and Kill). The menu and buttons allow you to build multi-effect distortions. The Add button adds a distortion to the menu. The On button is a toggle that turns a selected distortion on or off. The Kill button removes a distortion from the List drop-down menu. The Move Overlay, Opacity, and Mutation State features work as they do in Squizz's two other modes.

TIP | *The Human Software Web site at www.humansoftware.com includes some interesting examples of how the Envelope and Grid modes operate.*

Squizzing Movies

Want to indulge your desktop Spielbergian inner self? Squizz lets you make nifty morphing animations using any or all of its three modes. Making QuickTime movies with Squizz is easier than you might think. To access the movie-making feature, just click the Movie button, and the Frame Library dialog box will load, as shown in Figure 32-5.

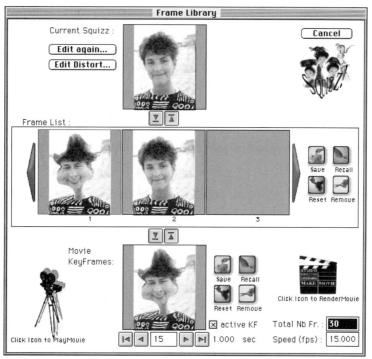

Figure 32-5: Yes, you too can make your pal's head explode! Are there practical applications? Who cares? This is too much fun!

You'll probably want to begin by setting the total number of frames and the playback speed (in frames per second) at the bottom right of the Frame Library dialog box. Squizz lets you create morphing animations through a process known as *key framing*. Key framing automatically interpolates an image from one frame to the next. For example, you might drop an original image into frame one and then drop another image into a frame at the end of the movie. Squizz will use its key framing smarts to blend the images together over the frames in between. This is often referred to as *tweening* or *inbetweening*. Squizz allows you to tween using distortion or color.

Here's how it works in Squizz. Load your original image into the Frame List by clicking the down arrow underneath the Current Squizz preview. Then save the Frame List. Edit the original image by applying some distortion, and save it to the Frame List as well. Save the Frame List again, just to be safe. Type the number *1* in the text entry box at the bottom of the screen. This is the first frame of the movie. Select the first image in the Frame List, and click the down arrow beneath it to load the image into the first frame. Next, type the last frame number in the text entry box, select the second image in the Frame List, and click the down arrow beneath it to load the image into the last frame. You now have two key frames.

Click the Render Movie icon to name and create the movie. Squizz provides a range of movie dimensions and types in addition to providing control over playback speed, compression options, and quality. Movies can be rendered in 256 or 16.7 million colors. Once your movie is finished rendering, you can view it with the QuickTime player by clicking the Camera icon.

TIP *Squizz is a good companion for folks creating multimedia work with Macromedia Director. Its tweening capabilities can quickly create intermediate cast members.*

chapter 33

Human Software's Textissimo

Creator

The Human Software Company

Purpose

Cool text and path effects

Platforms

Macintosh

Hardware/software requirements

8 to 9MB of RAM (in addition to what has been allocated to Photoshop), Piggy Plug-In Patch

URL/contact info for creator of plug-in

http://www.humansoftware.com
The Human Software Co.
14407 Big Basin Way
P.O. Box 2280 Saratoga, CA 95070-0280
408/399-0057 voice
408/399-0157 fax

Products that the plug-in works with

Adobe Photoshop 3.0.5 (or later), Adobe Illustrator, Macromedia FreeHand, and QuarkXPress

Want to create unique type treatments with infinite adjustability? Human Software's Textissimo is a powerful text and path special effects generator that's worth looking into. Although Textissimo's interface can be daunting to the new user, the plug-in offers a healthy selection of preconfigured effects to get you started.

Who Should Use Human Software's Textissimo?

Human Software's Textissimo appeals to multimedia artists, graphic designers, Web developers, desktop publishers, broadcast designers, and other folks who love to craft cool effects with type and images in Adobe Photoshop. The more familiar you are with Photoshop's Channel OPerationS (CHOPS), the happier you will be with Textissimo.

What Human Software's Textissimo Does

Textissimo provides a complete text and path effects workshop. The plug-in takes control of Photoshop's CHOPS to create effects that range from the workhorse chromes, marbles, and metallics through wild, otherworldly delights. In the bad old days, mastery of the channel operations was a black art. Textissimo provides you with a set of keys to the castle. While this software is not the easiest special effects generator to use, once you learn which key fits each door, you'll be amply rewarded.

Why Use Human Software's Textissimo?

Are you always hungry to create new, unique, and exciting text and path effects? Human Software's Textissimo opens up your special effect repertoire by allowing infinite variations upon a wide range of preset effects. The package comes with over 130 preconfigured effects, approximately 70 gradient effects, more than 100 seamless tiles, and a host of background images.

TIP *Textissimo needs all the RAM and computer speed it can get. The plug-in gets bogged down while accessing its files from CD-ROM, as well. One way to speed up Textissimo's performance—short of buying the fastest box you can afford—is to copy all of its effects and tiles from the installation CD-ROM to your hard drive.*

How Human Software's Textissimo Does It _____

Textissimo operates as an acquire filter. To access it, choose File | Import | Textissimo from Photoshop's menu bar. If you've flipped through the chapters on the other Human Software plug-ins, you'll notice that Textissimo shares much of the same interface. The Textissimo splash dialog box, shown in Figure 33-1, allows you to jump into its Effects, select whether to Scan the CD for Effects, specify a Scratch disk, and Quit the plug-in.

Figure 33-1: The Textissimo splash dialog box provides yet another billboard on the digital highway.

When you choose Effects, you're greeted by the New Background dialog box, shown in Figure 33-2. This dialog box lets you set the Document Size (in pixels or millimeters), Resolution, and Mode (RGB or CMYK) in addition to letting you select a file to use as a background image.

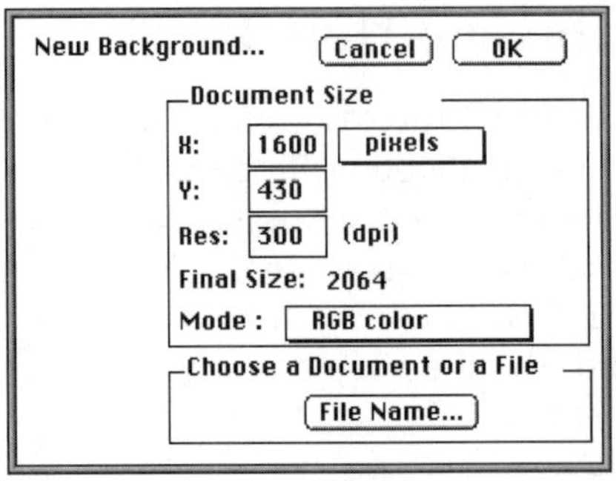

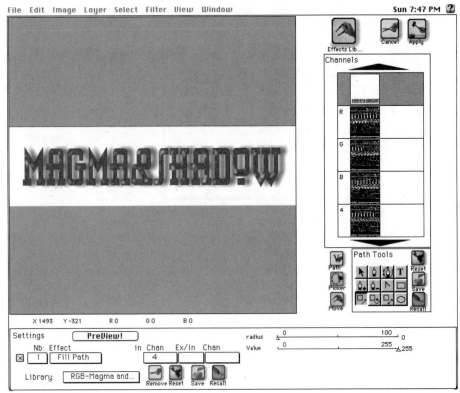

Figure 33-2: Textissimo lets you start with a blank background or use an existing image.

After you click the OK button, Textissimo scans the CD-ROM for its preconfigured effects (assuming you have that option selected in the splash dialog box) before opening up its main dialog box, shown in Figure 33-3.

Figure 33-3: Textissimo's dialog box may seem daunting at first. Give it time, and it will grow on you.

Creating Paths

In short, Textissimo works by letting you first create a path, to which you then apply an effect. Unlike Alien Skin's Eye Candy and WildRiverSSK—which work on paths *within* Photoshop and have the ability to perform similar effects—Textissimo operates far more independently of Adobe Photoshop. Unfortunately, this means that Textissimo will not allow you to import existing paths from Photoshop.

Here's a rundown on Textissimo's 12 path tools:

- **Select**. This tool is used to select and move existing points as well as to adjust curves.

- **Bezier**. Need that familiar Bezier drawing tool? The Bezier tool mimics the vector drawing tool found in so many applications. Hold down the Option key to draw a straight line.

- **Polygon**. Want to create polygon objects composed of straight lines? This tool lets you click-click-click away.

- **Text**. Use this tool to create your vector type. Textissimo is designed to vectorize PostScript Type 1 fonts.

- **Add Point**. Want to add an extra control point to a path? Select this tool and click on the path at the location where you want to add the new point.

- **Subtract Point**. Need to delete an existing control point from a path? Select this tool and click on the point you want to remove.

- **Corner**. Want to change a point from a curve to a corner? This tool lets you switch a control point from the default linked tangent mode, thus allowing two independent tangents.

- **Rectangle**. Just click and drag to draw a rectangle.

- **Move**. Need to move an entire path? Just click and drag.

- **Rotate**. To rotate a path, click a pivot point, and then drag around the pivot point to spin the path.

- **Resize**. To resize a path, click a pivot point; and then drag away or toward the pivot point to make the path larger or smaller.

- **Ellipse**. Just click and drag to draw an ellipse.

Let's set some type with Textissimo to see how the plug-in functions. When you click the Text tool button, the Text Input dialog box appears, as shown in Figure 33-4. This dialog is limited, as it provides only the bare essentials.

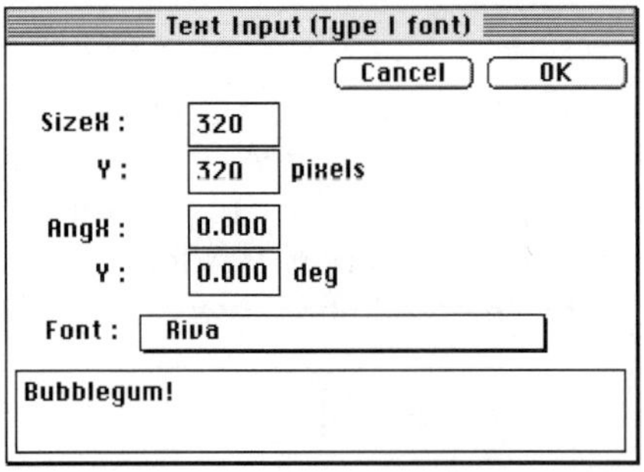

Text Input (Type I font)

Cancel   OK

Size X :   320

Y :   320   pixels

Ang X :   0.000

Y :   0.000   deg

Font :   Riva

Bubblegum!

Figure 33-4: The Text Input dialog box allows you to specify size, angle, and font.

A number of things we all take for granted—such as spacing controls and font previews—are noticeably absent. Type in a word or two, specify the size, angle, and font, and then click OK. Now click the pointer at the exact position where you want the text to be placed. The text will appear, as shown in Figure 33-5. If you need to reposition the text, click the Move Path tool button (it's the bottom left button in the bank of 12 buttons), and then click and drag the text path.

If you're not satisfied with the text as it sits, you can use the path editing tools to resize, rotate, or adjust individual control points. And if you're really not happy with a path, just click the Reset button to delete it. The Save and Recall buttons allow you to save a path and recall an existing path.

Figure 33-5: Don't worry if your text looks like it has been encrusted by barnacles. Those are only the control points! The more intricate the typeface, the more you'll see.

Applying Effects

Once you have a text path on screen, it's time to get into the fun stuff. The Library drop-down menu at the bottom of the Textissimo dialog box allows you to choose from scads of preconfigured effects. When you find one that suits your fancy and you release the mouse button, a dialog box appears asking if you want to save the previous effect. You have three choices:

- **No** renders the effect in the preview area.

- **Yes** allows you to save and name the effect before Textissimo renders the effect in the preview area.

- **Cancel** returns you to the main dialog box, without applying the effect.

Does that text still look like it's encrusted with barnacles? When you render the effect to the preview area, Textissimo will show both the effect and the path. To turn the path view off, click the Picker button to show just the rendered text, as shown in Figure 33-6.

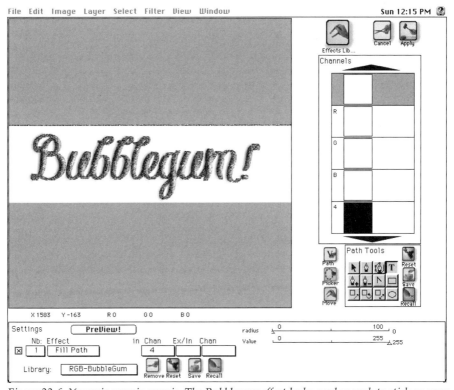

Figure 33-6: Yummie ummie ummie. The Bubblegum effect looks good enough to stick on your shoe.

If you're pleased with the effect you've rendered, click the Apply button to create a full resolution file. The Final Document Size dialog box will appear, as shown in Figure 33-7, enabling you to resize your image. You may also want to save your custom effect recipe (more on that, momentarily). When the render is complete, it will appear in a new Photoshop window.

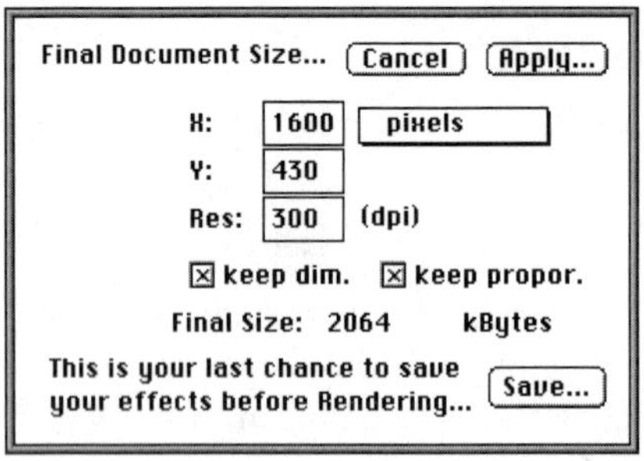

```
┌─────────────────────────────────────────────┐
│ Final Document Size...  [ Cancel ] [ Apply... ] │
│                                              │
│        H:   [ 1600 ]  [ pixels         ]     │
│        Y:   [ 430 ]                           │
│      Res:   [ 300 ]   (dpi)                   │
│        ☒ keep dim.   ☒ keep propor.          │
│      Final Size:  2064     kBytes             │
│   This is your last chance to save  ┌───────┐ │
│   your effects before Rendering...  │ Save..│ │
│                                     └───────┘ │
└─────────────────────────────────────────────┘
```

Figure 33-7: The Final Document Size dialog box is your last chance to check the dimensions and proportions of the full render.

If you're an inveterate tweaker, you'll be in hog heaven with Textissimo. After you've selected a preconfigured effect, you can go in and fiddle until the sows come sauntering home. The most amazing part of this plug-in is its ability to adjust individual channel operations. For example, if you want a stronger drop shadow than what's offered by a preconfigured effect, you need only go to the step that controls the operation and make the appropriate adjustments. This should appeal to folks who are intimately familiar with how the CHOPS work.

The scrolling Channels menu lets you preview individual channels. You can view the composite image and specific colors as well as other channels. Once you've gotten a handle on what each channel looks like, check out the Settings menus at the bottom of the Textissimo dialog box. The first menu, labeled Nb, is the number of the effect. The second menu allows you to select which effect you want to use (or alter). The third menu controls which channel the effect will take place in (up to 30 channels). The fourth menu determines whether the effect is internal, external, or off. The fifth menu specifies the out channel.

Textissimo lets you fiddle with the following effects: Copy, Add, Subtract, Difference, Multiply, Maximum, Minimum, Invert, Fill, Blur, Emboss, Lut, Black-White Points, Posterize, Adjust Brightness, Adjust Contrast, Adjust HSL, Offset, Displace, Displace With, ColorMatrix, Gradient, Load Image, Load Texture, Load Path, Fill Path, and Cube Path. As you select different effects, the controls for each effect will appear at the bottom right of the Textissimo dialog box. After making a change, click the Preview button to render the effect. Once you've created the coolest effect recipe in the world, you can stow it away with the Save button so that you can recall it for use at a later date as a preset effect.

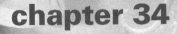

chapter 34

MetaCreations Kai's Power Tools 3

Creator

MetaCreations

Purpose

Special effects

Platforms

Windows 95/NT, Macintosh

Hardware/software requirements

Same as Photoshop

URL/contact info for creator of plug-in

http://www. metacreations.com
MetaCreations, Inc.
6303 Carpinteria Avenue
Carpinteria, CA 93013
805/566-6200 voice
805/566-6385 fax

Products that the plug-in works with

Any application that is Photoshop 3.0 plug-in compliant

Many Photoshop users will tell you that Kai's Power Tools is the reason to buy Photoshop. This set of filters by MetaCreations (formerly HSC Software Corp. and then MetaTools) would be more appropriately named "toys" instead of "tools." Warning: Exploring Kai's Power Tools's innovative interface and experimenting with its effects can be highly addictive!

Who Should Use Kai's Power Tools 3?

Kai's Power Tools 3 appeals to anyone who wants to make Photoshop more fun to use! Web and multimedia designers will find the Texture Explorer and Seamless Welder particularly invaluable when creating seamless background textures.

What Kai's Power Tools 3 Does

Kai's Power Tools 3 adds 18 special effects to Photoshop's Filter menu. Some help with everyday Photoshop tasks such as image touch-up, while others create delightfully bizarre visual effects.

Why Use Kai's Power Tools 3?

If you like wild, acid-trip-like effects, you're at the right place. Conservative Photoshop users can also benefit from Kai's simpler but indispensable effects, which are not found in the standard Adobe Photoshop filters.

How Kai's Power Tools 3 Does It

Kai's Power Tools 3 has three user interfaces for its plug-ins. There is a Standard interface for the most popular filters, a Compact interface for filters with less options, and the Lens f/x interface for filters that modify individual pixel values. The following table lists all of KPT3's plug-ins and which interface is available for each.

Standard KPT Interface	KPT Gradient Designer 3.0
	KPT Interform 3.0
	KPT Spheroid Designer 3.0
	KPT Texture Explorer 3.0
Compact Interface	KPT 3D Stereo Noise 3.0
	KPT Glass Lens 3.0
	KPT Page Curl 3.0
	KPT Planar Tiling 3.0
	KPT Seamless Welder 3.0
	KPT Twirl 3.0
	KPT Video Feedback 3.0
	KPT Vortex Tiling 3.0
Lens f/x Interface	KPT Edge f/x 3.0
	KPT Gaussian f/x 3.0
	KPT Intensity f/x 3.0
	KPT Noise f/x 3.0
	KPT Pixel f/x 3.0
	KPT Smudge f/x 3.0
	KPT Glass Lens 3.0*
	KPT Twirl 3.0*

*These filters were made accessible from the Lens f/x interface because they are fun to play with in this environment. If you want to do more than play, you should use the Standard interface versions, since the Lens f/x preview does not match the end result for the two effects.

TIP *Note that all of the Lens f/x filters have "f/x" in their names. If you want to use a Lens f/x filter and you aren't sure which one, remember that you can access any of the Lens f/x filters from the interface without having to exit the interface and go back to the Filter menu.*

Let's take a look at the user interfaces in the package before we delve into the individual filters.

The Standard KPT User Interface

The Standard interface appears as a 640 by 480 pixel window that blocks out most of the screen (see Figure 34-1). Most of the user interface controls found on the Standard KPT interface can also be found on the other interfaces, although they may be implemented differently. In addition to the common elements, there are always controls specific to each plug-in. The common controls are as follows:

- **The Kai logo.** Either gives you a preview of what your effect will look like or allows you to view more of the image you are working on.
- **The Help button.** Displays documentation for the filter set in a separate window.
- **The Options menu.** Lets you access some global options for KPT, as well as options specific to the plug-in being used.
- **The Info bar.** Provides context-sensitive help for the interface controls and indicates the settings of parameters as you change them.
- **The Presets menu.** Allows you to access the standard preset effects that come with the software as well as effects that have been created and saved by the user.
- **The Control buttons.** Allow you to add or remove presets and exit the KPT interface with or without applying the selected effect.

The Compact KPT User Interface

The Compact user interface is a smaller version of the Standard interface (see Figure 34-2). It contains all of the previously mentioned controls except for the elements relating to Presets, since the Compact UI filters do not use them. In addition, the following controls are available:

- **The Preview window.** Lets you click and drag to set specific effect options in addition to being able to preview the effect.
- **The Mode panel.** Lets you select different versions of the same effect.
- **The Glue panel.** Controls the way in which the effect is applied. These glues are very similar to the layer modes in Photoshop, which control how one layer looks when on top of another.
- **Opacity panel.** Controls the opacity of the effect. This is similar to the Photoshop Layers Opacity slider.

KAI LOGO   HELP BUTTON   OPTIONS MENU

INFO BAR   PRESETS MENU   CONTROL BUTTON

Figure 34-1: The Standard KPT interface and the locations of the common interface elements.
Note: *While we haven't annotated the other screen shots in this book, KPT's interface deserves some closer scrutiny. We thought that throwing a few arrows and labels onto the KPT interface might make things a bit clearer.*

PREVIEW WINDOW

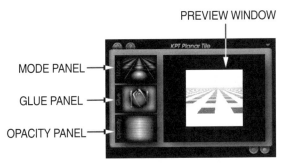

MODE PANEL

GLUE PANEL

OPACITY PANEL

Figure 34-2: KPT's Compact user interface offers lots of control while taking up only a small amount of screen real estate.

KPT's Lens f/x User Interface

The Lens f/x interface appears as a virtual lens that you can drag around an image to preview its effect on different areas. It is especially fun to play with because you can also drag the lens over menus and the desktop to see what the effect looks like. The controls specific to this interface are:

- **Intensity and Opacity controls.** Sliders on the left side of the lens. The Opacity control works the same as the Opacity panel in the Compact interface. The Intensity Control slider lets you determine the amount of the selected effect.

- **Direction control.** Allows you to control the direction of the effect. This control is not available for all of the Lens f/x filters.

- **Lens f/x menu.** Lets you switch from one Lens f/x filter to another without having to leave the interface.

- **Preview button.** Lets you toggle between viewing the center of your image through the lens or viewing whatever is currently under the lens.

- **Options gauge.** Gives you a pop-up menu of options for the selected effect. This control is only available for KPT Pixel f/x 3.0 and KPT Glass Lens 3.0.

- **Reset button.** Sets all of the controls to their default settings.

- **Glue gauge.** Works the same as the Glue panel in the Compact interface.

- **Mode gauge.** Works the same as the Mode panel in the Compact interface.

- **Label area.** Provides context-sensitive help just like the Info bar in the Standard and Compact interfaces.

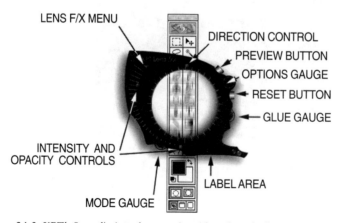

LENS F/X MENU
DIRECTION CONTROL
PREVIEW BUTTON
OPTIONS GAUGE
RESET BUTTON
GLUE GAUGE
INTENSITY AND OPACITY CONTROLS
LABEL AREA
MODE GAUGE

Figure 34-3: KPT's Lens f/x interface previews the selected effect—no matter what you drag the lens over!

How the KPT Spheroid Designer Does It

The KPT Spheroid Designer looks like, as the manual states, ". . . a bunch of spheres dropped onto an old, stale brownie." Regardless of how it looks, this filter is amazingly powerful. The following controls are specific to the Spheroid Designer:

- **The big ball.** Lets you preview the end result of your work. You can also click and drag on the ball to change the position of all of the lights at once.

- **The lamps.** Let you control the options for each light. Click and drag to change the position of the light, or simply click and release to turn the light on or off. Underneath each lamp are controls for Light Polarity, Light Intensity, Highlight Intensity, and Light Color.

- **The global controls.** The three spheres in the lower left corner. The first control allows you to control the curvature of the sphere. The second control allows you to control the ambiance by clicking and dragging on the Y-axis and the glossiness by clicking and dragging on the X-axis. The third control changes the transparency of the sphere.

- **The four dots.** Appear next to the global controls. Let you change the properties of the ambient light. Specifically, they control the Light Diffusion, Diffuse Hue, Ambient Intensity, and Ambient Hue settings.

- **The Bump Map panel.** Shows you the selected texture for the sphere. Clicking and dragging on the panel will change the texture's placement on the sphere.

- **The Bump Map menu.** Allows you to select preset textures or import grayscale bitmapped images for custom textures.

- **Four more dots.** Appear next to the Bump Map panel. Allow you to control the polarity, height, rotation, and zoom of the sphere's texture.

- **The Mutation tree.** Appears as a series of seven dots in the upper left corner. Clicking on a dot on the upper end of the "tree" will totally randomize the properties of your sphere. Clicking on the lower dots will make the randomization more subtle.

- **The Mutation menu.** Appears next to the Mutation tree. Allows you to control which properties of the sphere are to be randomized by the Mutation tree.

- **The Memory dots.** Appear in the upper right corner. Let you quickly save your settings without having to save a custom sphere to the Preset menu. Click on a dark dot to save your current settings in it. Click on a lit dot to revert to its settings. Option-click on a lit dot to clear its contents.

- **The Apply bubbles.** Appear in the bottom left-hand corner. Control whether a single sphere is output or multiple spheres.

- **The Apply menu.** Allows for many options of arranging multiple spheres.

- **The Presets menu.** Contains some truly weird spheres for your enjoyment. Was that an eyeball? Yuck!

Genesis Editor

When Genesis Packing is selected from the Spheroid Designer's Apply menu, the Genesis Editor controls the arrangement of the sphere output.

The Genesis Editor yields yet another interface and set of controls to learn. Here's what they do:

- **The Preview area.** Shows what your arrangement will look like. While you are changing settings, the preview changes to black and white temporarily to speed up redrawing.

- **The Control labels.** Appear in each corner of the interface. Open up a set of control dots for each aspect of an arrangement attribute.

- **The Amount Control dots.** Control the Total Spheres, Branch Deviation, Secondary Branching, and Initial Branching settings.

- **The Spacing Control dots.** Control the Branch Length, Branching Deviation, Spheres per Branch, and Kinkiness settings.

- **The Angle Control dots.** Control the Rotation, Branch Twist, Branch Spread, and Branch Angle settings.

- **The Size Control dots.** Control the 3D Offset Vertical, 3D Offset Horizontal, Shrink/Grow, and Zoom settings.

- **The Film Strip.** Allows you to save Genesis Editor settings into multiple "key frames" to be animated. The frames of the Film Strip work similarly to the Memory dots of the Spheroid Designer's interface.

- **The red dots.** Let you render and save your animation (the bigger dot), or simply preview it (the smaller dot).

- **The Color Swatch.** Indicates the selected background color. Click on the Color Swatch to select a new color.

- **The Presets menu.** Contains some preset sphere arrangements to experiment with.

TIP *Write it down! The Genesis Editor does not save presets, and the Film Strip frames are cleared after each session, so there is no real way to save your settings. If you really like the way you have something set up, you should make a record of the settings.*

How the KPT Gradient Designer Does It

You can create an infinite variety of colored gradients with the Gradient Designer, and with much more control than Photoshop's built-in gradient tools. Here's the lowdown on the interface:

- **The Preview window.** Shows you what the gradient will look like when applied. Clicking and dragging in this window moves the center point for the effect.

- **The Gradient bar.** The main control by which gradients are made. To change the color and/or opacity of a particular location in the gradient, click and hold on that location on the Gradient bar. A color/opacity picker will appear. Keep holding the mouse down and move the cursor to the color or opacity setting you want to select. Release the cursor and you will be able to preview your changes immediately.

- **The Gradient bracket.** Determines the editable portion of the gradient. The bracket can be resized with the mouse and repositioned at any location on the gradient.

- **The Channel arrows.** Located on the right-hand side of the Gradient bar. Clicking on the top arrow lets you select the RGB information from a preset gradient while retaining the other gradient information. Clicking on the bottom arrow does the exact opposite.

- **Gradient modifiers.** Let you tweak the properties of any portion of a gradient selected with the Gradient bracket. Click and hold to adjust a setting. Moving the mouse left will decrease the value, while moving the mouse to the right will increase it. The available modifiers are Hue, Saturation, Brightness, Contrast, Blur, Squeeze, and Cycle.

- **The Algorithm panel.** Sets the shape of the gradients application. The available settings are Linear Blend, Circular Sunburst, Elliptical Sunburst, Radial Sweep, Square Burst, Rectangular Burst, Angular Shapeburst, Circular Shapeburst, Angular Pathburst, Circular Pathburst, and Gradients on Paths.

- **The Looping panel.** Controls the direction and distortion of the gradient's application. Assuming that "A" represents the left-hand side of the gradient and that "B" represents the right-hand side, the available looping options are Sawtooth A->B, Sawtooth B->A, Triangle A->B->A, and Triangle B->A->B. The available distortion options are No Distortion, Pinch Right, Pinch Left, Pinch Inward, and Pinch Outward.

- **The Repeat panel.** Lets you loop your gradient from one to 10 times by clicking and dragging.

- **The Opacity panel.** Controls the overall opacity of the effect when you click and drag left or right. Clicking and holding makes a pop-up menu appear. This menu changes the image in the Preview window so that you can test your gradient in different situations.

- **The Glue panel.** Lets you apply the effect with various channel operations similar to Photoshop's Layer modes.

- **The Direction panel.** Changes the angle of the gradient when the Linear Blend or Radial Sweep algorithms are selected.

How the KPT Texture Explorer Does It

The Texture Explorer is one of the most popular components of Kai's Power Tools. With this filter, you can produce a multitude of gorgeous patterns in a small amount of time. Here are the controls for this simple yet elegant interface:

- **The Source texture.** The large square on the right-hand side of the screen. It shows what the output of the filter will look like if you were to accept the current settings. Clicking and dragging in this window will move the texture.

- **The Derivative textures.** Appear all around the Source texture. Each is based upon the Source texture, but all are a degree different. Clicking on a Derivative texture makes it the current Source texture. The Derivative textures will then be based on the new Source texture, and so on.

- **The Mutation tree.** Lets you control the degree of mutation in the Derivative textures. Clicking on the high end of the tree mutates the textures a lot, while clicking lower end mutates the textures less. Clicking more than once on a Mutation Tree ball results in different textures derived from the same level of mutation.

- **The Color globe.** Next to the Mutation tree. Uses the same Source texture, but mutates the colors only for the Derivative textures.

- **The Gradient strip.** Displays the current gradient used by the Source texture. Clicking and holding on the Gradient strip brings up a pop-up menu where you can select a Gradient Designer preset for the current texture.

- **The Gradient modifiers.** Modify the gradient used by the Source texture. The controls appear and operate exactly the same as in KPT Gradient Designer. Once again, the modifiers are Hue, Saturation, Brightness, Contrast, Blur, Squeeze, and Cycle.

- **The Direction panel.** Changes the angle of the texture. Click and drag on the panel to change the Direction value.

- **The Opacity panel.** Determines the opacity of the texture's application to the current selection. Click and immediately drag left or right to change the setting. Click and hold on this panel to bring up a pop-up menu that sets the preview image behind the Source Texture.

- **The Glue panel.** Lets you apply the effect with various channel operations similar to Photoshop's Layer modes.

KPT Interform

Once you have created your own texture presets in Texture Explorer, combine them in Interform to create entirely new textures! You can animate them too! Here's how it works:

- **The Mother and Father panels.** Appear on the left- and right-hand sides of the screen. Show the two Source textures to be combined. Click, drag, and release to set the texture in motion. Click and release to stop the motion.

- **The Parental Motion menus.** Accessible via the black triangles underneath the parent textures. From these menus, you can select a preset movement type for the texture.

- **The Offspring panel.** Shows the result of the texture combination. Click and drag in this panel to make the Offspring texture more like the Mother texture or the Father texture.

- **The Blending menu.** Appears underneath the Offspring panel. Lets you select a "movement" for the Offspring texture. Instead of moving the texture, it actually changes the amount of influence between the parent textures just like clicking and dragging in the Offspring panel does. The difference is that with this menu, the influence can be set to constantly change.

■ **The Opacity panel.** Determines the opacity of the texture's application to the current selection. Click and immediately drag left or right to change the setting. Click and hold on this panel to bring up a pop-up menu that sets the preview image behind the Source texture.

■ **The Glue panel.** Lets you apply the effect with various channel operations similar to Photoshop's Layer modes.

■ **The Frame panels.** Allow you to save Interform settings into multiple "key frames" to be animated. Click on an unused frame to store the current settings. Click on a used frame to restore the settings in that frame. Option-click on a used frame to clear its settings.

■ **The Record Keyframes button.** Looks like a movie camera. Click on it to save your animation to a QuickTime movie.

■ **The Movie Options menu.** Located below the Record Keyframes button. It lets you select the size, length, looping, and fading options for the QuickTime movie.

The Other KPT Plug-Ins

The rest of the KPT filters are straightforward enough to not need in-depth explanations. Here are the functions of the simpler but no less important filters.

KPT 3D Stereo Noise

Remember those pictures at the mall in which you can see a 3D dinosaur if you cross your eyes for half an hour? Well, why go blind in public when you can do it in the privacy of your own home? The 3D Stereo Noise filter will turn any grayscale image into a true stereoscopic image. The effect works best when used with simple shapes.

KPT Page Curl

This filter lets you create the illusion of curled corners on your images. While this effect can be easily overused, it's quite convincing when applied sparingly.

KPT Planar Tiling

You can tile a selected image infinitely with this filter. The two types of tiling available are Parquet Tiling and Perspective Tiling. Parquet Tiling is like looking down at a floor from the ceiling, while Perspective Tiling is like standing on the ground looking off at the horizon.

KPT Seamless Welder

This filter makes a seamless tile from a selected area in your image. This is great for making background images for Web pages. The Seamless Welder works by checking the area outside each edge of your selection and blending it with the opposite side of your selected area. There is also a Reflective Weld option, which instead only uses data from inside the selected area.

TIP *Make it big! Since the Seamless Welder uses the space outside of your selection to make a tile, your working texture should be much larger than your selected area. Start out with a large canvas to avoid any error messages.*

KPT Twirl

The Twirl interface offers real-time previews of its swirling effect as the values are changed, as well as a Kaleidoscope mode. Flashbacks are included with the price of admission.

KPT Video Feedback

This plug-in simulates the effect of aiming a camera at the same screen that is displaying the camera's output. Real-time previewing of the effect is available with this interface as well. There is also a Telescopic Feedback mode that repeats elliptical images rather than the Video Feedback mode's rectangular images.

KPT Vortex Tiling

This effect can best be described as a tunnel in which your selected area is tiled upon the walls. The Pinch Vortex mode sucks your image into and through itself. Okay, so maybe you will find a use for it!

KPT Pixel f/x

Your image's pixels can be scattered around in various ways with this effect. The available modes are Diffuse More, PixelWeather 1, and PixelWeather 2. You are also allowed various ways to control the direction of the scattering effect.

KPT Glass Lens

This filter makes the selected area appear as if a glass lens were on top of it. Click and drag in the Preview window to change the direction of the light source. The three light modes available are Soft, Normal, and Bright.

KPT Gaussian f/x

This effect is similar to that of Photoshop's built-in Gaussian Blur. The differences are the exceptional real-time preview, additional controls (such as Opacity and Intensity), and additional modes. The available modes are Blur, Weave, Block, and Diamond.

KPT Edge f/x

The Edge f/x filter outlines shapes in an image based on contrasting pixel values. The three modes are Normal, Soft, and Directional. Selecting Directional edges causes a control ball to appear that can be used to change the direction of the effect.

KPT Intensity f/x

Need to pump up a photograph? This plug-in does a great job of adding "oomph" to images by increasing their contrast and saturation.

KPT Smudge f/x

This filter is useful for creating directional blurring effects. There is also a Drip mode available that creates an effect not unlike that of a bad copy machine.

KPT Noise f/x

Noise f/x allows for three different types of noise. Hue Protected mode makes the noise pixels a similar color to the image's pixels, resulting in a more subtle effect. Grime Layer mode is more extreme, adding dark noise to the image. Special Color mode allows you to select a specific color for the noise.

TIP | *Use it! If you've been using Photoshop for a few years, you may be more accustomed to using a lot of Adobe's built-in effects. Don't forget that Kai's versions are there too, and that they're cooler!*

chapter 35

M.M.M. Software's SISNIKK Pro Plug-in

Creator

M.M.M. Software

Purpose

Creates single-image stereograms

Platform

Macintosh

Hardware/Software requirements

Same as Photoshop

URL/Contact info for creator of plug-in

http://www.mmmsoft.com

Products that the plug-in works with

Photoshop 2.5.1, 3.0, 4.0

Did you ever walk past a crowd of folks at the shopping mall as they gazed goofily in the window of the frame shop? There's a good chance that they weren't entranced by the selection of frames; they were probably just amusing themselves by staring at the stereograms, craning to see a tiger leap out of a poster. Now you can create eye-popping stereograms of your own with M.M.M. Software's SISNIKK Pro.

Who Should Use SISNIKK?

SISNIKK is a boon for artists, designers, and other graphics professionals interested in creating single-image stereograms for print, Web, and multimedia projects.

What SISNIKK Does

Single-image stereograms are pictures that include hidden three-dimensional images. When someone stares at the stereogram, the three-dimensional images seem to pop out as if by magic. SISNIKK allows you to use Photoshop's Channels to create stereograms in any color mode, size, and resolution.

Why Use SISNIKK?

SISNIKK lets you quickly create single-image stereogram images with effects ranging from the easy to perceive to the deep and complex. Print applications range from little postcards to giant posters.

How SISNIKK Does It

SISNIKK consists of three plug-ins: SISNIKK Image Pro, SISNIKK Random Pro, and SISNIKK Special Pro. Each of the plug-ins delivers the illusion of depth and automatic smoothing but goes about its magic in a different way. Image Pro can be used to hide images within any pattern fill, while Random Pro can be used to hide images within a random dot pattern. Special Pro is an experimental filter that allows you to hide three-dimensional images within other pictures.

Working with SISNIKK is fairly straightforward. You'll want to have your monitor set at thousands or millions of colors (24-bit). To hide an image within a pattern, place the hidden three-dimensional image into the Depth Channel and the pattern into the Color Channels (RGB or CMYK), as shown in Figure

35-1. Select all the channels, choose Filter | Pajalnikk | SISNIKK Image Pro, choose the depth (normal, deep, or max) and start (left, center, or right), and then click OK. The plug-in will create the stereogram. Once it's finished, you can try it out by pressing your nose to your monitor while staring off into space!

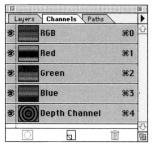

Figure 35-1: Place your pattern into the Color Channels and the 3D image into the Depth Channel and you're ready to go.

Want to hide a 3D image within a non-3D image? Follow the directions in the preceding paragraph but paste the (non-3D) image into the Color Channels before you apply the SISNIKK Special Pro filter. The Special Pro filter allows you to choose a depth (normal, deep, or max), start (left, right, or center), and either a direct or random dot.

Random pattern stereograms look a little like WildRiverSSK's TVSnow or Xaos Tools's Tube Time patterns. To create a random pattern stereogram, all you need to do is paste your 3D image into the Depth Channel, select all the channels, and choose Filter | Pajalnikk | SISNIKK Random Pro. Then choose your depth (normal, deep, or max) and color (halftone, fulltone, primary, or composite) and click OK.

TIP | *To create three-dimensional images for use with SISNIKK, you can use a full-blown rendering program—such as Specular Infini-D, Raydream Designer, and KPT Bryce—or you can use 3D plug-ins like Xaos Tools's TypeCaster, Vertigo's 3D Dizzy, or M.M.M. Software's very own (and very cool) HoloDozo.*

The demo version of SISNIKK Pro included on *The Photoshop Plug-ins Book* Companion CD-ROM is fully functional but works only with the images supplied by the developer. The best way to comprehend this plug-in is to actually experience it. Go ahead and give this one a whirl!

chapter 36

Xaos Tools's Paint Alchemy 2

Creator

Xaos Tools

Purpose

A unique brushing tool designed to enhance and alter electronic images

Platforms

Macintosh, Windows

Hardware/software requirements

Mac System 7 software or higher

URL/contact info for creator of plug-in

Xaos Tools, Inc.
55 Hawthorne Street
Suite 1020
San Francisco, CA 94105
415/538-7000 voice

Products that the plug-in works with

Any host application that accepts Adobe Photoshop plug-ins,
including the following programs: Adobe Photoshop 2.5.1, 3.0, Adobe
Premiere 3.0, 4.0,* Avid VideoShop 2.0, CoSA After Effects 2.0, 2.0.1,
Deneba Canvas 3.5.2, Equilibrium DeBabelizer 1.5.5, 1.6,* Fractal
Design Dabbler 1.0, Fractal Design Painter 2.0, 3.0, MicroFrontier
Color It! 2.3, 2.3.2, Pixel Paint Pro 3, Ray Dream Designer 3.0, Specular
Collage 1.1, Strata Vision 3D 3.0

* Paint Alchemy supports style animation in Adobe Premiere 4.0 and
DeBabelizer 1.6.

Want to add tactile qualities and natural media effects to your Photoshop images? Need to add a more "painterly" feel? Xaos Tools's Paint Alchemy 2 delivers multiple brush stroke capabilities in an easy-to-use yet extensive interface. The plug-in provides the utmost control over the coverage, color, angle, size, and opacity of each effect.

Who Should Use Paint Alchemy 2?

Xaos Tools's Paint Alchemy 2 is a treat for graphic designers and artists alike. The plug-in is intended for anyone seeking an interesting and different look using the simulated effects of natural media.

What Paint Alchemy 2 Does

Paint Alchemy 2 creates brush stroke effects on entire images or on selected parts of images. With complete control over brush opacity, size, and angle, the plug-in allows you to create a wide range of effects. Paint Alchemy 2 provides a host of features:

- **Preview options.** A large interruptible preview window with a moveable marquee selection lets you zero in on selected portions of your image. This enables fast previews and application of the brush stroke styles.

- **Convenient style settings.** The settings for each brush stroke selection are on individual floating palettes. They can be viewed either individually or simultaneously.

- **Brush stroke capabilities.** Brush strokes can be previewed over time and can also be dragged and dropped over the area to be affected on the main window, thus allowing the creation of unique brushes. Paint Alchemy has three paint-mixing options that allow you to create additional effects.

- **Animation options.** Style parameters can be animated over time on video clips in Adobe Premiere 4.0 and DeBabelizer 1.6.

Why Use Paint Alchemy 2?

When compared to the options available with Paint Alchemy 2, the standard Photoshop filters seem dull and overused. Paint Alchemy 2 allows you to breath life into lifeless images and can be used on illustrations and photographs alike. For example, you can turn a so-so sketch or photograph into a stunning oil painting or a mosaic. These qualities can be finessed, tweaked, and altered to give impressive and realistic effects. The brush settings, styles, opacity settings, angles, pixel setting alignments, and variations provide so many options that you will be sure to get the effect you're looking for every time.

How Paint Alchemy 2 Does It

Xaos Tools's Paint Alchemy 2 works wonders with just about any image or photograph. You can perform amazing enhancements in just seconds. By selecting any of the more than 70 standard effects and using only one brush type, you can get wide-ranging results. Figure 36-1 demonstrates four variations to the photograph of the kitty and stuffed animals. You will find that some effects deliver results that keep the photo or image identifiable just by changing the medium in which the art is rendered. And you will also find that some effects can be used to make a photograph into an entirely new piece of art, perhaps even a great background, which can be composited with other photos.

Figure 36-1: By simply selecting and applying various effects with Paint Alchemy, we were able to create four variations on the original photograph within seconds.

Merely selecting and applying brush types and effects can give nice results. Quite often, however, you'll want to tweak and change the various effects. Paint Alchemy provides a bevy of floating palettes that allow you to change the options for each effect: Brushes (standard and customized), Opacity, Size, Angle, Color, and Coverage. In the remainder of this chapter, we will examine each of the palette variation options to give a clear idea of just how much variation one can achieve with any given effect.

Using Paint Alchemy 2

To start Paint Alchemy 2, choose Filters | Xaos Tools | Paint Alchemy 2 from the Photoshop menu bar. You will be greeted with Paint Alchemy's interesting and user-friendly interface. The dialog box, shown in Figure 36-2, puts everything you need at hand to transform images easily:

- **Style Selection menu.** By selecting, saving, and deleting styles from the Style menu, you can customize which effects are available at any given time.

- **Brushes.** The main window displays eight brush types. You can choose from a brush in the preset style, or you can create and save your own brushes.

- **Palettes.** Palettes set the brush stroke options in five ways: Coverage, Color, Angle, Size, and Opacity. These are floating palettes that can be dragged away from the main dialog box or closed at any time.

- **Animating brush strokes.** When the Jitter Frames option is turned on, the random number generator will be automatically reseeded each time a style is applied.

- **Preview/Cancel/Apply.** A preview can be canceled or interrupted. To apply an effect to your image, just click on the Apply button.

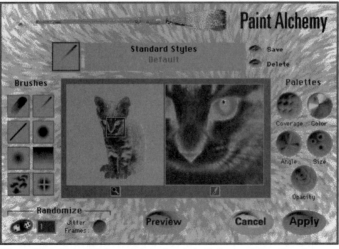

Figure 36-2: Paint Alchemy's interface is both fun and functional.

The Style Selection Menu

Let's take a run through Paint Alchemy's Style Selection menu.

Use a Preset Style

Use Paint Alchemy's main dialog box to select a style to apply to your image. Make sure your image is in RGB mode or you will find that Paint Alchemy is grayed out in the Filters pull-down menu. There are over 70 standard styles to choose from the Style menu. Figure 36-3 demonstrates how our kitty looks when painted with a soft pastel effect. We've used the Pastel Soft option (under the Standard Style menu) to create a very soft painterly effect. We previewed the selection before applying it to our image in the main window by moving the marquee area to be sure that all areas would be treated in the way we desired.

Figure 36-3: When a style is selected, it becomes the active style in the window. Click Preview in the main window to be sure that is the style you wish to apply. Once you decide to apply the style, click Apply and Paint Alchemy will render your image.

Save a New Style

To create a new style from one of the preset styles, adjust the appropriate palettes to achieve the desired effect. Then click Save to summon the Save Style dialog box, shown in Figure 36-4. Give the style a new name and click Save. The new style will become the active style in the pop-up menu.

The Brushes Palette

The Brushes palette lets you select an existing brush as well as create and save new brushes. Let's take a gander at the options.

Use a Preset Brush

Use any of the eight preset brushes by clicking on the appropriate icon. The brush you select will become the active brush. Figure 36-5 shows a nice example of the Oil Canvas blur default brush.

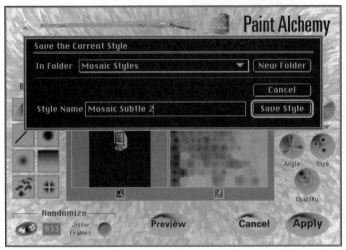

Figure 36-4: Here, the concentration and size of the brush style has been changed for the Mosaic Subtle 2 effect.

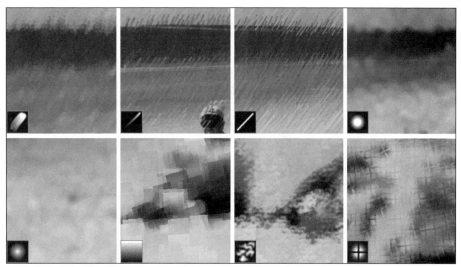

Figure 36-5: Here's a good example of the variety of effects that can be achieved by changing only the default brushes.

Create a Brush

Any application that can save files in PICT format can be used to create a brush. The grayscale image shown in Figure 36-6 was created in Photoshop in 128 X 128 pixels at 72 ppi. The sky is the limit for customized brushes. Try a few variations on one design before you decide. To bring up the Load/Save dialog box, hold down the Option key as you click on any of the preset brush icons. Figure 36-7 demonstrates the results of applying the custom brush.

Figure 36-6: A custom-made brush design created in Photoshop using grayscale mode.

Figure 36-7: And here's an example of artwork rendered with the custom brush.

Save a Brush

To save a newly created or custom brush, click the brush icon and hold down the Option key. This brings up the Load/Save dialog box, shown in Figure 36-8. Name your brush design. Once you've saved a brush, you will be able to use it whenever you choose, thus helping to provide continuity throughout a project.

Figure 36-8: The Load/Save dialog box.

The Coverage Palette

We demonstrated earlier how much the look of an image can change just by changing the type of brush stroke. The same principle is true for working with the other palettes in Paint Alchemy 2, including the Coverage palette, shown in Figure 36-9. You can change the Brush Density (number of brush strokes on an image), the Stroke Layering (the way the brush strokes are layered and mixed with the image), as well as the Horizontal and Vertical Placement Variation controls. The Coverage palette even lets you test out your coverage control options on a low-resolution image. When you apply it to a high-resolution/larger image, it will automatically scale the coverage to fit.

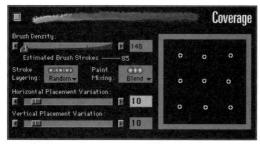

Figure 36-9: The Coverage palette.

Figures 36-10 through 36-12 illustrate how different settings in the Coverage palette affect an image. They have been set with various Brush Density settings and stroke layering. The images have also been rendered using different Paint Mixing techniques.

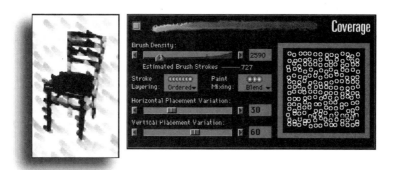

Figure 36-10: In this illustration, the coverage is not full; there is quite a bit of white space between pastel marks. The variation in both the horizontal and vertical placement of the strokes creates a slightly irregular pattern.

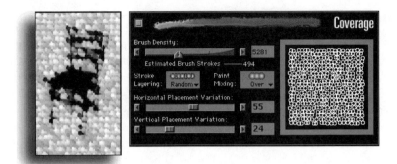

Figure 36-11: Here we have a fully covered background around the chair. Again, it has some variation in the horizontal and vertical placement of strokes. Instead of using the Blend Paint Mixing feature, we have chosen to use the Over Paint Mixture. This creates the effect of pastel marks coming out of the illustration.

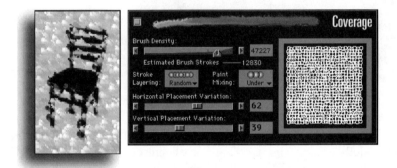

Figure 36-12: This example demonstrates very high levels of coverage, slightly higher variations in the horizontal and vertical stroke placement, and the Under Paint Mixture feature. With the controls set this way, we have created a slightly darker, more distorted image.

The Color Palette

The Color palette (see Figure 36-13) provides even more features than the Coverage palette. Here you can change the brush stroke color and the background color of a selection as well as vary a brush stroke color. When choosing a brush stroke or background color, you can either choose a color from your image (shown in the preview window) or from a solid color in the Apple color picker.

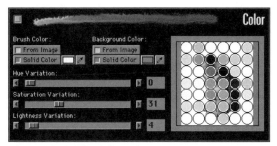

Figure 36-13: The Color palette.

Set a Brush Stroke Color

Decide which color selection method you want to use. Keep in mind that if you choose From Image, the brush stroke color is based on the colors of the underlying image. If you choose Solid Color, you can select a brush color in two ways. To use the Apple color picker, click the color swatch next to the Solid Color option, as shown in Figure 36-14. When the Apple color picker appears, select a color and then click OK. To select a color from your image, click the eyedropper, move it to the desired color, and click to set the color. You can select a color from any part of your screen.

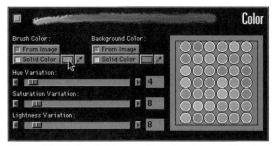

Figure 36-14: By clicking on the color chip next to the Solid Color/Brush Color option, you can choose any color to be your brush color. Here we have chosen a neutral tan color.

Set a Background Color

The background color that you set will be the fill color to the part of a selection that is left unbrushed. To set the background color, follow the steps for setting a brush stroke color (just make your choice under the Background Color menu for From Image or From Solid Color).

Vary a Brush Stroke Color

Now that you have chosen a brush stroke color and a background brush stroke color, you may want to vary those choices using hue, saturation, and lightness. The amount of randomness is determined by the value of the respective slider. A setting of 100 on each slider produces completely random brush stroke color; you will see no result when the setting is at 0. Figure 36-15 shows how the brush colors will change based on changes in the hue, saturation, and lightness.

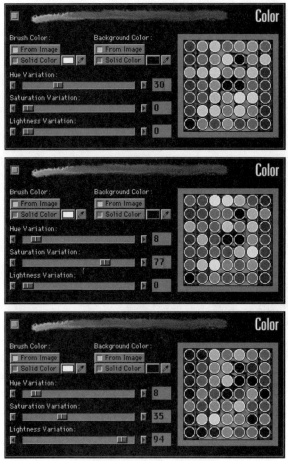

Figure 36-15: Notice the settings on the Hue Variation, Saturation Variation, and Lightness Variation sliders and how these settings change the colors in the preview window.

The Angle, Size & Opacity Palettes

The Angle, Size, and Opacity palettes, shown in Figures 36-16 through 36-18, have variation controls that are quite similar in nature. In the Angle palette, you define the angle at which brush strokes are applied. This can and will vary based on position or color information in the image. The Size palette controls the brush stroke size. The strokes can all be the same size or they can be made to vary based on position or on color information from the image. Using the Opacity palette allows you to determine the degree of transparency of the brush stroke. Opacity can be set to vary based on a number of options.

Figure 36-16: The Angle palette.

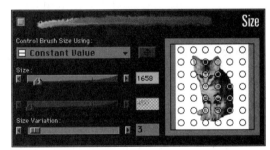

Figure 36-17: The Size palette.

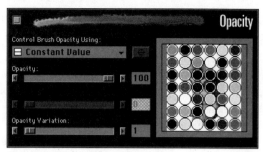

Figure 36-18: The Opacity palette.

For each of these palettes, you should use the preview window to see the angle, size, and opacity settings for the current brush. The arrows or circles across the front of the preview window will point toward the direction and show the size or opacity level in which the brush strokes will be made.

Setting Variations

You can vary a brush stroke by changing the angle randomly, radially, horizontally, and vertically along with adjusting the hue, saturation, and lightness of the images. Notice that each variation method you choose contains a set of sliders that let you control the angle variation more precisely. Simply change the location of the sliders to vary the method more or less than the standard setting.

There are so many different results you can get by setting any of these options. You can start with the default values and then create your own by changing any or all of the slider controls. Play around with them to get some astonishing results—with luck, one will be just what you were looking for!

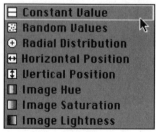

Figure 36-19: The Angle, Size, and Opacity palettes all have the same Control Brush options.

Control Brush Angles

Paint Alchemy provides total control over brush angles with the following options, as shown in Figure 36-19:

- **Constant.** Applies brush strokes to a selection at a constant angle. Change the angle by moving the Angle slider.

- **Random.** Applies brush strokes at random angles. The angle value can be set to fall within a range of values.

- **Radial Distribution.** Varies the brush stroke angle based on the distance from the center point to the outside edge of the selection. Adjust the center point using the controls in the Set Center dialog box.

- **Horizontal.** Varies brush strokes at varying angles from the left side of the selection to the right side of the selection.

- **Vertical.** Varies brush strokes angles from the top of the selection to the bottom of the selection.

- **Image Hue.** Determines the brush stroke angle by the hue of the image at the location of the brush stroke.

- **Image Saturation.** Determines the brush stroke size by the saturation of the image color at the location of the brush stroke.

- **Image Lightness.** Determines the brush stroke size by the lightness of the image color at the location of the brush stroke.

chapter 37

Xaos Tools's Terrazzo 2 & TubeTime

Creator
Xaos Tools

Purpose
Creates seamless tiles and textures and television snow patterns

Platforms
Macintosh, Windows

Hardware/Software requirements
Same as Photoshop

URL/Contact info for creator of plug-in
http://www.xaostools.com
Xaos Tools
55 Hawthorne St.
Suite 1020
San Francisco, CA 94105
415/538-7000 voice

Products that the plug-in works with
Adobe PhotoDeluxe, Adobe Photoshop 2.5.1, 3.0, 3.0.5, 4.0, Adobe Premiere
4.0, Adobe After Effects 3.0, Equilibrium DeBabelizer 1.6.5, Fractal Design
Dabbler 2.0, Fractal Design Painter 3.0, 4.0, Macromedia FreeHand 5.5, 7.0,
MicroFrontier Color It! 3.0, Ray Dream Designer 3.0, Specular Collage 1.1,
Strata MediaPaint 1.0

Do you need to use original seamless tiles for your designs? Tired of what you've seen on commercial CD-ROM collections? Xaos Tools's Terrazzo is one of the most powerful seamless-texture generators on the planet. In the wink of an eye, you can create scores of original seamless patterns.

Who Should Use Xaos Tools's Terrazzo?

Xaos Tools's Terrazzo is a blessing for anyone with the need or desire to create original seamless textures:

- Web designers often use the plug-in to create seamless background textures.
- Print designers use Terrazzo for publication or packaging design projects.
- Multimedia designers use it to generate textures for interface elements.
- 3D artists find Terrazzo to be extremely valuable for the creation of surface textures and bump maps.

The possibilities for Terrazzo extend into areas such as textile design as well.

What Xaos Tools's Terrazzo Does

Terrazzo creates wonderful seamless tiles from any bitmap image. The plug-in allows you to apply any one of 17 geometric symmetries—with control over opacity and feathering—to a selected area of an image. The resulting patterns can either be applied to the original image or saved as new PICT files.

Why Use Xaos Tools's Terrazzo?

With Terrazzo, you're never at a loss for a new scrumptious texture. While most folks purchase Terrazzo to create their own original textures, they soon find themselves using it for another reason. It's just great fun! Imagine having your own personal kaleidoscope, one that you can tweak and fiddle to your heart's content. A Terrazzo session is great therapy for stress-reduction. And it sure beats doodling on a notepad when you're on the phone!

How Xaos Tools's Terrazzo Does It _____

Working with Terrazzo is a terrific visual experience. You start with a source image—either greyscale, RGB, or CMYK—and fire up the plug-in by choosing Filter | Xaos Tools | Terrazzo 2. The playful interface makes texture creation a blast. The two big previews keep you constantly informed, as they display the original image alongside a rendering of the currently selected texture. Textures can be culled from nature, as in the giraffe hide in Figure 37-1, or from any image.

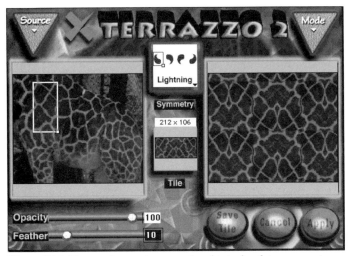

Figure 37-1: Terrazzo's easy-to-comprehend interface lets you create your own seamless masterpieces in minutes!

Let's take a quick look at each part of Terrazzo's interface:

- **Source pull-down menu.** Lets you choose a new source image and allows you to return to the current image (the Source pull-down menu is in the upper left portion of the window).

- **Mode pull-down menu.** Lets you select the manner in which the pattern is applied to the destination image. The choices include Normal, Lighten, Darken, Hue, Saturation, Color, Luminosity, Multiply, and Screen (the Mode pull-down window is in the upper right portion of the window).

- **Symmetry pull-down menu.** Lets you visually select from Terrazzo's 17 geometric patterns.

- **Tile preview.** Displays the currently selected tile.

- **Source Image preview.** Displays the original image along with the selection area (the Source Image preview is at the left side of the window).

- **Destination Image preview.** Provides a preview of how the currently selected options will appear in the destination image (the Destination Image preview is at the right side of the window).

- **Opacity slider.** Governs the percentage of opacity in the pattern as it is applied to the destination image.

- **Feather slider.** Controls the feathering percentage between tiles.

- **Save Tile button.** Allows you to save the tile as a new image rather than writing over the original source image.

- **Cancel button.** Lets you exit Terrazzo without making any changes to the original source image.

- **Apply button.** Makes the specified changes to the original source image and exits Terrazzo.

What's Your Motif?

With a source image open, you'll want to start by choosing a selection area. Terrazzo refers to this live portion of the image as a *motif.* The motif can be moved around the image by clicking and dragging. You can change the size of the motif by clicking on its handle (at the lower right corner). With Continuous Preview on, Terrazzo will provide instant feedback as you alter the selection area.

All the symmetries allow you to change the size of the motif. The Gold Brick symmetry, however, allows you to change the shape as well. The handle at the upper right corner of this motif area resizes the width, while the handle at the lower left governs the height and shape.

TIP *If you're running on an older (slower) computer, you may want to turn Continuous Preview off to speed up Terrazzo's responsiveness. You'll find the Continuous Preview setting on the Mode drop-down menu.*

Applying Symmetries

Terrazzo uses the magic of geometry to create its masterworks. You don't have to fret if you just squeaked by your high school geometry class, however. The plug-in does all the math for you! All you have to do is pick and choose between the 17 symmetric patterns. While the patterns have clever, descriptive names—Gold Brick, Crab Claws, Pinwheel, Wings, Hither & Yon, Card Tricks, Honey Bees, Prickly Pears, Pinwheel, Primrose Path, Sunflower, Spider Web, Lightning, Storm at Sea, Winding Ways, Monkey Wrench, Whirlpool, and Turnstile—nothing beats a visual preview. Thankfully, the Symmetry menu, shown in Figure 37-2, provides a handy thumbnail of each pattern.

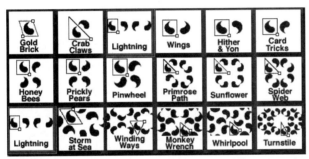

Figure 37-2: The currently selected symmetry will appear twice in the menu.

To select a symmetry, all you need to do is click it. No math required! While some of the symmetries may appear to be similar, each delivers a different result in the final rendered image. Terrazzo's documentation includes helpful examples of each of the symmetries.

Opacity & Feathering

Once you've selected an area from which to create the pattern and have chosen a symmetry, you're almost done. You'll probably want to fiddle with the Opacity and Feather settings to polish things off. The Opacity slider governs how the tiled image is applied with regard to transparency. If you don't want your pattern to be transparent, move the slider all the way to the right (100) to make it completely opaque. Move the slider to the left to increase the amount of transparency.

Careful use of the Feathering slider is essential when optimizing your seamless tiles. While you can get away with a feathering percentage of 0 on some images, many others demand that you apply at least a little feathering. In general, the less feathering you use, the better your seamless textures will be. Large feathering percentages introduce visible patterns that can ruin the illusion of seamlessness. Figure 37-3 shows an example of a pattern created from a photograph of a giraffe. The pattern uses the Lightning symmetry with a feathering percentage of 10.

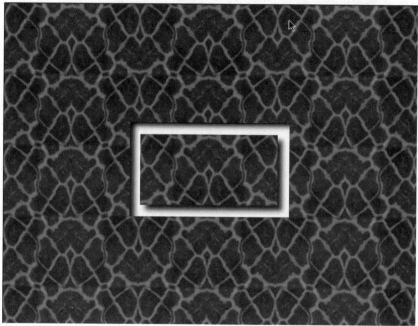

Figure 37-3: Yes, you too can rip off animal hides with a clean conscience.

Saving Textures

Although you can apply your textures to the original source image, more often you'll find yourself creating new image files. The Save Tile button allows you to quickly create a range of textures from a source image. Each time you make a significant change to the selection area, symmetry, or other options, you may want to save the tile for posterity.

Once you've created a range of Web page backgrounds, you can go back and preview them within a Web browser to choose the one that works the best. Since Terrazzo only saves tiles in PICT format, however, you'll have to convert them to GIFs or JPEGs before using them as Web page backgrounds. You can use Photoshop's built-in filters or, better yet, one of the excellent third-party filters, such as those from BoxTop and Digital Frontiers, covered earlier in this book.

TIP *Terrazzo's documentation includes a number of great tips. You'll find information on subjects such as creating black and white textures (great for spot color backgrounds), building paper textures for Fractal Design Painter, and working with Adobe Premiere. The docs are in Adobe Acrobat PDF format. Xaos Tools will send a printed manual upon request.*

Who Should Use TubeTime?

Designers of any ilk will groove on TubeTime's funky TV noise and snow patterns.

What TubeTime Does

Ever had the hankering to make your photos look as if they're being displayed on a vintage television replete with a set of aluminum-foil-encrusted rabbit ears? TubeTime does just that. This snazzy little plug-in, which is bundled with Terrazzo, delivers tons of fun (and even some useful effects)! It's the ticket for creating banding, comb effects, ghosting, scrambled reception, and snow. Let's take a look at TubeTime's interface, which is shown in Figure 37-4.

Figure 37-4: TubeTime's interface begs to be played with. And it's far more enjoyable than tweaking the antennas on your old portable TV!

How TubeTime Does It

TubeTime looks just like that old Philco black and white that belonged to your Uncle Louie. The preview screen is flanked by a host of controls. To the left of the screen, you'll see Help, Zoom, and Pan buttons. To the right of the screen, you'll see a host of sliders to control the size, brightness, horizontal distortion, and noise amount. These four sliders control the attributes of each of TubeTime's two video scan lines (the two lines have identical settings by default):

- **Size.** Sets the height of each scan line up to 25 pixels wide.

- **Brightness.** Adjusts the brightness of each scan line from black (-100) to white (+100).

- **Horizontal Distortion.** Pushes the image within the scan line to the left or right (specified in pixels) for ghosting or interference effects.

- **Noise Amount.** Controls the amount of snow, from nary a flake (0) to a whiteout (100).

The Greyscale and Tint controls are just below the four sliders. Selecting Greyscale converts a color image into greyscale while applying a color. The tint can be specified through either the eyedropper or a color picker. The Vertical Offset, Blend, Distortion, Phase, and Generation Decay effects are found below the preview screen. These controls allow you to tweak your image into the outer limits:

- **Vertical Offset.** Controls the comb effect by governing the range of vertical offset from none (0) to full (25).

- **Blend.** Applies the effect to your original image with full control over opacity.

- **Distortion.** When Horizontal Distortion is set to other than zero, you can apply scrambled signal effects.

- **Phase.** Use this with Adobe Premiere to create that all-too-familiar horizontal roll effect.

- **Generation Decay.** Controls the number of repetitions or strength of the distortion.

The three knobs at the bottom right of TubeTime's interface allow you to preview, cancel, and apply your effects. Once you've created the coolest video interference effect in the world, you can save the settings to apply to other images by using the Save feature, just above the Preview area.

Part V

Plug Into the Third Dimension

chapter 38

M.M.M. Software's HoloDozo

Creator

M.M.M. Software

Purpose

QuickTime 3D rendering

Platforms

Macintosh

Hardware/software requirements

PowerPC processor, 24MB of RAM recommended
(16 minimum), QuickDraw 3D 1.0.4 (included on installation CD),
CD-ROM drive

URL/contact info for creator of plug-in

http://www.mmmsoft.com

Products that the plug-in works with

Adobe Photoshop 3.0.5 (and higher), Adobe Premiere, Macromedia
Director 5.0 (and higher), and other programs that are compatible
with the Photoshop plug-in standard

Looking for a fun way to create basic three-dimensional shapes within Adobe Photoshop? Want to create wacky objects for your Web page designs and multimedia projects? Check out M.M.M. Software's HoloDozo! This package was the very first Photoshop plug-in to use Apple's QuickDraw 3D technology.

Who Should Use M.M.M. Software's HoloDozo?

M.M.M. Software's HoloDozo is a blast to use. While you might buy it to render three-dimensional effects within Adobe Photoshop, you'll find yourself firing it up as a welcome diversion, as well! The audience for this set of plug-ins includes Web and multimedia developers, artists, graphic designers, videographers, broadcast designers, and desktop publishers.

What M.M.M. Software's HoloDozo Does

Without a doubt, M.M.M. Software's HoloDozo is one of the most unique three-dimensional rendering applications ever developed. Its innovative HoloCube interface makes it flat-out fun to texture map and illuminate these 28 different primitive 3D shapes: HoloAtom, HoloBagel, HoloBow, HoloBox, HoloBrick, HoloCone, HoloCookie, HoloDome, HoloFit, HoloFizz, HoloGriz, HoloHat, HoloHorn, HoloKnee, HoloMol, HoloO, HoloPack, HoloPasta, HoloScrew, HoloSheet, HoloSlide, HoloSnail, HoloSnake, HoloSphere, HoloStick, HoloTorus, HoloTube, and HoloUfo.

Why Use M.M.M. Software's HoloDozo?

If your three-dimensional rendering needs are not complex, you'll want to take a look at HoloDozo. This set of 28 plug-ins makes quick work out of texture-mapping, manipulating, lighting, and rendering. The software provides real-time previews.

How M.M.M. Software's HoloDozo Does It

To render one of the 28 objects with a texture, load the texture into the current layer. Then choose Filter | HoloDozo | *filter name here* from Photoshop's menu bar. Figure 38-1 shows the HoloUfo 3D primitive being manipulated on one of our favorite beach scenes.

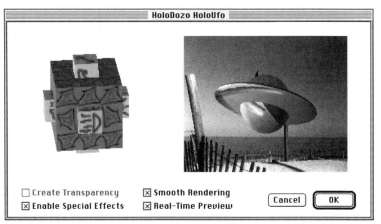

Figure 38-1: Call the Men in Black! The HoloUfo filter renders a fun flying saucer.

HoloDozo's interface is unlike anything you've ever encountered before. While you can reorient an object within its 3D space by clicking and dragging (like other 3D programs), the HoloCube is truly unique. There are no sliders or other conventional controls. To alter a setting, you merely tug on one of the six yellow bars that protrude from the surface of the HoloCube. Want to get at one of the controls on the other side of the HoloCube? Just drag the cube around!

The HoloCube lets you take charge of the following effects:

- **Ambient Light**. This control governs the overall room light.

- **Spot Light**. This control governs the highlight.

- **Fill Light**. This control governs the light in between the other two light sources.

- **Zoom**. This control lets you get a better look at the object—or not.

- **Squeeze**. This control squishes the object. To use this control, the Enable Special Effects check box must be selected.

- **Clipping**. This control lets you look into or through the object. To use Clipping, the Enable Special Effects check box must be selected.

There are four check box options:

- **Enable Special Effects**. Activating this check box allows you to use the Squeeze and Clipping features.

- **Create Transparency**. Use this when you want your 3D object to float on a transparent background. (You must be working on a layer to use transparency.)

- **Smooth Rendering**. With this option turned off, you'll get a chunky render. Turn it on, and you'll smooth things out.

- **Real-Time Preview**. This option allows you to watch your alterations as they are applied.

TIP *To speed up HoloDozo and improve rendering, check into a graphics card with QuickDraw 3D acceleration.*

chapter 39

Vertigo 3D Dizzy

Creator
Vertigo Technology Inc.

Purpose
Add 3D models to Adobe Photoshop

Platforms
Power Macintosh

Hardware/software requirements
Same as Photoshop, QuickDraw 3D 1.5.1

URL/contact info for creator of plug-in
http://www.vertigo3d.com
Vertigo Technology Inc.
1255 W. Pender Street
Vancouver, BC V6E 2V1
Canada
604/684-2113 voice
604/684-2108 fax

Products that the plug-in works with
Adobe Photoshop 3.0.5 or later

Looking for a quick and easy way to add 3D to your Adobe Photoshop designs? Take Vertigo 3D Dizzy for a spin, and you'll be flying through the third dimension in no time!

Who Should Use Vertigo 3D Dizzy?

Graphic designers, creative professionals, and digital designers who use Adobe Photoshop and are interested in an easy way to add 3D models to enhance their designs will find Vertigo 3D Dizzy an easy-to-use tool.

What Vertigo 3D Dizzy Does

Vertigo 3D Dizzy allows you to add 3D models to Photoshop images with ease. When you launch Dizzy, you launch the QuickDraw 3D environment. Dizzy runs within this environment, allowing for real-time interactive rendering. All QuickDraw-3D-compatible plug-ins—such as those from ThinkFish and LightWorks—are accessible right from within Dizzy. The plug-in ships with over 500 3DMF models from Viewpoint DataLabs and Vertigo and accepts any 3DMF model.

Why Use Vertigo 3D Dizzy?

Use Vertigo 3D Dizzy to get an edge on your competition. Impress your clients and your boss by creating supercool Adobe Photoshop designs that include 3D models.

How Vertigo 3D Dizzy Does It

Vertigo 3D Dizzy's simple and intuitive interface makes it the fastest way for designers to get into real three-dimensional rendering. With Vertigo 3D Dizzy, you can quickly and easily add 3D models within Photoshop. When you launch Vertigo 3D Dizzy from Photoshop's Filter menu, you'll feel right at home. The Vertigo 3D Dizzy interface looks and feels as if it belongs in Photoshop, as shown in Figure 39-1.

Vertigo 3D Dizzy is based on Apple's QuickDraw 3D technology. The plug-in lets you bring three-dimensional models right into Photoshop, allowing you to quickly create a 3D world within a 2D environment. Vertigo 3D Dizzy's implementation of QuickDraw 3D provides real-time interaction as you position and scale models, create custom lighting effects, and move the virtual camera to view your 3D scene from any perspective. Vertigo 3D Dizzy takes advantage of QuickDraw 3D's extensibility, supporting QuickDraw-3D-compatible plug-in renderers, such as ThinkFish's LiveStyles, to give you unlimited output options.

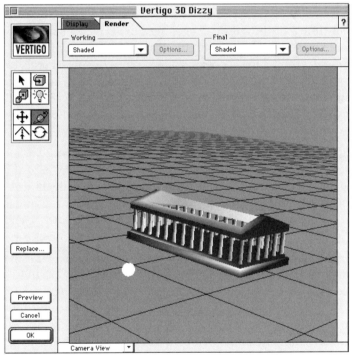

Figure 39-1: The Vertigo 3D Dizzy interface is simple and easy to use.

With Vertigo 3D Dizzy, you get real 3D without the steep learning curve. The familiar and easy-to-use interface gives you many ways to customize your 3D scene and get the look you want. Vertigo 3D adapts to fit your Adobe Photoshop selection, allowing you to work with the entire image, or just a portion. The plug-in can render models into Photoshop as a separate layer and fully supports Adobe Photoshop's transparency features. Here's a summary of Vertigo 3D Dizzy's strong suits:

- ■ **Supports 3DMF models**. Vertigo 3D Dizzy imports 3DMF models, assuring you an endless supply of new wireframes. 3DMF is a standard file format in the 3D industry and is consistent across Macintosh, Windows, and UNIX. This means you can import models made in any program that supports 3DMF. Vertigo 3D Dizzy comes with an extensive library of models made by Vertigo and by Viewpoint DataLabs, so you can get started right away. You can also download 3DMF models from the Web or create your own with any 3DMF-compatible modeling program.

- ■ **Real-time manipulation**. One of Vertigo 3D Dizzy's most attractive features is its ability to manipulate models in real-time. Once you've brought a model into Vertigo 3D Dizzy, use the object tools to move the model into any position and get the look you want. You can even change a model's size and proportions. Vertigo 3D Dizzy uses QuickDraw 3D to provide interactive rendering, which means for real precision you can see any changes to your model as you make them.

- ■ **Lighting effects**. It's easy to create dramatic looks with Vertigo 3D Dizzy's custom lighting capabilities. Add point lights, move them anywhere in the scene to create different effects, and see the results in real-time. The Color Picker allows you to change any light's color and intensity. Vertigo 3D Dizzy comes with built-in ambient light, which also features adjustable color and intensity, to shape your overall lighting effect.

- ■ **Virtual camera**. Vertigo 3D Dizzy is equipped with a built-in virtual camera so you can see your 3D world from any perspective. Simply select a camera tool, and drag it in the workspace to change your point of view. You can save custom camera views, giving you the option of trying a number of views before you decide on the one you want. Switching between different camera views gives you added flexibility when you are positioning your model and lights.

Have you ever had the unpleasant experience of getting lost in a typical 3D package? Vertigo 3D Dizzy goes a long way to avoid that feeling. The plug-in uses an optional grid to help you orient yourself in the 3D world. And if you've moved your camera or model such that you're having a hard time finding your way around, choosing a preset camera view will help you get your bearings.

■ **Rendering options**. Vertigo 3D Dizzy gives you a range of rendering options to help you work efficiently and get the look you want. You can specify both your working render (how your model is displayed while you work in Vertigo 3D Dizzy) and your final render (how your model is displayed in your final Photoshop image). And of course you can pre-view your final image before you add your model to Adobe Photoshop.

Vertigo 3D Dizzy comes packaged with built-in QuickDraw 3D, LightWorks, and ThinkFish LiveStyles rendering and can also support any third-party renderers designed to work with QuickDraw 3D. When you're conceptualizing and fiddling with an image, you'll want to use QuickDraw 3D's wireframe or shaded rendering for your working render for fast results. When it's time to create the final render, use the award-winning LightWorks renderer for photorealistic rendering. For a whimsical look, try a ThinkFish LiveStyles renderer.

TIP *Check out the ThinkFish Web site at http://www.thinkfish.com for the lowdown on LiveStyles rendering. If you purchase Vertigo 3D Dizzy, you can even pick up some free LiveStyles! ThinkFish's online store features a range of cool LiveStyles.*

chapter 40

Xaos Tools's TypeCaster 1.15 Plug-in

Creator
  Xaos Tools

Purpose
  3D type renderer

Platforms
  Macintosh, Windows

Hardware/Software requirements
  Same as Photoshop, Adobe Type Manager 3.8 or higher

URL/Contact info for creator of plug-in
  http://www.xaostools.com
  Xaos Tools
  55 Hawthorne St.
  Suite 1020
  San Francisco, CA 94105
  415/538-7000 voice

Products that the plug-in works with
  Adobe PhotoDeluxe, Adobe Photoshop 2.5.1, 3.0, 3.0.5, 4.0, Adobe
  Premiere 4.0, Adobe After Effects 3.0, Equilibrium DeBabelizer 1.6.5,
  Fractal Design Dabbler 2.0, Fractal Design Painter 3.0, 4.0,
  Macromedia FreeHand 5.5, 7.0, MicroFrontier Color It! 3.0, Ray
  Dream Designer 3.0, Specular Collage 1.1, Strata MediaPaint 1.0

Want to create cool three-dimensional type without resorting to a full-blown rendering program? Xaos Tools's TypeCaster allows you to craft gorgeous 3D type without leaving the Photoshop environment.

Who Should Use Xaos Tools's TypeCaster?

Artists and designers who need to create photo-realistic three-dimensional type for print, Web, and multimedia projects will find TypeCaster to be invaluable. TypeCaster is appropriate for all of these mediums since it renders at the resolution of the Photoshop file, whether it's a 300 dpi image for print or a 72 dpi image for the Web.

What Xaos Tools's TypeCaster Does

TypeCaster puts a 3D rendering engine into the conventional image-editing environment. It allows you to create amazing three-dimensional RGB type (from PostScript Type 1 typefaces), complete with texture maps and lighting control, without ever leaving Photoshop. It can even be used to create 3D type animations when used with Adobe Premiere, Adobe After Effects, and Equilibrium DeBabelizer.

Why Use Xaos Tools's TypeCaster?

Have you ever found yourself frustrated at the complexity of learning how to use a 3D rendering program or put off by the costs associated with buying a full-blown renderer? Xaos Tools's TypeCaster is a wonderful alternative for artists and designers who just need to add some 3D type to their artwork. The interface is easy to understand and the learning curve is far from steep. This plug-in will have you creating stunning 3D type in just minutes! Figure 40-1 shows a simple design that was created shortly after we started fiddling with the plug-in.

Figure 40-1: Yes! Professional-looking 3D type can be rendered by mere mortals.

How Xaos Tools's TypeCaster Does It

TypeCaster uses a simple and intuitive interface. When you choose Effects | Xaos Tools | TypeCaster, the main TypeCaster window will appear. Take a quick look around. If you've ever struggled with complex 3D rendering programs, you'll have to agree that TypeCaster offers a refreshingly simple interface. There's no lack of power however, as the plug-in delivers serious 3D capabilities.

Let's take a look at how you might go about creating some 3D type with TypeCaster.

Setting & Positioning Type

TypeCaster allows you to work with one line of text at a time. To begin, type your words into the text box and choose a font from the drop-down list. Once you've entered the words and selected a font, the type will appear as a wireframe as shown in Figure 40-2. If you don't see the type right away, you'll probably have to zoom around the window to find it.

Figure 40-2: The basic TypeCaster interface is easy to grasp.

Navigating around the window and manipulating the 3D type within the space is about as easy as it gets. The row of tools at the left side of the preview area provides the following controls:

- **Zoom.** Works like you think it should. Hold down the option key to zoom out.

- **Pan.** The "grabber hand" lets you reposition the background image in the preview frame.

- **Move.** Repositions the text over the background image.

- **Rotate.** Lets you manipulate the text upon its x, y, and z axes. You can perform free rotations by just clicking and dragging on the text, or you can hold down the option, command, or Ctrl keys to constrain movement to the x, y, or z axis, respectively.

- **Resize.** Interactive control used to make your text larger or smaller. As you click and drag to the left, the wireframe will expand. To make the wireframe smaller, click and drag to the right.

- **Extrude.** Controls the depth of the extrusion. As you click and drag to the left, the extrusion will grow deeper. To thin the extrusion, click and drag to the right.

- **Preview.** Lets you preview a selected area (rather than the entire block of text).

With the type specified, you'll want to position it within the image, size it, set its extrusion, and rotate it. You can perform all of these operations interactively with the tools, or you can click the Position button to summon the Position dialog box, shown in Figure 40-3.

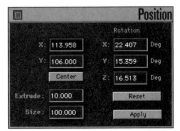

Figure 40-3: The Position dialog box allows you to take total control over your 3D type, to the thousandth!

Controlling Type Attributes

TypeCaster allows you to assign different materials to the *face, bevel,* and *extruded* surfaces of your three-dimensional type. While the face is the most important surface of the three—from the standpoint of legibility, as it carries the basic shape of the letters—you'll want to pay careful attention to each. Too wide a bevel, too deep an extrusion, or too muddy a material (on any of the three surfaces) can result in illegible type.

Controlling Face Attributes

To set the face material, you can drag materials from the scrolling preview at the right of the main dialog box to the Face texture preview box (see Figure 40-4). You can also access the Face dialog box by double-clicking on the Face texture preview box. The Face dialog box, shown by Figure 40-4, is used to specify a number of important attributes. You can assign a texture from an image file or solid color in addition to controlling its transparency. Texture wrapping can be controlled letter by letter, by the widest letter, or by the length of the entire sentence. You can specify the diffuse and specular lighting colors and assign a bump map with full control over the percentage of relief. The Update View button lets you quickly preview the changes for just the Face attributes. You can even preview your changes with the lights on or off.

Figure 40-4: The Face dialog box (shown here) and the Extrude dialog box use the same basic interface. Clicking the little arrow button on the right side toggles each dialog box between terse and verbose modes.

Clicking on either the From Image button or the texture preview box brings up a dialog box to import bitmap files for use as textures. TypeCaster comes with over 200 textures. You can also use your own bitmap files for textures or bump maps. Once you've created the perfect combination of texture, bump map, and lighting, you can save it as a preset material.

Controlling Extrusion Attributes
How deep do you want to go? TypeCaster provides control over extrusion depth interactively in the main dialog box or with three-digit precision in the Position dialog box. The Extrude dialog box governs the texture attributes and shares an interface similar to the Face dialog box.

Controlling Bevel Attributes
Although the Bevel dialog box, which is shown in Figure 40-5, appears to be similar to the Face and Extrude dialog boxes, there are three important additions. The Width slider controls the size of the bevel, while the Angle drop-down menu allows you to choose from Flat, Concave, or Convex bevel shapes. These bevel shapes can be subtle or obvious, depending on how wide you choose to make them. The Back Bevel check box lets you assign a bevel to the back face of your typographic designs.

Figure 40-5: The Bevel dialog box lets you add the finishing touches to your three-dimensional type.

Applying Lighting

Once you've specified the font, size, orientation, extrusion, bevel, and materials, it's time to start fiddling around with the spot lighting controls. Clicking on the Lights button in the main window brings up the Lights dialog box, shown in Figure 40-6. Adding and deleting lights is a straightforward affair. To add a light, just click the Add Light button. New lights are placed in the center of the preview area. After you've added a new light, click and drag it to where you want it to appear and watch as the preview box updates itself dynamically.

Figure 40-6: The Lights dialog box allows you to assign up to 10 lights per text object.

It's important to keep in mind that all light is not white. Varying the lighting colors is one key to achieving dramatic results. To change the color of the light, double-click on it to access the system color picker. After you've chosen the color of the light, you'll want to adjust its intensity with the slider. If you want to place the light behind your type, click the Send Back button. To delete a light, select it and then click the Delete Light button. Working with lighting is one of the most daunting tasks in 3D rendering. TypeCaster does a laudable job of turning it into a pleasant experience.

TIP | *The Auto Refresh button is only functional on older Macs. Power Macintosh machines are fast enough to refresh the Lights preview automatically.*

Saving Projects

TypeCaster allows you to save entire projects as well as individual face attributes. This enables you to create timesaving presets that are invaluable when working on 3D designs that will be used repetitively. Click on the Save button in the main window to save by project name. You can create separate project folders as well.

To load a project, click on the Project menu and select it. Be sure to check out the Sample Projects folder to learn how to create specific effects.

chapter 41

Andromeda Series 2 – 3D Filter

Creator

Andromeda Software

Purpose

Three-dimensional texture wrapping effects

Platforms

Macintosh, Windows

Hardware/software requirements

Same as Photoshop

URL/contact info for creator of plug-in

http://www.andromeda.com
Andromeda Software, Inc.
699 Hampshire Road
Westlake Village, CA 91361
805/379-4109 voice
805/379-5253 fax

Products that the plug-in works with

Mac: Adobe Photoshop 2.0.1 or later, other programs that support the Photoshop plug-in standard; Windows 95 or NT: Adobe Photoshop 3.0.5 or later, other programs that support the Photoshop plug-in standard

Looking for an easy way into the three-dimensional world? Just need to map textures to basic shapes within Photoshop? The Andromeda Series 2 - 3D Filter provides you with the tools you need to surface wrap bitmaps around objects to create everything from packaging mock-ups to surreal scenes.

Who Should Use the Andromeda 3D Filter?

Andromeda's Series 2 - 3D Filter is ideal for anyone who wants to create basic 3D effects within Adobe Photoshop, including graphic designers, artists, Web and multimedia developers, desktop publishers, videographers, broadcast designers, and photographers.

What the Andromeda 3D Filter Does

Andromeda's Series 2 - 3D Filter does a wonderful job of mapping textures to cylinders, boxes, planes, and spheres, allowing you to create some magnificent 3D effects.

Why Use the Andromeda 3D Filter?

Do you want to create basic three-dimensional artwork but don't have the time, patience, or funds to afford a full-blown 3D rendering application? Perhaps you only need to mock up some packaging designs or create some nifty Web page graphics? Andromeda's Series 2 - 3D Filter is a great 3D solution for folks who don't need the power or complexity of the big 3D apps.

How Andromeda's 3D Filter Does It

Andromeda's Series 2 - 3D Filter functions within a multimode dialog box. The dialog box provides complete control over the model (Surface, Colors, Grids, and Photo) and render (Viewpoint, Shading, and Display) attributes. Let's take a look at the controls provided by each of these seven modes.

Model Surface

To paraphrase Henry Ford, you can have any 3D object you want, just as long as it's a cylinder, box, plane, or sphere. Thankfully, you can manipulate these basic shapes into many variations. For example, a cylinder can become a flattened penny, or a sphere can be squished into a grape. While this doesn't offer the same flexibility afforded by 3D renderers such as Infini-D and Ray Dream Designer, it may be just enough to get your job done. Figure 41-1 shows the Andromeda Series 2 - 3D Filter in Cylinder mode.

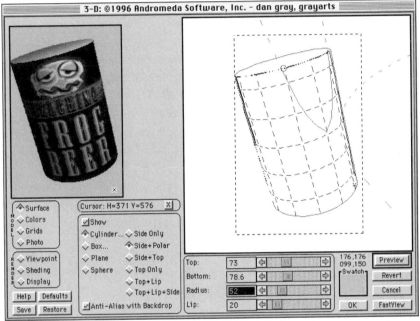

Figure 41-1: With Andromeda Series 2 - 3D Filter's Cylinder mode, you can preview your own personal beer labels.

Here are the options provided by each of the four objects.

- **Cylinder.** You can adjust size using the Top, Bottom, Radius, and Lip sliders. The texture can wrap using one of six methods: Side Only, Side+Polar, Side+Top, Top Only, Top+Lip, and Top+Lip+Side.

- **Box.** You can adjust size using the X, Y, and Z sliders. The texture can wrap using one of four methods: Wrap Corner, Cutout X, Cutout Y, and Cutout Z.

- **Plane.** You can adjust the Left, Top, Right, and Bottom sliders to set the size, or you can click the Autosize button to automatically size the plane to the image.

- **Sphere.** You can set the size of your orb with the Radius slider.

Model Colors

You can take command over six key color attributes: Backdrop, Grid, Dropout, Surface, Host Foreground, and Host Background. To change a color, use the sliders or enter the RGB percentages numerically; then click the appropriate Swatch to Button. To move a color from a button to the Swatch, click the appropriate Button to Swatch button.

TIP

Want to pull a color from the model to examine the RGB values or to copy it into one of the color attributes? Reposition the x cursor in the preview window to bring the color underneath the x cursor into the swatch.

Model Grids

Going after that techie-grid look? You can add a grid to either a surface or photo-wrapped object. Sliders control the width, spacing, number, and length of the gridlines. Figure 41-2 shows the Andromeda's Series 2 - 3D Filter dialog box in Grid mode with a plane object and no texture.

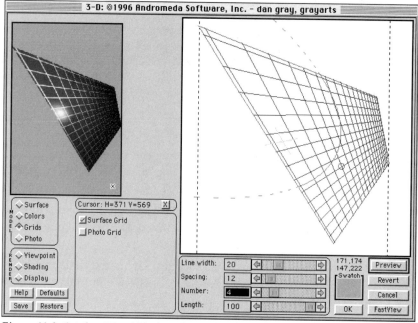

Figure 41-2: Get that 3D grid look in the wink of an eye!

Model Photo

Wrapping a bitmap image around a 3D object is perhaps 90 percent of the fun of 3D rendering. By taking a flat image and affixing it to a sphere, cylinder, or rectangular object, you can create artificial life. You can apply an image just once, or you can tile it to create a motif. Figures 41-3 and 41-4 show the same silly bitmap wrapped in two different ways. Photo mode lets you shift or scale your image to fit. Tiling is especially effective when you work with seamless textures. You can drop the dropout color and other colors as well.

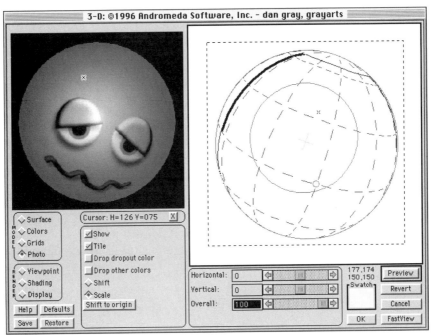

Figure 41-3: Apply a face to a sphere just once, and you can create a fun avatar for The Palace, our favorite virtual world chat environment.

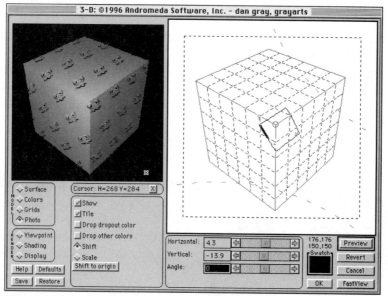

Figure 41-4: Tile that same face to a rectangle, and you'll end up with some wacky wrapping paper, just for fun.

Render Viewpoint

The Render Viewpoint controls let you reposition your three-dimensional objects. The dialog box provides different controls for Rectangular, Cylindrical, and Spherical objects.

- Rectangular objects can be spun with the X- and Y-axis sliders. They can be moved in and out with the Z-axis slider.

- Cylindrical objects can be spun with the Radius and Longitude sliders. They can be moved in and out with the Z-axis slider.

- Spherical objects can be spun with the Latitude and Longitude sliders. They can be moved in and out with the Distance slider.

Render Shading

You can render your 3D objects with or without the benefit of shading. Rendering without shading, however, loses much of the impact of the medium. Proper lighting position helps add drama to your renderings. When you click the Enable check box, you can alter the Light Source, which Andromeda refers to as the Point of Light (P.O.L.), and Lighting Effects. The Light Source can be configured for Rectangular, Cylindrical, and Spherical objects.

- Set Rectangular P.O.L. with X-, Y-, and Z-axis sliders.
- Set Cylindrical P.O.L. with Radius, Longitude, and Z-axis sliders.
- Set Spherical P.O.L. with Latitude, Longitude, and Distance sliders.

Bright Surface and Photo lighting are essential effects. Sliders for Ambient Light, Spread, and Glare help you add a realistic touch.

Render Display

The Render Display options let you alter a number of key rendering attributes. The Shift mode governs the relationship of the model to the camera, with the Horizontal, Vertical, and Angle Shift sliders controlling how the image is rendered within the frame. As you might suspect, the Horizontal slider moves the model left and right (on the X-axis), the Vertical slider moves the model up and down (on the Y-axis), and the Angle slider rotates the model (on its Z-axis) in a clockwise or counterclockwise manner.

The Scale mode offers Horizontal, Vertical, and Overall sliders. The Horizontal and Vertical sliders allow you to squish or expand the object on its respective axis, while the Overall slider lets you make the object proportionally larger or smaller.

chapter 42

Plastic Thought QuickSpace 3D

Creator

Plastic Thought

Purpose

Brings QuickDraw 3D models into Photoshop

Platforms

Macintosh, Windows 95/NT

Hardware/software requirements

Mac: System 7.6 or higher, 16MB of RAM, PowerPC processor, QuickDraw 3D 1.5.1; Windows: 16MB of RAM, Pentium processor, 16- or 24-bit display card, QuickDraw 3D 1.5.1

URL/contact info for creator of plug-in

www.plasticthought.com
Plastic Thought
11207 - 103 Ave.
Edmonton, AB T5K 0V9
Canada
403/429-5051 voice
403/426-0632 fax

Products that the plug-in works with

Photoshop 3.0 (or later), Illustrator 6.0 (or later), PhotoDeluxe

Tired of your boring old collection of two-dimensional clip art? Looking for the latest in three-dimensional Photoshop plug-ins? Plug into Plastic Thought QuickSpace 3D! This groovy package lets you rotate, size, position, and render QuickDraw 3D models in Photoshop layers for some awesome effects. While you may still have to search for that killer image, getting the right angle is just a twist away.

Who Should Use Plastic Thought QuickSpace 3D?

Plastic Thought QuickSpace 3D lets you quickly spice up your Adobe Photoshop images with 3D models. The audience includes designers, artists, and desktop publishers as well as Web and multimedia developers

What Plastic Thought QuickSpace 3D Does

Plastic Thought QuickSpace 3D loads a single QuickDraw 3D model and allows it to be rotated, scaled, positioned, and rendered. The plug-in puts the currently selected layer into the background for easy positioning. Once you have your scene looking the way you want it, QuickSpace allows you to choose different renderers for varying quality levels and effects. The package even includes 200 QuickDraw 3D models to get you started.

Why Use Plastic Thought QuickSpace 3D?

Have you ever had the perfect image but at the wrong angle? Perhaps you had the front of the object but really needed the backside? QuickDraw 3D images—such as the stylized Plastic Thought Active Art collection—are photo-realistic or stylized like traditional stock images or clip art. You can rotate them for viewing at any angle, enabling you to create your artwork in the exact manner you envision it.

How Plastic Thought QuickSpace 3D Does It

Let's take a look at the QuickSpace 3D interface. Choose Filter | Plastic Thought | QuickSpace from Photoshop's menu bar. The QuickSpace dialog box will appear, as shown in Figure 42-1. You'll note a row of 10 buttons running down the left side of the dialog box. Each button illuminates as you click on it, letting you know that it's the active button. Let's take a look at what the buttons do, starting from the top:

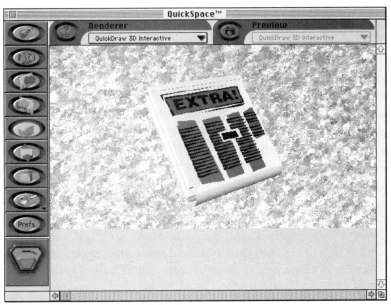

Figure 42-1: The QuickSpace dialog box.

- ■ **OK.** Click this button to commit the image to the current layer.

- ■ **Cancel.** Click this button to go back to Photoshop without rendering the model.

- ■ **Open.** If QuickSpace is selected twice in one Photoshop session, the last model is automatically opened. Click this button to get a model other than the one that is currently open.

- ■ **Save.** Click this button to save a PICT of the current view of the model—but it does not render the image into the current Photoshop file.

- ■ **Rotate.** Need to put a new spin on things? Click this button to spin the model in any direction. The model can be rotated sideways as well as up and down. The model is manipulated by positioning the mouse over the model and then clicking and dragging. Moving left or right swivels the model along its Y-axis. Moving the mouse up or down turns the model along its X-axis. To rotate the model on its Z-axis, click and drag outside of the model.

- ■ **Zoom.** Click this button to make the model larger or smaller. Clicking and dragging the model downward makes it larger, while dragging it upward makes it smaller.

- ■ **Move.** Want to move the current object? Just click and drag. If the current layer has elements, they will show in the background.

- ■ **Magnify.** Select this button to reduce or increase the size of the current view.

- ■ **Preferences.** The Preferences dialog box provides options for Illumination (Phong, Lambert, or Null), Interpolation (None, Vertex, or Pixel), Backfacing (Both, Remove, or Flip), Fill (Filled, Edges, Points), Clear Color, and Background (Hide or Show).

- ■ **Progress Indicator.** When the current view is being rendered, the progress indicator visually illustrates how much time is left. Click the camera icon or the OK button to start the progress indicator.

At the top of the dialog box, you'll see the Renderer and Preview drop-down menus. QuickSpace ships with the standard QuickDraw 3D Interactive renderer, which is quick, and the photo-realistic LightWorks SuperLite renderer, which offers high-quality anti-aliasing, transparency, soft shadows, and texture map rendering. You can use any QuickDraw 3D renderer with QuickSpace 3D, including the ThinkFish LiveStyles renderer. The LiveStyles renderer provides a stylized, hand-drawn effect (while removing all texture). You can even make your 3D art look like a blueprint.

Clicking the camera icon next to the Interactive Preview drop-down menu renders the model for preview and starts the progress indicator. While clicking OK also starts the progress indicator, it renders the model into Photoshop. If you click the camera icon, it displays the current layer with the rendered model within QuickSpace. The model can still be moved, resized, and rotated. After the model is previewed and the position, size, and angle are satisfactory, you can click OK to perform the final render into Photoshop.

Setting Preferences

The Preferences dialog box, shown in Figure 42-2, allows for a number of important settings. While the default preferences should suffice for the majority of models, let's take a look at what each of the options provides:

Figure 42-2: Not sure of which preferences to set? If in doubt, go for the default settings.

■ **Illumination.** Rather than go into too much detail, we will just tell you that Phong gives the best results, Lambert delivers mid-range results, and NULL does not interpret the lights.

■ **Interpolation.** This setting controls how detailed the model should be with the applied texture (the "paint" on top of the wireframe that defines the model). The None setting is not very detailed, Vertex is semi-detailed, and Pixel is very detailed. This also affects how quickly the model moves and is rendered.

■ **Backfacing.** If the backfacing is not shown, this speeds up manipulation of the model (since the backside is not being displayed at the present angle). However, if the front is not completely defined, "holes" may show through. If a model has problems, then Backfacing should be set to Both. Occasionally, a model is brought in with the backside flipped; Flip fixes this.

■ **Fill.** The Fill option lets you decide if the texture will fill the space (usual settings) or if just the edges or points will be shown.

■ **Clear Color.** This setting affects the color that the model anti-aliases to. The default is the surrounding pixels of the layer in the background of QuickSpace.

■ **Background.** This setting lets you show the selected layer background of QuickSpace.

QuickSpace 3D at Work

Here's a good example of why you might want to use QuickSpace 3D. Let's say you have to design a catalog, or perhaps a Web site, for FunkyStuff shop. The folks at FunkyStuff really want their products to be showcased from all sides. In this example, the basic design was laid out in Photoshop. The FunkyStuff design staff has selected a model from PlasticThought's ActiveArt collection, as shown in Figure 42-3, which remarkably is a stylized version of an old radio featured in their catalog. (OK, so we're stretching it a bit, but you get the idea!) As you can see in Figure 42-4, the radio had to be spun and rendered three times.

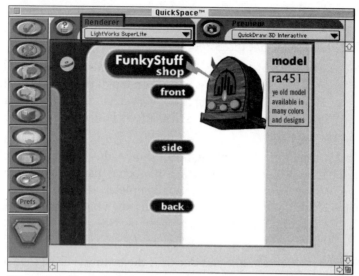

Figure 42-3: Here's the front view of the FunkyStuff Shop's antique radio within QuickSpace 3D.

Figure 42-4: One model can be quickly rotated to many views.

Part VI

Appendices

appendix A

About the Companion CD-ROM

The Companion CD-ROM included with your copy of *The Photoshop Plug-ins Book* contains many valuable plug-ins. In addition, if you are connected to the Internet, the CD-ROM's connectivity feature also serves as your passport to discuss Photoshop plug-ins issues with members of the Photoshop community.

To View the CD-ROM

- Macintosh—Double click on the LAUNCHME icon after opening the CD on your desktop.
- Windows 95/Windows NT—Double click on the RUNME_32.EXE file from Windows Explorer.

You'll see a menu screen offering several choices. See "Navigating the CD-ROM" below for your options.

Navigating the CD-ROM

You can access the Companion CD-ROM whether or not you are connected to the Internet. If you are not connected to the Internet, your options include viewing the Software section to learn more about using software on the CD-ROM and browsing through Ventana's Hot Picks to find out about other Ventana titles or learning more about us.

If you are connected to the Internet, you may utilize the CD-ROM's connectivity features. These include chat room Photoshop discussions, real-time communication with other Photoshop users (including a "quick message" feature which will alert you to incoming messages), and access to a complete listing of Photoshop-related events.

To take advantage of these exciting community features, first-time users must be sure to set their user preferences and obtain a user password. Once you've set your preferences and gotten a password, come on in to join the Photoshop crowd.

For optimum Windows performance:

1. Copy the RUNME_32.EXE AND THE RUNME_32.INI files to the same directory on your hard drive.

2. Open the RUNME_32.INI file in a text editor such as Notepad.

3. Find the section in the .INI file that reads:

```
[Memory]
;ExtraMemory=400
;Amount of kBytes over and above physical memory for use by a projector.
```

4. If your computer has enough memory to do so, delete the semicolon from the ExtraMemory line, and change the ExtraMemory setting to a higher number.

5. Save the changes to the RUNME_32.INI file, and close the text editor.

6. With the CD-ROM still inserted, launch the viewer from the hard drive.

If the viewer still does not run properly on your machine, you can access the material on the CD-ROM directly through Windows Explorer (Windows 95).

For optimum Macintosh performance:

1. Copy the Launch Me file to your hard drive.

2. Click once on the Launch Me file.

3. Select Get Info from the File menu.

4. If your computer has enough memory to do so, change the amount in the Preferred Size field to a higher number.

5. Close the info box.

6. With the CD-ROM still inserted, launch the viewer from the hard drive.

If the viewer still does not run properly on your machine, you can access the files on the CD-ROM directly by double-clicking on its icon on the desktop.

Software

Andromeda Filters	Demo versions of Andromeda Software's Filters, including: Series 1 Photography Filters, containing 10 special effects lenses; Series 2 3-D Filters, offering surface wrapping, lighting and shading control, and viewpoint control for images; Series 3 Screens Filters, which convert grayscale into mezzotints, mezzograms, line screens, and patterns and specialty screens; Series 4 Techtures, offering 900 hand-rendered, realistic techtures, maps, and environments to explore and modify; and the Velociraptor Filter, which lets you create incredibly realistic or stylized motion trails. Visit http://www.andromeda.com for more information.
Alaras Apertura	An import/export plug-in for Adobe Photoshop. You have the ability to quickly open, edit, and save any smaller area of a large image at full resolution, in a matter of seconds. With Alaras Apertura you can browse through folders of images as thumbnails to select the right image, directly read scitex native media in Photoshop, and even virtually eliminate "Scratch disk full" messages. If you are a scitex user, you can also instantly perform last-minute LW corrections, including typeset text changes, without reRIPping your job. When you've got to get to press, this can be a lifesaver.
Alaras Mixxer	An Adobe Photoshop color transformation filter plug-in that empowers you to make sophisticated color corrections, such as UCR, ghosting, color contaminant removal, and radical color changes, very efficiently. Instant before and after previews and unlimited color swatches makes experimentation a snap.
Andromeda Series 4 Textures	A demo version of the Andromeda Series 4 Textures, offering 900 hand-rendered, realistic techtures, maps, and environments to explore and modify. To find out more about Andromeda Software's products, visit http://www.andromeda.com. Key Features include: Multi-platform compatibility; preset menus, novice and expert modes, and preference libraries.
Chromassage	Chromassage creates wild colorization effects within Adobe Photoshop and allows you to try out thousands of color combinations in the blink of an eye. Colors can be manipulated with "jog wheels" that let you rotate and shift hues. Swap colors from 26 built-in palettes. ➡

	Randomize, invert, reverse, and "steal" colors from existing documents, or infect the image with a "virus of chroma." Chromassage is ideal for use with designs intended for multimedia or artwork destined for high-profile fabric printing and fine art. For more information about Second Glance Software, check out http://www.secondglance.com.
Chromatica	Chromatica is a plug-in for Photoshop and compatible applications that lets users select objects instantly, recolor with greater precision, blend edges automatically, and create spectacular color effects.
Cinematte	Cinematte is a Photoshop plug-in that allows users to create photo-realistic transparencies and mattes. Cinematte provides blue/green screen compositing and simplifies creation of qps clipping paths. Visit http://www.novadesign.com for more information about Nova Design's products.
CSI PhotoOptics	A collection of eight photographic color manipulation filters for Adobe Photoshop. These filters give the user an intuitive interface and additional controls over colorization, contrast, exposure, and color cast treatment, along with some special effects such as noise generation and infrared simulation. The CSI PhotoOptics filters are the first filters for Photoshop that are based on Photographic methods for contrast, exposure, and color correction.
DeBabelizer Pro for Windows	Equilibrium's DeBabelizer Pro for Windows 95 and NT 4.0 is a comprehensive automated application for anyone working with graphics, animations, and digital video in multimedia, Web, and desktop productions. With its intuitive interface, digital designers can easily perform any number of graphics processes to an unlimited number of images or frames. Users can also create an optimized SuperPalette for an entire batch of stills or movies, and output everything to over 90 point-mapped file formats. Additionally, Wizards are set up to automate many popular processes such as optimizing images for digital video or preparing graphics for Web delivery. DeBabelizer Pro for Windows also supports most Photoshop Import, Filter, and Export plug-ins. The multi-image file capabilities of DeBabelizer Pro are awesome! Multiple frames can be converted into AVI movies and optimized for any target platform with full compression support.

➡

Debabelizer Toolbox for Mac	DeBabelizer Toolbox is an essential tool for anyone working with computer graphics. This award-winning product combines graphics processing, palette optimization, and translation in one program. With easy "Watch Me" scripting and batch features, thousands of images can be processed automatically to specifications. A true production powerhouse, DeBabelizer Toolbox translates between 70+ bit-mapped graphics, animation, and digital video formats, including DOS/Windows, Amiga, Sun, XWindows, Alias, Electric Image, SoftImage formats, and more. DeBabelizer Toolbox supports Photoshop and third- party Acquire, Filter, and Export plug-ins, as well as AppleScript. It includes dozens of image-editing and palette-manipulation tools, including SuperPalette, which automatically creates the best palette for a series of images. DeBabelizer Toolbox complements all paint, scan, and image-processing programs.
Eye Candy 3.0	A demo of the new set of Photoshop plug-ins from Alien Skin Software. Eye Candy 3.0 (formerly known as The Black Box) is the answer to serious Photoshop users' prayers. These filters create special effects in seconds that would normally require hours of hand tweaking. You have probably heard experts explain complex 12-step processes for creating 3D bevels or flames. Now you can stop trying to follow those frustrating recipes and simply use Eye Candy. Version 3.0 makes professional effects even easier by giving you flexible previews and a thumbnail for rapidly navigating your image. Visit http://www.alienskin.com.
Genuine Fractals Demo	Compresses RGB images into scalable fractal image format (FIF) files and opens FIFs in Photoshop. With Genuine Fractals, you can 1) Work in medium-resolution original files for hi-res output; 2) Compress to small file sizes for storage and transmission; and 3) Render multiple output sizes from the same compressed file and get the same high quality at all scales.
GIFmation	GIFmation is a powerful GIF animation application. Advanced color reduction and palette handling, sophisticated transparency tools, the most file format support including QuickTime and Photoshop layers conversion, browser compatibility checking, the top optimization for lightning fast downloads, and many other time-saving capabilities, in an intuitive and easy to use interface make GIFmation the right tool for the job. Macintosh. This is a limited version.

➡

GIF/JPEG SmartSaver 1.1	A non-destructive WYSIWYG image optimization utility, GIF/JPEG SmartSaver features side-by-side image previews and file size comparisons. Allows you to reduce colors in GIF images, using Netscape Navigator and Internet Explorer safe palettes. Lets you quickly reduce colors in GIF images to ensure the ideal compression/quality ratio from JPEG images. Batch processing of images at different color and compression ranges offers fast fine-tuning for perfectly optimized images.
HoloDozo	HoloDozo is a set of 28 plug-ins for Photoshop, Premiere, Director 5.0, and other Photoshop-compatible host applications that frees you from the time-consuming drudgery of 3D work. Each of the plug-ins contains one 3D primitive onto which you can apply any imaginable texture. Manipulating and lighting these 3D objects is a snap with the unique Holocube, an innovative three-dimensional interface. To find out more about products from M.M.M.Software, visit http://www.mmmsoft.com.
HVS JPEG 2.0	Award-winning filter plug-in that gives Web developers the smallest, best-looking JPEG files in the industry. Makes 8-bit files look like 24-bit, but downloads up to 70% faster. Full-featured, 7-day unlockable demo. Visit http://www.digfrontiers.com for more information on this and other Digital Frontiers software.
HVS Color Demo for Mac 1.27	HVS is the award-winning color-reduction Export plug-in for Photoshop 3 and 4. This demo will give you an idea of the color reduction quality, but it's not unlockable, and it inserts a watermark in the center of images. An unlockable demo of the next-generation HVS ColorGIF 2.0 will be available soon. Visit http://www.digfrontiers.com for more information.
HVS Color Demo for Windows 1.27	HVS is the award-winning color-reduction Export plug-in for Photoshop 3 and 4. This demo will give you an idea of the color reduction quality, but it's not unlockable, and it inserts a watermark in the center of images. An unlockable demo of the next-generation HVS ColorGIF 2.0 will be available soon. Visit http://www.digfrontiers.com for more information.
Intellihance 2.0	Intellihance gives users the ability to produce professional-looking photos in Adobe Photoshop automatically. A revolutionary photo-enhancement filter that optimizes photo images in a single step, Intellihance allows users

➡

	to optimize image saturation, sharpness, contrast, brightness, and despeckle, all with one mouse click. Intellihance includes preference controls to modify the intelligent enhancement engine. This is a proven tool that will save you hours of time; it's the ultimate "make better" button. For more information about this and other Extensis products, visit http://www.extensis.com.
Kai's Power Tools	A demonstration version of MetaTools, Inc.'s Kai's Power Tools 3.0. KPT 3.0 is available as a 32-bit native application extension for the Intel-based Windows 95/NT platforms, as well as for the Apple Macintosh/Power Macintosh platforms. Kai's Power Tools 3.0 is a unique and powerful collection of extensions that expand the power of image-editing applications which support the Adobe plug-in specifications.
LaserSeps Pro (Mac 68K, PowerMac)	An export filter for Adobe Photoshop that creates stochastic screens for process color separations. Since there are no screen angles involved, problems with registration, moiré patterns, and rosettes are dramatically reduced. Files are output in industry-standard DCS 2.0 format and support advanced features such as white plate and underprint masks. Ideal for the textile industry. For more information about Second Glance Software, check out http://www.secondglance.com.
PANTONE	MC-P/CoCo enhances Photoshop's color correction and image control capabilities. Channel 24 gives Photoshop the DCS 2.0 file format option. With PANTONE MC-P/CoCo, you can individually correct up to 16 colors and accurately preview images on the monitor.
PhotoCell	PhotoCell is a plug-in that converts Photoshop layers into animation files for multimedia use on the World Wide Web and beyond. Multi-Layer files can be output in QuickTime or Animated GIF formats, creating animations of unprecedented depth and realism. For more information about Second Glance Software, check out http://www.secondglance.com.
PhotoGIF	PhotoGIF is a Macintosh file-format plug-in for Adobe Photoshop 3.0 or higher. PhotoGIF provides unsurpassed capability for creating and editing highly optimized, Web-ready GIFs and GIF animations. PhotoGIF is a must-have tool for Web graphics creation. Visit http://www.boxtopsoft.com to find out more.

Photoshop Plug-ins SDK	Adobe's Software Development Kit (SDK) for Photoshop Plug-ins contains reference material, specifications and protocols, technical notes, sample code, development tools, and software application(s)—a tool set for taking full advantage of Adobe technology. For more information, go to http://www.adobe.com/supportservice/ devrelations/sdks.html on the World Wide Web.
Premiere Plug-ins SDK	Adobe's Software Development Kit (SDK) for Premiere Plug-ins contains reference material, specifications and protocols, technical notes, sample code, development tools, and software application(s)—a tool set for taking full advantage of Adobe technology. For more information, go to http://www.adobe.com/supportservice/ devrelations/sdks.html on the World Wide Web.
ProJPEG	ProJPEG is a Macintosh file-format plug-in for Adobe Photoshop 3.0 and higher. ProJPEG provides an unsurpassed capability for creating and editing highly optimized, Web-ready JPEG and progressive JPEG images. Visit http://www.boxtopsoft.com to find out more.
PhotoSpot	PhotoSpot is a series of filters and export functions designed to facilitate spot-color separation from within Photoshop. Special color-reduction filters enable the artist to control the separation process from 2 to 500 colors. For more information about Second Glance Software, check out http://www.secondglance.com.
Photographic Edges 3.0	A demo version of Auto F/X's Photoshop plug-in compatible graphic design product. Visit http://www.autofx.com for more information.
Photo/Graphic Patterns 1.0	A demo version of Auto F/X's Photoshop plug-in compatible graphic design product. Visit http://www.autofx.com for more information.
Phototools 1.1	PhotoTools from Extensis is a collection of eight productivity and "everyday effects" plug-in tools that address many of the most requested features from a variety of Photoshop users. For more information about this and other Extensis products, visit http://www.extensis.com.
ScanPrepPro	ScanPrepPro is an Adobe Photoshop plug-in that automates image processing. Whether you start from an initial scan or an existing image, ScanPrepPro prepares your image for output using an intelligent agent for lithographic information. Just specify the source of the image, its condition, and your desired output, and ScanPrepPro does the rest.

SISNIKK	SISNIKK Pro provides Photoshop plug-ins for high-quality single image stereograms. To find out more about products from M.M.M.Software, visit http://www.mmmsoft.com.
Terrazzo with Tube Time	A powerful, interactive Adobe Photoshop plug-in for creating limitless tileable textures and patterns from any source imagery. Some key features include: the ability to create dramatic effects while seamlessly working within your host application; and elegant, easy-to-use interfaces with push-button simplicity.
Typo/Graphic Edges	A demo version of Auto F/X's Photoshop plug-in compatible graphic design product. Visit http://www.autofx.com for more information.
The Ultimate Texture Collection 1.0	A demo version of Auto F/X's Photoshop plug-in compatible graphic design product. Visit http://www.autofx.com for more information.
Vertigo 3D Dizzy	Vertigo 3D lets Adobe Photoshop users easily add 3D models to their designs. Users can change the orientation and size of models and add lights before positioning the models in Photoshop. Check out Vertigo Technology, Inc. at http://www.vertigo3d.com.
WildRiverSSK 1.0	An exciting new suite of plug-in filters for Adobe Photoshop from WildRiver Systems Software of Japan. This sophisticated new arsenal of tools puts seven powerful filters in an artist's box of tricks—enhancing, with amazing speed, the possibilities to create. Running as plug-ins for Adobe Photoshop 2.51 or greater, on the Macintosh and PPC platforms, the WildRiverSSK filter suite offers seven filters for use in image editing with RG and Grayscale models.

Technical Support

Technical support is available for installation-related problems only. The technical support office is open from 8:00 a.m. to 6:00 p.m. Monday through Friday and can be reached via the following methods:

- Phone: (919) 544-9404 extension 81
- Faxback Answer System: (919) 544-9404 extension 85
- E-mail: help@vmedia.com
- FAX: (919) 544-9472
- World Wide Web: http://www.vmedia.com/support
- America Online: keyword Ventana

Limits of Liability & Disclaimer of Warranty

The author and publisher of this book have used their best efforts in preparing the CD-ROM and the programs contained in it. These efforts include the development, research, and testing of the theories and programs to determine their effectiveness. The author and publisher make no warranty of any kind expressed or implied, with regard to these programs or the documentation contained in this book.

The author and publisher shall not be liable in the event of incidental or consequential damages in connection with, or arising out of, the furnishing, performance, or use of the programs, associated instructions, and/or claims of productivity gains.

Some of the software on this CD-ROM is shareware; there may be additional charges (owed to the software authors/makers) incurred for their registration and continued use. See individual program's README or VREADME.TXT files for more information.

appendix B

More Great Plug-ins!

Pulling this book together was no easy feat. Dealing with the constantly changing world of Photoshop plug-in development was our biggest challenge. As with any book that contains more than a handful of chapters, the logistics of naming and numbering the individual production elements can be a painstaking task. In a book like this, with hundreds of files, it can be monumental. This edition of *The Photoshop Plug-ins Book* contains 42 separate chapters, with a number of these chapters covering more than one plug-in.

About halfway through this process, it became apparent that we would not be able to accommodate every single commercial plug-in package with its own chapter. There were just too many new plug-ins out there! So we decided to include this appendix in a noble attempt to cover as many plug-ins as humanly possible. While we won't go into depth, we'll provide a quick overview of each plug-in.

Auto F/X Photo/Graphic Patterns

Texture Effects
Macintosh, Windows
http://www.autofx.com
Auto F/X
Black Point Association
HCR-73, Box 689
Alton Bay, NH 03810
603/569-8800 voice
603/569-9702 fax

Want to apply a texture or pattern to your Photoshop artwork? Auto F/X's Photo/Graphic Patterns comes with 1,000 easy-to-apply textures, including paper, metal, and fabric. Like Auto F/X's other offerings, Photo/Graphic Patterns comes complete with a well-illustrated color manual that allows you to quickly select the right effect.

ChromaGraphics MagicMask

Image masking
Macintosh, Windows 95/NT
http://www.chromagraphics.com
Chroma Graphics, Inc.
577 Airport Blvd.
Suite 730
Burlingame, CA 94010-2020
415/375-1100 voice
415/375-1118 fax

Image masking is one of the hottest areas of Photoshop plug-in development. Magic Mask uses patented ImageGenetics technology developed by Chroma Graphics and includes a color brush tool, a density tool, and a very cool MagicLasso tool.

Cytopia PhotoOptics

Color correction and photographic effects
Mac, Windows 95/NT
http://www.cytopia.com/
Cytopia Software, Inc.
812 Ninth Avenue
Redwood City, CA 94063
415/364-4594 voice
415/364-4592 fax

Are you looking to re-create traditional photographic color corrections? Cytopia PhotoOptics provides the tools you need to create sepia tones and other colorization techniques because it mimics traditional photographic gel and filter effects. The Cytopia PhotoOptics filters include CSI Levels, CSI GradTone, CSI HueSlider, CSI Monochrome, CSI PhotoFilter, CSI Negative, CSI PseudoColor, and CSI Noise. The package comes with handy presets for immediate productivity.

TIP *Juggling lots of Photoshop plug-ins? Check out Cytopia's Plug-In Manager for Macintosh!*

DigiEffects AgedFilm

Old movie effects
Windows 95/NT
http://www.digieffects.com/
DigiEffects
818 Monterey Boulevard
San Francisco, CA 94127
415/841-9901 voice
415/841-1207 fax

Want to make your images appear like they were culled from an old film? DigiEffects AgedFilm provides control over 19 crucial parameters, including dust, hair, vertical scratches, tint, luminance flicker, film response, grain control, and missing sprockets. The plug-in works with still images as well as video sequences and movies. You can animate all of its effects for multimedia and video applications.

Digimarc PictureMarc

Digital Watermarking
Macintosh and Windows
http://www.digimarc.com/
Digimarc Corporation
521 SW 11th Avenue
Suite 200
Portland, OR 97205
503/626-8811 voice

Want to protect your digital images? Digimarc's PictureMarc plug-ins let you hide and detect watermarks in your files. These invisible marks allow you to identify the owner of a digital image, thus protecting copyright and avoiding any possible infringement. Digimarc has been aggressive about bundling PictureMarc; the plug-ins are shipped with applications including Adobe Photoshop and Corel Photo-Paint.

digital showbiz flux collection

Special effects
Windows 95/NT
http://www.dsb.com/
digital showbiz, ltd.
28 Belgravia St.
Penzance, Cornwall TR18 2BJ, UK
44 1736 362 964 voice
44 1736 330 083 fax

This is a collection of Photoshop plug-ins for wild special effects. The flux collection filters include blast, bright noise, bubbles, cassini, center mirrors, electrosphere, gears, isotope, linear transmission, mirrors, mosaic ripple, psychedelic, radial mosaic, radial noise, radial smox, radial transmission, radial warp, radiCal, spider, tiler, and warp. The company sells exclusively online through software.net, atonce.com, and other online vendors.

Human Software OttoPaths

Path and text effects
Macintosh
http://www.humansoftware.com
The Human Software Co.
14407 Big Basin Way
P.O. Box 2280
Saratoga, CA 95070-0280
408/399-0057 voice
408/399-0157 fax

Want to set text on a path within Photoshop? Human Software OttoPaths takes a cue from your favorite vector drawing package. With OttoPaths, you can set text on arcs, circles, polygons, and other groovy paths, all without leaving the Photoshop environment.

IBM VRBA Watermarking

Visible watermarking
Windows
http://www.software.ibm.com/is/dig-lib/

Looking for a way to add visible watermarks to your 24-bit color images? The IBM VRBA Watermarking plug-in uses the Windows clipboard to allow you to add 8-bit grayscale watermarks with control over intensity and granularity.

inTouch JPEGiT!

Progressive JPEG support
Macintosh, Windows 95/NT
http://www.in-touch.com/
inTouch Technology Corporation
1383 Washington Street
Newton, MA 02165
617/332-6800 voice
617/332-1685 fax

Do you need to create the tight JPEG images? inTouch Technology JPEGiT! allows you to save images in the Progressive JPEG format, in addition to providing a higher level of control over standard JPEG exports.

Knoll Software CyberMesh

Creates 3D DXF files from grayscale images
JKnoll@aol.com
415/453-2471 voice

Looking for a spiffy new way to create 3D models? Knoll Software CyberMesh turns grayscale images into 3D/DXF files.

MicroFrontier Pattern WORKSHOP

Pattern fill and creation
Macintosh
http://www.MicroFrontier.com/
MicroFrontier, Inc.
P.O. Box 71190
Des Moines, IA 50325-0190
515/270-8109 voice
515/278-6828 fax

Are you a pattern nut? Take a look at MicroFrontier Pattern WORKSHOP. This inexpensive package consists of two components, Pattern Fill and Pattern Edit, along with a library of 160 patterns. You can alter the existing patterns or create your own patterns by sampling 64 X 64 pixel areas from your images. MicroFrontier sells additional pattern libraries, as well (there are seven libraries as of this writing).

Monarch Design Systems Plaids & Stripes

Plaid and stripe patterns
Macintosh, Windows NT/95 under development
http://www.monarchcad.com/
Monarch Design Systems
74-10 88th Street
Glendale, NY 11385
718/894-8520 voice
718/416-0330 fax

Need to create some groovy plaid or striped patterns? If you're in the apparel, textile, interior design, or home furnishing industries, Monarch Design Systems Plaid & Stripes might just be the ticket. The plug-in functions as an acquire module and comes with a library of woven designs. You can alter the size of the pattern as well as the stripe direction and spacing with control down to the thread level.

Total Integration

http://www.totalint.com/
Total Integration, Inc.
600 North First Bank Drive
Palatine, IL 60067
847/776-2377 voice
847/776-2378 fax

Total Integration has developed a number of plug-ins targeted at the pre-press, printing, and publishing industries:

Epilogue V2.1

Macintosh

Need to bring any PostScript or EPS file directly into Adobe Photoshop? Total Integration offers Epilogue V2.1, an Adobe PostScript Level 2 acquire module. This is the real thing: a true Adobe Configurable PostScript interpreter (CPSI) RIP! Epilogue provides support for OPI, DCS, and APR scenarios.

FASTedit/Deluxe

Macintosh

Want to speed up the process of retouching huge images? Total Integration FASTedit/Deluxe lets you open up individual layers (or portions thereof) as well as sections of an image. By opening up a smaller chunk of the file, you'll need less RAM and spend less time waiting for the image to load. Once you've made your changes, FASTedit/Deluxe saves them back into the original file. The plug-in can work with the following formats: DCS, EPS, Macromedia xRes LRG, Photoshop 2.5 & 3.0, Scitex CT, Targa, and TIFF.

FASTedit/IVUE

Macintosh

Do you work with both Live Picture and Adobe Photoshop? Did you ever wish that Photoshop could open Live Picture's IVUE file format? If so, your prayers have been answered! Total Integration FASTedit/IVUE lets you use the same technology found in FASTedit/Deluxe to acquire and export IVUE files.

HandShake LW

Macintosh

Looking to extend the functionality of your Scitex system without breaking the bank? The Total Integration HandShake LW plug-in allows you to open and save files in the Scitex Handshake linework (LW) format. The plug-in opens LW files as CMYK images in Photoshop.

Ultimatte PhotoFusion

Blue screen compositing
Macintosh
http://www.ultimatte.com/
Ultimatte Corporation
20554 Plummer Street
Chatsworth, CA 91311
818/993-8007 voice
818/993-3762 fax

Want to drop your studio shots onto a new background? Ultimatte PhotoFusion allows you to acquire blue or green screened images using Ultimatte's patented algorithms. It creates foreground masks that maintain fine details, including hair, shadows, and reflections, allowing you to build complicated composite images.

Vertigo HotText

Three-dimensional text and path rendering
Power Macintosh
http://www.vertigo3d.com
Vertigo Technology Inc.
1255 W. Pender Street
Vancouver, BC V6E 2V1 Canada
604/684-2113 voice
604/684-2108 fax

Looking for the latest way to create three-dimensional text and paths within Photoshop? Vertigo HotText allows you to build awesome 3D artwork with control over custom textures, lighting, and camera angles. You can even flow text along 3D paths.

Wacom PenTools

Pressure-sensitive drawing effects
Macintosh and Windows
http://www.wacom.com/
WACOM Technology Corporation
501 S.E. Columbia Shores Blvd.
Suite 300
Vancouver, WA 98661
360/750-8882 voice
360/750-8924 fax

If you have a Wacom digitizing tablet, check out Wacom's hot new PenTools plug-ins! The package includes Brush-on Noise to selectively add noise, Super Putty (just like its namesake), 3-D Chisel to carve cool bevels and etches, Pen Duster and Despeckler to clean up images, and Virtual Airbrush for the ultimate in spray-on control.

appendix C

How Plug-ins Work

This appendix is intended to provide a basic overview of Photoshop plug-in technology rather than serve as an in-depth programming guide. We're truly fortunate to be able to include Adobe's Software Development Kits (SDK) for Photoshop and Premiere on *The Photoshop Plug-ins Book* Companion CD-ROM. If you're ready to dive headlong into the programming code, you'll find the Acrobat PDF versions of Adobe's SDK Guides to be an invaluable resource.

So What's a Plug-in?

Plug-ins are supplementary programs that extend a host application. A host program—in this case, Adobe Photoshop—loads plug-in programs in and out of memory as needed. By not being hard-coded into the base application, plug-ins allow for a range of flexibility. Most importantly, plug-ins can be updated at will without the need to upgrade the entire application. This can greatly extend the life cycle of a program revision.

In the case of Adobe Photoshop, there are eight specific plug-in module types. Here's a rundown of what each module does, an example or two of each type of module, along with their Macintosh file types and Windows file extensions:

- **Color picker.** Want to add a new way to select color? This module allows you to use a custom color picker (other than the system or Photoshop color picker).
Macintosh File Type: 8BCM
Windows File Extension .8BC

■ **Import.** Need to bring artwork in from an image acquisition device or an unsupported file format? This module lets you create hooks to scanners, digital cameras, and other devices.
Examples: Umax VistaScan and Human Software CD-Q
Macintosh File Type: 8BAM
Windows File Extension .8BA

■ **Export.** Want to save your files in the latest Web format? This module allows you to build export plug-ins for unsupported file formats. The Export module should be used for "one-time-only" (degenerative) exports. It can also be used to create drivers to print to Macintosh printers that lack standard Chooser controls.
Examples: Second Glance LaserSepsPro and Ulead SmartSaver
Macintosh File Type: 8BEM
Windows File Extension .8BE

■ **Extension.** These modules are hidden beneath the surface of Photoshop. Extension plug-ins are used to initialize devices such as drawing tablets and handle the start-up and shutdown of said devices.
Examples: Adobe Pressure Support and Multiprocessor Extension
Macintosh File Type: 8BXM
Windows File Extension .8BX

■ **Filter.** Want to jazz it up? These are the most common of all the plug-in modules. They're the pixel tweakers that allow you to alter a selected area of your image.
Examples: Kai's Power Tools and WildRiverSSK
Macintosh File Type: 8BFM
Windows File Extension .8BF

■ **Format.** Need to open or save files in an unsupported format? This module type is similar to the import and export modules, although it differs a bit. The Format module allows you to bring files into Photoshop with the Open command and save files with the Save As and Save a Copy commands (as opposed to using the Import and Export commands, respectively). You'll want to use the Format module when building plug-ins for non-degenerative file formats.
Examples: BoxTop ProJPEG and PhotoGIF
Macintosh File Type: 8BIF
Windows File Extension .8BI

■ **Parser.** Here's another one that's similar in intent to the Import and Export plug-in modules. The difference is that the Parser module is most often used to deal with conversion vector-to-raster file format conversion. Examples: Adobe Illustrator Paths Parser and EPS Parser
Macintosh File Type: 8BYM
Windows File Extension .8BY

■ **Selection.** Want to grab a piece of that image? You can use selection modules to specify which pixels are selected, via pixels or paths. Example: Human Software OttoPaths
Macintosh File Type: 8BSM
Windows File Extension .8BS

Want to Create Your Own?

To create a plug-in, you'll need to be able to program in the C or C++ programming language. Plug-in developers often use Metrowerks CodeWarrior for Macintosh development and Microsoft Visual C++ for Windows development. If you're proficient in C or C++ code and are interested in creating your own plug-ins, you'll definitely want to tear into the Adobe Photoshop Plug-in SDK documentation that we've included on *The Photoshop Plug-ins Book* Companion CD-ROM.

Photoshop plug-in development has deep Macintosh roots. Most developers create their plug-ins in a Mac environment before porting the code to Windows. With the lion's share of the Photoshop user base still using Macs, this makes sense. As of this writing, only a minority of commercial Photoshop plug-ins have been developed in the Windows environment.

Some techie-background: The Macintosh is little-endian, while the Wintel world is big-endian. This means that the bytes need to be flipped when porting from platform-to-platform. You don't want to do this by hand! Thankfully, the Photoshop 4.0 SDK includes Visual C++ projects to automate the conversion process. The projects allow you to originate plug-ins from the Windows side without having to have a Macintosh to build static (PiPL) resources. If you're not a C or C++ programmer but still want to try your hand at creating custom plug-ins, you're not out of luck. Check your original Photoshop Installation CD-ROM for the Filter Factory plug-in. Filter Factory allows you to hack out your own filters without knowing an advanced programming language. You'll still have to mess with some math, but the results can be well worth wrinkling your brow and scratching your head.

There are some wonderful Filter Factory resources on the World Wide Web where you can find some great information and great filters. Be sure to check out:

- **Greg's Factory Output**
  http://mars.ark.com/~gschorno/gfo/

- **Filter Factory FAQ**
  http://www.fhd-stuttgart.de/~ws01/fffaq.htm

- **PC Resources for Photoshop - Filter Factory FAQ List**
  http://www.netins.net/showcase/wolf359/fffaq.htm

- **The Plugin Head**
  http://pluginhead.i-us.com/

Seven Steps to Quality Color

Throughout this book, we've focused on ways to increase your productivity and raise the quality level of your output through the use of plug-ins. In this appendix, we'll touch on seven steps to quality color that you can follow whether your computer is loaded up with plug-ins or not. These seven steps apply to new scans as well as to color-correcting a previously scanned file. They are a fundamental guide to performing quality color separations.

1. Get Your Workstation up to Snuff

Your workstation needs to be up to the task at hand. Running Adobe Photoshop places serious demands on your Mac or PC. Don't expect to redeploy a computer that's been liberated from the accounting department without making some alterations.

- **Load up on RAM.** Your computer should have plenty of RAM on hand to maximize performance of the scanner software, Photoshop, and plug-ins. The oft-repeated rule of thumb is that system RAM should equal 3X your average Photoshop image.

- **Get a real video card.** Preferably, the monitor should display millions of colors. A high-performance display card should carry a minimum of 4MB of video RAM. You can get away with less RAM, however, when running at lower resolutions—lowering the resolution setting often allows you to raise the bit-depth.

- **Calibrate your monitor.** You can accomplish this in many ways. If your budget is tight and you want to keep things simple, take advantage of the Knoll Gamma control panel utility that comes with Adobe Photoshop. Simply output a file and make a proof. Open the file in Photoshop, compare the color quality to the proof, and then adjust the Gamma controls accordingly.

- **Work under proper lighting.** The workstation needs to be in a low-light environment to take full advantage of the Gamma control. A monitor shield protecting the screen from light reflections is another must. You can always rig one up out of cardboard. The next logical question at this point is, "How do I view a color proof if I'm working in a low light environment?" Simple—have a desktop lightbooth positioned on either side and toward the rear of the monitor. This will let you view a proof or original under the proper lighting conditions and compare the color to that of your monitor.

Even under the most successful conditions, the monitor-to-proof relationship will only be around 85 percent. This is due to the projected light of the monitor and the reflected light of the proof. All colors viewed on a monitor consist of red, green, and blue (RGB) combinations, while the colors on a standard proof consist of cyan, magenta, yellow, and black (CMYK). Each has its own color gamut. Even when the RGB and CMYK are properly calibrated to each other, you will not achieve a 100 percent identical match.

2. Scan It!

Most professional-level image acquisition devices share basic similarities. Drum scanners, flatbed scanners, transparency scanners, and even digital cameras all provide some type of software to control color separations.

Taking advantage of these tools is a primary challenge for everyone from the highly skilled drum scanner operator through the greenest graphic designer. Have you ever looked at a wall of television sets in an electronic store, where every TV set produced slightly different color? Scanners are the same way. Before you can manipulate any scanner medium, you must first understand the scanner's personality.

Therefore, the next logical step is to scan (at the scanner's default setting) a variety of originals—35mms, 4X5s, 8X10, high key, low key, anything that shows an assortment of color. Performing this task before doing any live production scanning can save time and money; you won't have to scan jobs multiple times to get it right. Of course, every scanner will have its own calibration method that should be adhered to also.

Evaluating these test scans to their originals will allow you to better understand how the scanner sees different subjects. Let's assume, for example, that all the images have a red cast and are heavy. Now you as the operator have some experience with the scanner and can anticipate this color cast prior to scanning.

Some scanners allow you to adjust overall brightness and cast, and often allow you to save these settings. If this is the case, you can reduce the overall tone, take out a little red, and then save the adjustments so that they can be used as a standard starting point for every subsequent scan.

3. Follow the Numbers

Looking at the numbers when scanning is the final assurance of good quality. Even with a calibrated monitor and scanner, you will need to establish proper numbers in key areas of the scan. This is especially important in the highlight and shadow areas, since most color monitors fall short when showing good highlight and shadow detail.

Typical white highlight values should be about equal amounts of yellow and magenta with a little more cyan. For example: 3-5C, 2-3M, 2-3Y. "Why are the numbers unbalanced and not equal?" you ask? It's all in the inks. As a rule, all process color inks are contaminated in some fashion.

Cyan, magenta, and yellow inks printed in equal percentages will reflect more red light. This results in a reddish color cast. To compensate, you'll need to unbalance the inks by increasing the cyan amount. An average midtone gray will be around 50C, 42M, 42Y. This same relative balance applies to the highlight and shadow as well.

The shadow values will vary depending on the type of paper that the image will print on. Newsprint values will normally be the lightest, with percentages around 70C, 65M, 65Y, and 70-80K. Commercial work should have percentages around 90C, 85M, 85Y, and 85-95K. Looking for these key areas of white, black, and gray and then establishing reliable numbers will eliminate some of the guesswork involved in scanning.

4. Contrast

Once you've established those numbers, you'll want to analyze contrast. With the balance of the color separation in order, you can examine the overall brightness of the image. By the way, if there is not a white, black, or gray point to examine, simply skip that step in the process.

The best way to establish good contrast is to ask yourself a few key questions. Contrast is best defined as the separation between light and dark areas.

- Can the whites be whiter without losing much detail? If the answer is yes, you can use one of many controls either on the scanner or in Photoshop to reduce the tone values in the white areas.

- Can the shadow area be darker without plugging up the detail? In some cases, by making the shadows dark, the whites appear whiter, resulting in more contrast.

- Use caution when adjusting contrast with slider-type controls. These controls are okay, but you need to watch the numbers because the white areas can easily be reduced to nothing and the black areas may go solid, resulting in an unwanted appearance.

5. Selective Color Adjustment

Selective color adjustment is one of the last steps in completing a color separation. Selective color adjustment allows the user to adjust CMYK values within colors—for example, reducing the cyan value in the red without affecting any other colors such as blues and yellows.

Up to this point, we adjusted the white, black, gray, and contrast of the image. These four steps in the process will change the appearance of the image dramatically. After adjusting these four steps, the colors in the image should typically improve. If they do not, however, selective color adjustment is necessary.

To understand selective color adjustment, you'll need to understand wanted and unwanted colors. For example, the wanted colors in red are magenta and yellow. The unwanted color is cyan. Cyan and black control saturation in red. The only way to brighten a red that consists of solid magenta and yellow is to reduce the cyan and/or black.

Some scanners provide you with this capability directly in the scanner software. If your scanner does not, Photoshop has a selective color adjustment that also allows correction in whites, blacks, and grays.

6. Look Sharp

Sharpness can either be applied on the scanner or after the initial scan. It's a good idea to apply sharpening after the final tone adjustments. Unsharp masking (USM), as it is often referred to, works by examining where light and dark gray levels meet. The process then creates a fringe effect between the light and dark gray levels.

Think about an image of a person wearing a white shirt and black slacks. The point where the shirt and slacks meet is a prime example of where USM will apply a fringe effect. The white area will take on a slight white line where it meets the dark slacks. The dark area will take on a black line, creating the illusion of sharpness. Because you've adjusted the tones throughout this process, it's best to apply USM when the tones are close to their final setting.

7. Specify the Right Resolution

Choosing the proper resolution before making the final scan can save valuable time and storage space. The rule of thumb is that the resolution should be 1.5-2 times the line screening. For example, an image printed at 150 LPI should be scanned in at 225-300 pixels per inch. You may have read that anything more is a waste of time. In most cases this is true; however, not all images are created equal! Most high-end scanners allow the operator to scan at a high res mode to improve overall quality.

Images with lines or patterns can benefit from a higher input resolution. For example, the vent of a monitor that is made up of horizontal lines may look jagged with the normal suggested resolution. Increasing the resolution to 350 pixels can reduce the jaggedness.

It may take a while for you to earn your wings and feel really comfortable with color. By following these seven steps, you'll surely transcend your previous attempts. There is no substitute for time in the pilot's seat; the longer you work with color, the better you'll get. With these guidelines, however, you're assured of a smooth takeoff—just remember to keep an eye on those instruments!

Index